Alexander of Aphrodisias
On Aristotle Metaphysics 1

Alexander of Aphrodisias

On Aristotle's *Metaphysics 1*.

Translated by

W. E. Dooley, S.J.

Alexander, of Aphrodisias.

Cornell University Press

Ithaca, New York

First published 1989 Cornell University Press.

Library of Congress Cataloging-in-Publication Data

Alexander, of Aphrodisias.
[Hypomnēma eis to meizon A tōn meta ta physika Aristotelous.
English]
    Alexander of Aphrodisias on Aristotle's Metaphysics 1 / translated
by W. E. Dooley.
    p. cm.
    Translation of: Hypomnēma eis to meizon A tōn meta ta physika
Aristotelous.
    Bibliography: p.
    Includes indexes.
    ISBN 0–8014–2235–3
    1. Aristotle. Metaphysics. 2. Metaphysics. I. Dooley, W. E.
II. Title. III. Title: On Aristotle's Metaphysics 1.
B434. A926 1989
110—dc 19   88–47752
                                                                                CIP

Printed in Great Britain

Contents

Acknowledgments

The editor and translator would like to thank all those who have helped with their valuable comments on this volume: Jacques Brunschwig, Gail Fine, M.M. Mackenzie, Bruce Perry, David Robinson, Christopher Rowe, Robert Sharples and Christian Wildberg. We are further grateful to Robert Sharples for providing the main part of the Introduction and Bibliography.

The present translations have been made possible by generous and imaginative funding from the following sources: The National Endowment for the Humanities, an independent federal agency of the USA; The British Academy; The Jowett Copyright Trustees; The Royal Society; Centro Internazionale A. Beltrame di Storia dello Spazio e del Tempo (Padua); Liverpool University; and by the collaboration of I. Hadot (Paris), CNRS (Paris), and the Institute of Classical Studies (London).

We further wish to thank Eric Lewis, John Ellis and David Barlow for their help in preparing the volume for press.

IÔANNÊI ADELPHÔI · PHILIAI

Introduction

Richard Sorabji and
Robert W. Sharples

The commentary on *Metaphysics* 1

In the first two chapters of *Metaphysics* 1, Aristotle asks what is philosophy and in particular philosophical wisdom (*sophia*), and how is it related to philosophy? He answers that it is a knowledge of causes, or rather of explanations, including God, who is a cause or explanation in one of the few distinguishable ways. The remaining eight chapters examine the account given of cause or explanation by his predecessors.[1]

Alexander of Aphrodisias was the greatest expositor and elaborator of Aristotle's philosophy. But his commentary on this book has a curious feature: over half is devoted to the two chapters in which Aristotle discusses Plato. From this we learn not only about Alexander, but also far more than we could from Aristotle's text itself about Aristotle, Plato and Plato's Academy. Aristotle's battery of objections against the theory of Ideas is spelled out, with fragmentary quotations and paraphrases from four of his lost works, *On the Ideas*, *On the Good*, *On Philosophy* and *On the Pythagoreans*. There is an expanded account of the 'unwritten doctrines' which Plato developed late in his career, according to which the Ideas are numbers, namely the One and the Indefinite Dyad.

[1] The following is a summary of the contents of Aristotle's chapters:
(1) To show that philosophical wisdom (*sophia*) is a knowledge of causes, Aristotle passes in review lower types of cognition.
(2) It is a knowledge of first causes, ultimately of God, who is a final, rather than an efficient, Cause.
(3), (4) Anticipations of the doctrine of four causes by the Presocratics: material and efficient causes.
(5) Pythagorean material causes and the Eleatics on cause.
(6) Plato on Forms as formal causes and on the material and formal causes of Forms.
(7) Earlier thinkers support the distinction of four causes, although they treat formal and final cause inadequately.
(8) Criticism of the Presocratics on cause.
(9) Criticism of the Platonic theory of Forms and its later development, and of the arguments for it.
(10) The inadequacy of earlier treatments of cause.

1

From the many arguments for the theory of Ideas, and sometimes from the arguments against it, we learn much more about what Plato's circle hoped for from the theory and therefore about how the Ideas were conceived. The deliberations recorded are more detailed than anything in Plato's dialogues or in the modern litera-ture, and students of the theory of Ideas will find profit in expanding their researches not only to the fragments of Aristotle, which have been increasingly studied of late, but to the whole of Alexander's discussion.

Alexander and his commentary

Alexander's commentary on Aristotle's *Metaphysics* was the work chosen for the volume introducing the whole of the Berlin series of editions of the Greek commentators on Aristotle.[2] It is the most substantial commentary on the *Metaphysics* to survive from antiquity, and many of its interpretations enter explicitly or implicitly into the subsequent series of commentaries right down to the present century.

Alexander, who was known to later generations as 'The Commen-tator' *par excellence* until Averroes took over that title,[3] wrote at the end of the second century AD and the beginning of the third. He was appointed as a publicly-funded teacher of Aristotelian phil-osophy by the emperors Septimius Severus and Caracalla between 198 and 209 AD.[4] If his post was in Athens, it will have been the one that the satirist Lucian represents at an earlier date in his sketch *The Eunuch* as open to public competition involving a eunuch, among others.

Alexander's voluminous writings included numerous commen-taries on Aristotelian texts, some of which survive while others were incorporated in later commentaries and so are now known to us only at second-hand. In all his works Alexander's aim is to present Aristotle's doctrine and to interpret statements and texts of Aristotle in the light of what Aristotle says elsewhere; unlike some later commentators, he is not influenced by commitment to some other doctrine, whether Platonist or Christian.

Alexander's interpretations of Aristotle are not, indeed, always free from the influence of the philosophical context in which he wrote. He takes account of the views of other philosophical schools,

[2] M. Hayduck (ed.), *Alexandri Aphrodisiensis in Aristotelis Metaphysica commen-taria*, Berlin 1891 (*CAG* 1). This is the standard edition. There was an earlier edition by H. Bonitz, Berlin 1847.

[3] cf. Simplicius *in Phys.* (*CAG* 9–10) 707,33; 1170,13; 1176,32; Philoponus *in An. Pr.* (*CAG* 13,2) 126,30.

[4] Alexander, *de Fato* (*Suppl. Arist.* 2,2) 164,1–3 and 13ff.; cf. R.B. Todd, *Alexander of Aphrodisias on Stoic Physics*, Leiden 1976, 1 n.3.

but he does not see his task as being to interpret them as a historian would, giving an account of what their proposers intended by them; rather, he shares with Aristotle the belief that there is a single objectively true account of the world, and regards rival theories as more or less accurate approximations to the understanding of this. (Stoic logic, for example, is for Alexander in some respects just misguided; but whether his judgments of particular Stoic logical theories are positive or negative, he is always judging them in the context of Aristotelian syllogistic as the norm.) And, just as Aristotle, not least in *Metaphysics* 1, tends to regard his predecessors as making successively closer approximations towards the truths he himself has expressed clearly, so Alexander tends to equate objective truth and Aristotelian doctrine; sometimes he makes appeals to what is clear or obvious, or to common and natural opinions, which are in fact appeals to Aristotelian theory.[5]

Nevertheless, as with Aristotle himself, Alexander's commitment to there being a single true Aristotelian account of how things are is combined with a great deal that is provisional and open-ended in his discussions of particular points; it is indeed a characteristic of his works that he presents various possible solutions to a problem, often without clearly indicating his choice among them. His discussions of Aristotle, together with those of his predecessors, were part of the process that tended to turn Aristotle's thought into an Aristotelian *system*; but the systematisation is in Alexander far from complete or conclusive.

Alexander's commentary on books 1–5 of the *Metaphysics* is preserved for us in its genuine form. The proportionately much shorter commentary on books 6–14 is, in its present form, by Michael of Ephesus (eleventh–twelfth centuries AD).[6] It is debated how much of the genuine commentary by Alexander it incorporates, and what the relation is between Alexander's original commentary and citations preserved in Arabic quotations. There is a variant recension of the commentary on books 1 and 2 and the first couple of pages of that on 3 in two MSS, Hayduck's L and F; this seems to be the work of a much later adapter who omitted some of what Alexander wrote and incorporated scholia from other sources.[7] In the commentary on book 1, Alexander is naturally much concerned with Aristotle's predecessors; his commentary is not such a mine of

[5] cf. R.W. Sharples, *Alexander of Aphrodisias On Fate*, London 1983, 18 and nn.; a notable example at *de Fato* 8. 172,17–19.

[6] Michael's name actually appears in one MS, and his authorship is generally accepted. Cf. K. Praechter, reviewing *CAG* 22,2 in *Göttingischen Gelehrten Anziegen* 168, 1906, 861–907, at 882–96; also, recently, L. Tarán, *Gnomon* 53, 1981, 750, and P. Thillet, *Alexandre d'Aphrodise*, lvi–lviii.

[7] So Hayduck, above no. 2, ix, who argues that the adaptation is later than the commentary on the *Metaphysics* by Asclepius (sixth century AD).

information about them as Simplicius' *Physics* commentary, but it
has preserved important evidence relating to Aristotle's objections
to Plato's theory of Ideas and to works now lost in which Aristotle
dealt with this topic in more detail than in *Metaphysics* 1 itself.

Alexander already raises some of the objections to Aristotle's
attacks that have been made repeatedly since – for example, against
Aristotle's apparent disregard of the Demiurge in the *Timaeus* as
an efficient cause,[8] even though Alexander naturally sees his duty
as being to defend Aristotle against these objections.

[8] Alexander *in Metaph.* 59–60.

Translator's Preface

This translation is made from the Greek text edited by Michael Hayduck, *Alexandri Aphrodisiensis in Aristotelis Metaphysica Commentaria* (*CAG* 1: Berlin 1891), with the exception of the excerpts from Aristotle's *Peri Ideôn, On Ideas*, in Chapter 9 of the commentary, where I have followed Dieter Harlfinger's edition (see Bibliography). Departures from Hayduck's text are given in the notes as they occur, and are listed consecutively under Textual Emendations.

Hayduck's vulgate text is based principally on Codex A (thirteenth century, Hayduck, fourteenth century, Hadot[1]), supplemented by Codex M (sixteenth century). In addition, however, he prints extensive extracts from two other manuscripts, L and F, under the heading *altera recensio* (hereafter *alt. rec.*). This latter text of Alexander's commentary on Books 1 and 2 of the *Metaphysics* differs widely, as Hayduck notes, from that of AM: at times it contracts or omits entirely what is contained in the vulgate version, at times greatly expands this – '*additamentis*', says Hayduck, '. . . *aut bonis aut inanibus aut supervacaneis*' (Praefatio, ix). In a number of instances, however, the reading of LF is an essential aid to interpretating the vulgate text, or at least provides a clue to Alexander's meaning, so that I have included translations of such passages in the notes.

Square brackets [ ] in the translation enclose words, not found specifically in the Greek text, that seem necessary to an adequate understanding of the thought. I have attempted to be judicious in the use of this device, lest the translation become an interpretation, but Alexander's often compacted form of expression necessitates certain interpolations to make the translation intelligible. The modern divisions of the text of *Metaphysics* into chapters within a book have been retained in the translation, although they are, of course, not found in Alexanders' commentary.

I am grateful to Dr R.W. Sharples for his detailed discussion of certain vexed passages on which I consulted him; a number of his suggestions have been incorporated in the text without specific acknowledgment. My debt to the editor, Richard Sorabji, is very

[1] For a detailed description and discussion of A (= Paris gr. 1876), see Ilsetraut Hadot, Note supplémentaire to her article, 'Recherches sur les fragments du commentaire de Simplicius sur la Métaphysique d'Aristote' in *Simplicius: sa vie, son oeuvre, sa survie*, Berlin 1987, 242–5.

great, not only for his encouragement during the progress of the work but for his many valuable comments, as a result of which both text and notes have been notably improved.

Textual Emendations

The following departures from Hayduck's text have been adopted in the translation. These emendations are also recorded in the footnotes at the point of their occurrence in the text.

2,25–28. Punctuating with a full stop after *ti* (25), and transposing *dia toutôn didaskei hêmas* to 25 from 28.

9,1. *ou dêlon* for *eudêlon* (Brandis).

9,33. *einai* for *eti* (Ascl.).

13,6–8. Placing the interrogation mark after *prôta tina legein einai* (7) rather than after *tina legein einai* (8).

13,20–21. *hôste ei eisi . . . malista an eiê* for *hôste eisi . . . malista d' an eiê* (Bonitz after S).

17,16. *ktêsin* (*Met.* 982b29) for *gnôsin*.

21,32. *en têi . . . apodosei* omitted (Hayduck after Bonitz).

23,20–21. *en têi genesei* for *en tois . . . genesin* (Bonitz).

25,21. *tôi to presbutaton timiôtaton* for *tôi timiôtaton presbutaton* (Bonitz).

30,1. Omitting *to*, bracketed by Hayduck.

30,4. Omitting *gar*, bracketed by Hayduck.

38,5. Supplying *pantôn tôn ontôn arkhas* for the lacuna (Brandis).

38,7. *hoion gên kai ta alla ha epênenke* for *hoion gês kai tôn allôn epênenke*.

39,19–20. *kat' arithmous tinas* for *kat' arithmon tina* (Ascl.).

45,1. *ou mên hen ê oukh hen* for *ou mên hen ê mê on* (LF).

46,11. *mekhri hou* for *mekhri ou* (Hayduck).

47,12. *exô tôn loipôn duo* for *exô toutôn* (LF).

50,14. *tôi mê menein ta auta* for *tôi mêde einai tauta* (Ascl.).

56,3. *par' autou* for *pros autou* (Bonitz).

57,31–32. *arithmou ep' arithmôi genomenou* for *arithmoi ep' arithmou genomenoi* (A).

62,1–2. Transposing the lemma printed here to 62,10 below.

63,10. *agathon* for *agatha* (Bonitz).

66,4. Supplying *atelesteron de to* for the lacuna.

69,9. Supplying *hoion te* after *einai* (Ascl.).

74,15. *tauta* for *tauta*.

75,6. *hôste* for *hôn ta* (Hayduck), with the bracketed *te* omitted.

75,8. *to* for *tou* (Bonitz).

76,17–18. *ê ho . . . aitia*. Substituting for the corrupt text the Latin version (S).

82,11. *ek tôn pros ti* for *kai tôn pros ti* (Harlfinger).

83,16. Deleting *kai eikôn* (Harlfinger).

84,1. *eti te* for *eti* (Harlfinger).

84,4. *ekeino* for *ekeina* (Harlfinger).

85,11. *prôtôi* for *tetartôi* (Harlfinger).

85,22. *khôriston ti* for *te* (S).

88,9. Supplying *ideas eisagei kai ou tôn ousiôn* before *monôn* (Hayduck).

90,1. *autôn* for *ousiôn* (LF).

90,6. *to einai* for *kai auto* (Bonitz after L).

90,14. *aidiou ousês hê duados metekhousa* for *epei aidiou hê duas metekhousa duas estin* (Hayduck).

91,12. *monê ousia* for *monêi ousiai* (Bonitz).

91,13.17.27. *taûta* for *tauta*.

92,6. *einai* after *pantôn* (Brandis).

92,23. *autêi têi phusei* for *têi autêi phusei* (Bonitz).

93,24. *tôi kata* for *to kata* (Bonitz).

96,20. Adding *dunaton* after *einai* (Bonitz).

98,4. *merous* for *meros* (Harlfinger).

100,35–36. *eti kataleipomenou tropou* for *tous eti kataleipomenous tropous* (Bonitz after S).

101,3–4. *hoti to paradeigmata legein autas einai kai houtô metekhein* for the text as printed (Hayduck after S).

103,18. Reading *poiein* after *phusin* (Bonitz).

105,9. *metekhei* for *metkhon* (Hayduck).

105,9–10. *hôste eiê an anthrôpou ou monon ho autoanthrôpos alla kai to autozôion paradeigma* for the text as printed (Hayduck).

105,22–23. *to gar legein ... atopôtaton* transposed as parenthesis after *zôion estin* (20).

109,16. *ê allou tinos, ho ti pot' an êi en autois* (Ascl.) inserted after *en autois*.

113,3. *ha* for *ho*.

113,8–9. Omitting *hetera genê estai*.

113,9–10. *ha pôs* for *haplôs* (Bonitz).

113,13. Supplying *ta gar metaxu onta tinôn kata koinônian tina kai oikeiotêta metaxu ti esti* after *arkhôn* (Hayduck after S).

114,5. *tôn en têi duadi monadôn eis tên monada anakhthêsetai* for *tôn ... anasetai* (Bonitz after S).

114,6. *polu gar hautai ekeinês an* for *pollai gar hautai ekeinên an* (Brandis).

115,14. *allo ti* before *mallon* (Bonitz).

115,18–21. *oukh hôs* for *hôste* (18) and *all' hôs* for *all' oukh* (20) (Ascl.)

116,4–5. *eti te ousia hekastou kuriôs to eidos, hoi de arithmoi hulês ouk eidous logon hexousin* for *eti ... hexousin* (Ascl.).

116,8–9. *tou toioutou henos suntheseôs* for *tou toioutou suntheseôs* (Ascl.).

116,20. *onta* for *on* (Brandis).

122,5. *allo khôris* for *allo peri* (Ascl.).

127,18. *hen* for *aei* (Bonitz).

127,22. *mêkous kai epipedou kai stereou* for *tôn mathêmatikôn*.

134,4. *ekeinai* for *ekeina* (Bonitz).

134,19. *tôn proterôn* before *peri* (LF), *aitiôn eirêkotôn* (Bonitz).

136,6. *an* for *oun* (Bonitz).

Alexander of Aphrodisias

On Aristotle Metaphysics 1

Translation

The Commentary of Alexander of Aphrodisias on [Book 1] (Alpha Meizon) of the *Metaphysics* of Aristotle[1]

CHAPTER 1

980a21 All men by nature desire to know.

Knowledge (*gnôsis*)[2] is perfection (*teleiotês*) of the soul (*psukhê*):[3] in general of the soul that merely knows, but to a greater degree of the rational (*logikos*) soul, and still more of the rational soul whose end (*telos*) is theoretical knowledge (*theôria*);[4] and the perfection of

---

[1] Title: *Alexandrou Aphrodiseôs hupomnêma eis to meizon A tôn meta ta phusika Aristotelous*. This form of the title, but with the names of Alexander and Aristotle omitted, is common to books 1 to 5. The remaining books, the work of ps.-Alexander, have *skholia* for *hupomnêma*.

[2] More important terms are transliterated at their first occurrence, thereafter only if the translation differs notably from that first given.

[3] 1,4. This statement is clarified by Alexander's remark, in his commentary on ch. 16 of *Metaphysics* 5, that each thing is called *teleios* (either 'complete' or 'perfect') when it possesses the excellence proper to it (410,30–1). Thus the excellence proper to soul is knowledge either as the developed capacity (*hexis*) of its cognitive power, or the activity (*energeia*) of actually knowing. In a more fundamental sense, however, the perfection of the soul is the rational power itself (*DA* 99,13). Robert Todd cites the present text as an instance of Alexander's use of *teleiotês* in an ethical sense distinct from a metaphysical sense in which *teleiotês* means *entelekheia* or *eidos* (actuality on form) ('Lexicographical notes on Alexander of Aphrodisias' philosophical terminology', *Glotta* 52, 1974, 214, n. 29). By contrast, the metaphysical sense is found in Alexander's account of how the act of knowing is produced: the thing known is *eidos kai teleiotês* of that which knows, the intellect (*in Metaph.* 2 155,23–4).

[4] A progression is implied here, one that Alexander describes in the *DA* (81,13–22), where 'the scientific and theoretical intellect' is said to be engendered only at a mature stage of human development. The characteristics of *theôria* as a form of knowledge are discussed in the commentary on the first section of Book 2 (138,26–149,13); and the superiority of *theôria* over *praxis* (action) is dealt with in the same place, and in the following sections of the commentary on Book 1. This superiority is shown by the fact that its *energeia* (activity), which is directed towards divine objects, is the activity of the intellect, the most precious of the powers of the soul (*in Top.* 236,24–6); indeed, when men attain the intermittent exercise of *theôria* of which they are capable, they perform an activity similar to that of the gods, and are thus made like them (*in An. Pr.* 6,7–8). In this wide sense, then, *theôria* is *sophia*, the wisdom that is the object of the present inquiry; as such, it is equivalent to, or comprehends, theoretical philosophy as a whole (*in Metaph.* 2 138,28–9). But the term *theôria* is also used in the more limited sense of 'speculation', as at 55,13; 120,21; and 121,28, where I have so translated it. On the supposed etymology of *theôrein*, see n. 8.

each thing is in every case its good (*agathon*), and in its good each
thing has both its being (*to einai*) and its preservation.[5] For this
reason Aristotle introduces[6] the general statement that 'All men by
nature desire to know', i.e. by their very nature they love knowledge
10   because knowledge is their perfection. And as the most obvious sign
of this [truth] he adduces the love we have for our senses (*aisthêsis*);[7]
for we delight in our senses because it is through them that we
acquire knowledge of sensible things. But even apart from this fact,
we cherish our senses for themselves, and in particular the sense
of sight more than the other senses; indeed, without regard to action
15   or activity, 'We prefer seeing (one might say) to everything else'
[980a25]. More than the other senses, then, this sense of sight
enables us to know not only one another but also the divine heavenly bodies (*sôma*). Indeed, as Plato says, it is through this sense
that 'we procured philosophy' [*Tim*. 47B]; for when we fix our gaze
on the heavens and contemplate their order (*taxis*) and ineffable
beauty (*kallos*), we arrive at a notion (*ennoia*) of the one who
20   fashioned them (*ho dêmiourgêsas*).[8] Moreover, through no other

---

[5] 1,6–7. 'The appropriate end of each thing is both its good and its beauty', *in
Metaph*. 5, 347,24; cf. 2,160,12: 'In all things that come to be according to reason or
nature, the good is end.' These texts refer in the first instance to the end achieved
through natural generation or artistic production, but the principle holds also for
the order of immanent activity, which has its end in itself. Thus the soul is ordinated
to knowing, and finds its completion and perfection in the exercise of its highest
power, whose end is *theôria*. The statement that a thing has its being in its good
may perhaps be interpreted by reference to a passage in the *de Anima* in which
Alexander distinguishes *to einai* and *to eu einai*: the theoretical intellect does not
contribute simply to man's existing, as do the nutritive and sensitive powers, but to
his existing in an excellent way: 'for the good [is found] in what is perfect' (81,15–20).
On *to einai* in contrast to *to eu einai*, see further 121,19 and n.358.

[6] In his commentary, Alexander rarely refers to Aristotle by name; I have supplied
'Aristotle' throughout without the usual square brackets. In citing the text of Aristotle on which he is commenting, Alexander sometimes uses the present tense,
sometimes a past tense: 'he says' or 'he said'. For the sake of uniformity, I have
given all such citations in the present tense, except when the reference is clearly to
a prior text.

[7] 1,10. The term *aisthêsis*, of frequent occurrence, has three meanings. (i) The
sense power or faculty, translated as 'sense, senses', but also as 'sensory power' (e.g.
133,29ff.). (ii) The act of sensing, translated as 'sense perception'. (iii) The content
of perceptual activity as a form of knowledge distinguished from *epistêmê*. In many
texts, this meaning is combined with, or indistinguishable from, the second meaning,
so that 'sense perception' serves to translate this meaning as well, although on
occasion 'sense knowledge' may be preferable. (See Greek–English Index for specific
citations for all meanings.) *Aisthêtos* is regularly translated as 'sensible', but in a
few instances (e.g. 51,24; 134,2) as 'perceptible'. The very common term *ta aisthêta*
is regularly translated as 'sensible things'; but when the context shows that the
term refers to these things as objects of perception, it is translated as 'sensible
objects' (e.g. 1,22; 11,13; 133,28).

[8] 1,18–20. cf. *in Sens*. 11,21: 'The sight [of the heavenly bodies] led us to seek even
the first cause, which is responsible both for their order and for their movement'.
His reference to Plato's *Timaeus* perhaps suggested to Alexander the term *ho dêmi-*

sense do we experience things[9] in the way in which we do through this sense; hence Aristotle also says that sight 'reveals many differences' [980a27] in sensible objects (*ta aisthêta*). For there are many differences (*diaphora*) of colour between the extremes of white and black, such as grey, auburn, bright and darker red, and pale yellow;[10] but there is no large number of such differences between hot and cold or dry and moist.   2,1

By this consideration, knowledge is shown to be more estimable (*timios*) than action (*praxis*). Again, this point is evident not only from the fact that every action is referred to some end other than itself; indeed, those very actions associated with the virtues (*aretê*),   5 which seem of all actions the ones to be chosen for their own sake, have obviously a reference to something else. For animate beings (*zôion*) who have no passions (*pathos*),[11] such as is the case among

---

ourgêsas, but we should not suppose that this agent is Plato's demiurge – for Alexander, the artificer of cosmic order is nature itself, as will be seen from the text quoted below. (In his commentary on the *Topics*, Alexander gives as an example of faulty definition, 'God is *dêmiourgos* of the things that are', on the ground that the things of which god is said to be *dêmiourgos* are unlimited and in motion (440,23–5).) The notion of philosophy in the present text is expanded in the introduction to Alexander's commentary on the *Prior Analytics*: 'The knowledge of every chance thing is not worthy of philosophy (there are certain things, in fact, of which it is better to be ignorant), but [only] the knowledge of things divine and precious, and these are things of which nature is the artificer (*dêmiourgos*), since it is a kind of divine art; for from the very name it is clear that *theôrein* has for its object the vision and knowledge of divine things, for it means, "to see the things that are divine (*theia*)". For this reason we say that theoretical philosophy is knowledge of divine things and of things that come to be, and are constituted, by nature . . .' (3,17–23). On nature as a divine art, see below, 103,4–104,18, with the notes to that passage.

[9] 1,20–1, *sumpaskhomen tois pragmasin*, where *pragmasin* might be instrumental dative with the sense, 'are we so affected by things'. But the usual sense of *sumpaskhein* in this construction is 'to be affected or influenced along with another', especially with reference to the mutual interaction of body and soul; thus Aristotle (?) *Physiogn.* 805a5–6, 'the body is influenced by the affections of the soul', and Alexander (?) *Mantissa* 117, 14–16, 'nor is the soul affected along with the body as if it were something other [than the body] and separated [from it] . . ., but that which is affected is the composite. . . .' By analogy with this mode of expression, he may here mean that in seeing, we take on the *pathè*, accidental modifications, of the things seen, such as their gradations of colour.

[10] 1,22–2,1. Alexander's explanation of the statement that 'Sight reveals many differences', differs from the reason given by Aristotle in *de Sensu* 437a6–10, where sight is said to report many differences because all bodies have colour, so that in perceiving colour we also perceive the common sensibles: qualities, that is, perceptible by more than one sense; and thus Alexander interprets the statement in his commentary on the *de Sensu*: 'This sense perceives size and movement and shape and number through its apprehension of colour' (*in Sens.* 12,27–9). In his *de Anima*, Alexander explains that different colours result because of the greater or lesser transparency of bodies (*DA* 45, 9–26).

[11] 2,6, *pathê*. On the multiple senses of *pathos* in Aristotle, see Christopher Kirwan, *Aristotle's Metaphysics, Books Gamma, Delta, Epsilon*, Oxford 1971, 171; and Martha Nussbaum, 'The Stoics on the extirpation of the passions', *Apeiron* 20, 1987, 130,

the gods (*hoi theoi*), have also no need of the actions associated with the virtues;[12] it is therefore on account of the passions that we, since we are by nature subject to passion (*empathês*), must choose these actions: because, that is, of their reference to the passions 10 and their training and control of them.[13] Now it seems obvious that no theoretical knowledge or science (*epistêmê*)[14] is referred to something else; at any rate, the knowledge of things constituted by

---

n. 2, on its meaning in various contexts. In the present commentary, the term occurs chiefly in the sense of 'property', whether essential or accidental; see Greek–English Index for the citations. For *pathos* as an emotive movement of the soul, Kirwan gives 'feeling', and William Fortenbaugh 'emotion' ('Theophrastus on emotion', *Theophrastus of Eresus*, New Brunswick N.J. 1985, 226, n.2); but I believe that the stronger term 'passion' is required in passages such as the present one. Cf. Alexander *DA* 13,4, 'We are overcome by the passions', and *Mantissa* 118,8, 'The warfare of the passions against reason'.

[12] 2,6–7. 'If we ought to say anything about the beings above us, we must not suppose that any activity belongs to the gods other than that [of *theôria*]; for to say that they act in accordance with any of the other virtues should not be conceded in any way, if in fact the virtues, for their part, have to do with the passions, imposing measure and order on them, whereas the divine is without passion (*apathês*): *in An. Pr.* 5,22–6; cf. *in Metaph.* 5, 'Divine things are without passion in the unqualified sense' (390,23). In the *de Fato*, however, Alexander seems to imply that the gods do have the moral virtues, if not the actions proceeding from them: we praise those in whom the virtues are present by nature, as we do in the case of the gods (197,26–30; Sharples, 77). But as he subsequently says, good things such as the virtues are naturally present in the gods, not acquired by personal effort, so that they merit honour but not praise. See further 18,7–8, and n. 75.

[13] 2,8–10. To be *empathês* is to have the capacity for rejoicing and sorrowing and fearing and desiring (*in Top.* 163,4). The therapeutic effect of the ethical virtues on these passions is described in the text quoted in the preceding note, and is explained at greater length in Alexander's (?) *Ethical Questions* under the question, 'Whether the virtues are to be chosen for their own sake' (146,14–29): they cannot be, because we must choose them to rid ourselves of passions that are without measure (*metron*). This idea is developed with respect to the particular moral virtues, each of which introduces *summetria*, due measure or proportion, into the excesses of the passions (id. 149,17–150,22). Thus the virtues 'are forms of a certain kind, and they bring order into the soul as forms [produced by art] give shape to matter', ps.-Alexander *in Met.* 7, 495,29–30.

[14] In commenting on a passage in the *Topics*, Alexander remarks that Aristotle 'is using the term *epistêmê* in a somewhat popular sense instead of *gnôsis*' (283,21), this latter being the generic term for 'knowledge', as at 1,4 above. Alexander too employs *epistêmê* in this loose sense; in such cases I translate it simply as 'knowledge', except when it occurs in conjunction with *gnôsis*, where I give it as 'understanding'. When Alexander uses *epistêmê* in its more restricted and technical sense to describe the apodeictic knowledge achieved by scientific demonstration, I translate the singular as 'scientific knowledge', or as 'science' if there is reference to a particular form of such knowledge; and the plural as 'sciences'. (Kirwan, however, thinks that 'science' is now too specialized, and adopts 'discipline' as the translation of *epistêmê*: op. cit., 76.) See Greek–English Index for specific citations to both senses of the term. According to Simplicius, Alexander distinguished *to eidenai* and *to epistasthai*, 'for we are said to know (*eidenai*) the objects of sense perception and of opinion, and the immediate premises, none of which we cognize through demonstration'; but this terminology is inapplicable to things known in virtue of scientific knowledge (*epistêmê*): *in Phys.* 1,1; 12,14–20.

nature[15] is to be chosen for its own sake, just as a number of other forms of knowledge as well.[16] That knowledge is more estimable than action might be shown not only by this [argument], as I said, but also by the following. If two men are concerned with the same thing, one of whom only knows it while the other is making or doing it, the one who only knows how the thing ought to be [made   15 or] done is more estimable than the one doing or making it. But if knowledge is without qualification (*haplôs*) better and more estimable than action (for master-workers are more estimable than the skilled workers,[17] those who know rather than those who do or make [something]), then knowing too is without qualification better and more estimable than acting. But if knowledge is superior to action even in matters that call for action (*ta prakta*), it is clear that what ranks highest as knowing is most estimable, and this is   20 just what knowledge of the principles (*arkhê*) provides most of all, and this knowledge is called 'wisdom' (*sophia*); wisdom, therefore, is most estimable.

[15] 2,11, *ta phusei sunestôta*. This expression is frequent in Alexander, who takes it from Aristotle, e.g. *Phys.* 192b13, 193a36, 250b15, 254a31; *Metaph.* 1043a33, 1041b30. Translators of these passages from Aristotle give *phusei* either as 'naturally' or 'by nature'. In translating Alexander, I adopt the latter to indicate the active role that, according to him, nature plays in the constitution of natural things.

[16] 2,3–12. Throughout his commentary on ch. 1, Alexander assumes that the reader is familiar with Aristotle's distinction between theoretical and practical knowledge, and his division of the sciences into the theoretical in contrast to the practical and productive. The theoretical sciences include 'physics' or the philosophy of nature, referred to in this text, mathematics, and 'wisdom' or metaphysics, the subject of the present treatise. The practical sciences are ethics, politics, and economics; these have as their object *praxeis* in the precise sense of human actions, and are differentiated from the productive sciences or arts, whose objects are extrinsic to the agent and his action. Alexander explains the distinction between theoretical and practical sciences at some length in Book 2, 145,3–19; here he merely implies one basis for the distinction, that of the finality of the two types of knowledge. Theoretical knowledge has no end other than knowledge itself, or the truth which this knowledge reveals, whereas the end of practical or productive knowledge is the right performance of the actions to which it is directed, so that this sort of knowledge is not its own end. The theoretical and practical sciences also differ, however, in a more fundamental way with regard to their respective objects: those of the theoretical sciences are necessary and immutable, those of the practical sciences contingent and variable.

[17] 2,17, *tekhnitês*. This term is regularly translated 'artisan'; see n.29. Here, however, Alexander uses it as the equivalent of Aristotle's *kheirotekhnai*, 'manual workers' (*Metaph.* 981a31). 'Artisan' is also inappropriate at 5,11.21.23 below, where Alexander contrasts men of experience with *tekhnitai* who are without practical experience in a skill. This distinction subverts the usual sense of *tekhnitês*, who is understood to be one who possesses expert knowledge and actually works at his craft.

980a27 By nature animals are born with sense perception.

Aristotle has stated that man loves his senses too not only for
the sake of their usefulness but also for the sake of knowing,
25 because sense perception (*aisthêsis*) too contributes something to
his knowledge. By what he now [says] he is teaching us[18] that
man does not have knowledge merely through sense perception,
but that he possesses something more in relation to knowledge
in comparison with other animals (*zôion*), namely reason (*logos*),[19]
whose proper (*idios*) act is to know, and that on this account man
is more perfect than the other animals, and that wisdom is the knowledge everyone thinks to be most estimable. At the same time he
3,1 also confirms the reasonableness of his previous assertion that men
love their senses for the sake of knowing as well. [In the present
text] he also explicates the ordering of the powers (*dunamis*)[20] of
the soul that belong to the senses, an order by which the more perfect animals are also distinguished and separated from those less
5 perfect. [He shows] too that because man possesses something
more in comparison with other animals, namely reason, he is in
this respect more perfect than the other animals. In Aristotle's
intention, all these considerations point to his account (*logos*)
of wisdom and to [his attempt] to show who the wise man (*ho
sophos*) is.

He says that among animals having only sense perception, those
are more perfect that in addition to sensing can also remember
what they perceive; such animals 'are more intelligent and capable
10 of learning' [980b1] than those that cannot remember. He uses the
term 'intelligent' (*phronimos*) in a somewhat popular sense; in the
proper sense, in fact, *phronêsis* (practical wisdom) [deals] with the
objects of deliberation and [is found] in the act of deliberating (*to
bouleuesthai*), and is called 'a state (*hexis*) of capacity to deliberate',
although in another sense the rational power itself is also called
phronêsis. In addition to these meanings, exactness (*akribeia*) and

---

[18] 2,25–8. To account grammatically for the *hoti*-clauses at ll. 25 and 27, I punctuate with a full stop after *ti*, l. 25, and transpose *dia toutôn didaskei hêmas* to this
place from l. 28.

[19] See Greek–English Index for the multiple senses of *logos*, and for specific
citations for each of these senses.

[20] 3,3, *dunamis*. To emphasize the dynamic character of this term when it
refers to the sources of activity within the soul, I translate it as 'power' in these
contexts. In other contexts, 'capacity' is more suitable, and 'potentiality' when
dunamis is contrasted with *energeia*, especially in the frequent *dunamei-energeiai*,
'potentially-actually' or 'in actuality'. (See Greek–English Index for specific citations to all these senses.) For a discussion of the options, see L. A. Kosman, 'Substance, being, and *energeia*', *Oxford Studies in Ancient Philosophy* II, Oxford 1984,
121, n.1.

differentiation among imaginings (*phantasia*)²¹ is also called *phron-êsis*, and the natural versatility in regard to the performance of 15
actions that is found in animals capable of remembering. Memory
(*mnêmê*) is 'the having (*hexis*) of an image (*phantasma*) regarded
as a copy (*eikôn*) of that of which it is an image' [Arist. *De mem. et
rem.* 451a15];²² for the impression (*tupos*)²³ in the imagination is
not sufficient for memory, but the activity that relates to it must
relate to the copy as well,²⁴ i.e. [it must be] from something else
that has happened,²⁵ as Aristotle has shown in his treatise *On
Memory* [id. 450b20–451a3].

He explains his use of the term 'more intelligent' by adding, '[and]
more capable of learning'. For his reason for saying that [animals] 20
are more capable of learning is that, because they are able to
remember, some of them can then even learn and imitate certain
sounds (*phônê*), as do many birds; others, such as dogs and elephants 4,1
among others, can even perform some actions [in response to
commands]. They could also have been said to be more capable of
learning with reference to their being more capable of knowing, for
the animals endowed with memory recognize what [they remember]
– having seen [an object, such an animal]²⁶ not only remembers it,
but can distinguish what is its own from what belongs to another. 5
By these considerations Aristotle shows at the same time that each

²¹ 3,13–14. The sense of this statement is given more fully in the *alt. rec.*: 'Of those
animals that have sense perception, some do not imagine, or do so in an obscure
way without differentiation, as grubs, while others imagine in a distinct and determinate way, so that they are able to judge shape and place, as the bee and the ant . . .'
(3). Note that Aristotle himself excludes the bee and the ant from the class of animals
having imagination (*DA* 428a10).

²² 3,15. Translation of David Ross, *Aristotle: Parva Naturalia*, Oxford 1955, 239.

²³ 3,17. Alexander explains the nature of this *tupos* in his *DA* 72,5–13: 'impression'
in the proper sense is something stamped into a material recipient, and the term is
used metaphorically to describe the residual trace left in us by contact with sensible
objects. At 68,4–10 of the same work he explains how this *tupos* is produced, criticizing the Stoic doctrine (68,10–21).

²⁴ 3,16–18. In Alexander's explanation, *tupos* (l. 17) replaces the *phantasma*
(image) of Aristotle's text (*Mem.* 451b24), and his *energeia* (activity) echoes Aristotle's *hotan energêi hê kinêsis* [*tou phantasmatos*] [ibid. 27]. A less literal translation
might better show the sense: 'The *tupos* must be actuated not only as impression
but also as likeness.'

²⁵ 3,18, *hôs ap' allou gegonotos*. *Gegonotos* can be taken, as in the translation, as
agreeing with *allou*, in the sense that the *energeia* producing the likeness is derived
from the event that produced the impression. It might also be understood as part of
a genitive absolute, [*tupou*] being supplied: 'because, that is, the impression is
derived from something else'. But since the purpose of these words is presumably to
explain why the *tupos* must be actuated *as an image*, a more intelligible reading
would be either *gegonuian* or *gegonuias*: 'i.e., a likeness [is what] is derived from
something else', or, 'because, that is, [a likeness] is derived from something else'.

²⁶ 4,3. There is a lacuna in the text before *idôn*, and the sequence after the lacuna
is singular. The reference therefore seems to be to one of the particular animals just
mentioned, e.g. a dog.

of the powers belonging to sense perception contributes something
to the store of knowledge in the animals that possess them, [the
process] beginning from sense perception. For the apprehension
(*antilêpsis*) [of something] through sense perception is itself a form
of learning; but [those animals] are more capable of learning that
can retain the movement[27] [proceeding] from the objects perceived
even when these objects are no longer present. There seems to be
10   a correspondence between imagination and sense perception, for in
animals that have the former of these [powers] the latter is also
present, as Aristotle says in the third book of *On the Soul* [427b15].

980b25 The animals other than man live by appearances and
memories.

Aristotle said previously, 'By nature animals are born with sense
perception'; but [now] he says that animals other than man 'have
15   but little share in experience' [980b26]. He is saying either that the
other animals have no such experience (*empeiria*) at all,[28] or that
it is present in some of them to a limited degree, something comparable to what he said about intelligence as well. He shows that man
shares in experience in addition to memory by saying that man has
art (*tekhnê*)[29] and reasoning (*logismos*), pointing out that art is
established from experience; and he calls 'reasoning' the reason
(*logos*) that deals with things that are to be done, those that are
20   properly the object of practical wisdom. That experience is proper
to man he shows by saying, 'Now from memory experience is produced in men' [980b28], and states clearly how experience is produced
from memory. For experience is already rational knowledge of some

---

[27] 4,9, *tên kinêsin*: i.e., the effect produced in the sense organs by the action on
them of the sensible object.

[28] 4,15–16. Since Aristotle goes on to say that it is men, and presumably only
they, who develop *empeiria* out of memory, Alexander suggests that *mikron* (*Metaph*.
980b27) understates the case, or is to be interpreted loosely. But as Ross points out,
what truly distinguishes men from other animals is art, not experience (*Aristotle's
Metaphysics* (2 vols), Oxford 1924, I, 117, hereafter referred to as 'Ross, *Metaphysics*').
Alexander's text is noted by Omer Ballériaux, 'En relisant le début de la *Métaphysique*', *Aristotelica*, Bruxelles 1985, 50, n. 23.

[29] 4,18. In modern usage, the term 'art' is usually understood to mean the 'fine
arts' such as painting, sculpture, etc., a sense that *tekhnê* does not have in Aristotle.
(But see Alexander, 80,4 below.) For this reason, some contemporary translators of
Aristotle render *tekhnê* as 'skill' or 'craft', and the cognate *tekhnitês* as 'man of
skill', 'craftsman', and the like. I prefer, however, to retain the older and familiar
terminology, 'art' and 'artisan'. For the definition of *tekhnê*, see 7,17 below, where
it is distinguished from *epistêmê*, scientific knowledge; but *tekhnê* is sometimes
used of theoretical knowledge (e.g. *Metaph*. 981b24, *hai mathêmatikai tekhnai*), and
Aristotle frequently speaks of the *tekhnai* as 'productive sciences' (see n. 16). *Tekhnê*
has also, for Aristotle, a wider sense than its usual meaning of the skill of the craftsman or physician; thus the dialectician employs a *tekhnê sullogistikê* (*Top*. 172a36),
and recitation and acting are *tekhnai*, 'and other arts as well' (*Rhet*. 1404a23).

sort, although inferior to art in this respect, that experience is
a kind of general knowledge of something remembered on many
occasions, which was the particular instance, whereas art is know-   25
ledge not only of this particular instance but of everything similar
to this, as of one thing. And as experience is related to memory,
which is knowledge of a thing or utterance that is numerically
one, so art and scientific knowledge are related to experience. For
experience is a drawing together, into a single [act of] comprehen-   5,1
sion, of the many particulars, i.e. of things perceived, that are
the objects of memory, while art is a bringing together of many
experiences. For from experience [comes] the knowledge that this
particular medicine was useful to those particular individuals
suffering from this particular disease, but from art comes the knowledge that for those suffering from a disease of such-and-such a sort   5
it is beneficial to use remedies of such-and-such a sort; and from
this [it follows] that art recognizes things similar to those learned
from experimentation. For it is the function of art to make infer-
ences based on similarity,[30] as Aristotle himself shows clearly by
his examples. 'This disease' stands for 'a disease of such-and-such
a sort', since the inference that art makes by reference to similarity
is applied to diseases as well as to their remedies. He does not say
that it is impossible to acquire art without experience, but that art   10
was initially discovered through experience, since, as he will say,
some men can be experts in an art although they lack experience. It
is clear, however, that (as Polus said) those who produce something
without experience achieve their end by chance, but not through
foresight (*pronoia*) or art [Plato *Gorg.* 448C].

981a12 With respect to action, experience does not differ[31] at
all from art.   15

By these words Aristotle shows at once that knowledge is more
estimable than action, and that wisdom properly so called [consists]
in knowledge, not in action. For if art is more estimable than
experience even though this latter is in no way inferior to art with
respect to action, and may in fact occasionally prove more effective
than art, but *is* inferior with respect to knowledge, it is clear from
this too that men hold knowing in greater esteem than acting. For   20

[30] 4,22–5,8. For a more detailed account of the progression from sense perception
of particular instances to a rudimentary comprehension of the universal, cf. Alexander's *DA* 83,2–13. That passage concludes: 'This comprehension (*perilêpsis*), and the
grasping of the universal by means of the similarity [found] among particular
perceptible objects, is thinking (*noêsis*); for the combining (*sunthesis*) of similar
things [into a unity] is already a function of intellect (*nous*).'
[31] 5,14. The lemma reads thus, while the modern text of *Metaphysics* has 'does not
seem to differ'.

if we call those expert in an art wiser than men of experience
because the former excel in knowing, it is clear that wisdom has
turned out to be understanding[32] and knowledge of some sort. Aristotle states clearly why men of experience are more effective in
action than those expert in an art who are without experience: the
25   doctor who treats Callias cures man *per accidens* because Callias
happens to be a man. Having said that artisans (*tekhnitês*) and wise
men are superior to men of experience by virtue of their knowledge,
and having established this point from the common conception
(*prolêpsis*)[33] (for he says that it is everyone's practice to call 'wise'
6,1   those who know), he adds [a statement about] what is most proper
to the man who knows. For he says that this is knowledge of the
cause (*aitia*), a point he establishes by showing that to know the
causes is what is most proper to wisdom, the subject of the present
treatise, and that the highest level of wisdom is the knowledge of
the first causes. By his example of the master-workers he shows
5   clearly that wisdom is, by common agreement, referred to knowledge, not to action, and that knowledge is something more estimable
than action. He shows, moreover, that art is superior to experience
by reason of its knowledge and understanding of the cause from the
fact that those who know are able to teach, but men of [mere]

---

[32] 5,22, *epistêmen kai gnôsin*. See n. 14.

[33] 5,27. To designate popular and commonly accepted beliefs about wisdom and
the wise man, Alexander uses the following terms: *prolêpsis*, 'conception' (cf. 9,20.29;
15,14); *ennoia*, 'notion' (8,25; 9,23.27); and in one instance *hupolêpsis*, 'supposition'
(10,20); this latter is Aristotle's term (*Metaph.* 982a6, 20). *Prolêpsis*, in the sense of
'preconception', was introduced by Epicurus; see Long and Sedley, *The Hellenistic
Philosophers* 1, Cambridge 1987, 88–9, and the text from Diogenes Laertius which
they cite (17E, 87), so that Alexander could presumably have known the term from
Epicurus. But the terms *koinai kai phusikai prolêpseis* or *ennoiai* are borrowed from
the Stoics; on their technical sense in Stoic philosophy see F. H. Sandbach, '*Ennoia*
and *prolêpsis* in the Stoic theory of knowledge', *Problems in Stoicism*, London 1971,
22–37; and Robert Todd, 'The Stoic common notions: a re-examination and reinterpretation', *Symbolae Osloenses* 48, 1973, 47–75. As Todd has shown, Alexander
uses the terms in their more technical sense in other places; but in the present
context, 'common and natural conceptions' or 'notions' are simply, as Alexander says,
starting-points which may lead to more formal proofs (9,19–20). ('. . . The doctrine
of the common notions . . . provided a convenient terminology with which the Aristotelian commentators could characterize 'consensus' arguments in Aristotle': Todd,
op. cit., 47.) At 9,22, Alexander also says that these starting-points have been given
to us 'by nature', but that statement should not be taken to mean that the common
and natural notions are innate truths; rather, they are vague generalizations derived
from experience, or from the social and cultural milieu in which one is reared. Thus,
in his commentary on the *Topics*, Alexander gives as an example of a *koinê ennoia*
the proposition – based, as he points out, on an induction – that every animal is
capable of moving and moves (558,24–7); and in his (?) *Ethical Questions* he speaks
of generally accepted moral convictions as common conceptions of mankind
(129,8–16 and 138,14–17). He also applies the term 'natural and common notions'
to propositions of another type, the self-evident first principles or axioms of demonstration; see e.g. *in Metaph.* 4, 317,34–5, and *in Top.* 18, 20–1.

experience cannot do so, and that teaching is [an activity] proper
to the man who knows. He also presents clear evidence from the   10
senses that knowledge of the cause is scientific knowledge and
wisdom: although the senses are more capable of apprehending
particular things, we do not call them kinds of wisdom because they
are not capable of apprehending causes.

981b13 It is natural that at first he who invented any art
whatever that exceeded the common perceptions of men [should
be an object of admiration].

If men did indeed always look with admiration on those who had   15
invented something new beyond the [merely] useful, because they
regarded the inventors as wise and as superior to the rest of
mankind, this very fact establishes and shows that knowledge is
something admirable and estimable. By what he says here, Aristotle shows at the same time the way to wisdom and the most
perfect knowledge, and how men arrived at wisdom, the theoretical   20
inquiry into the things that are most estimable: because, after the
discovery of things necessary to satisfy their needs, they then had
leisure to pursue a free[34] and more refined kind of thinking. He
includes among the utilitarian arts even those that provide pleasures, since it was because of their lack of pleasures (*hêdonê*) and
their need for them and for relief from toil that men began to seek   7,1
the means of producing these. The end of such arts too is a kind of
action, for the pleasures [resulting] from theoretical knowledge do
not make pleasure their end, but possess it as their [natural]
concomitant.[35] That the mathematical sciences also originated from
experience Aristotle points out by [his reference to] the priests in   5
Egypt. Because they had leisure, they first acquired experience
through their observations of celestial phenomena, then established
an art; and in this way geometry too was initially discovered from
the surveyor's art.[36] And just as arts of this sort were discovered by
men who had leisure, so leisure is also required for their exercise.

[34] 6,21. Wisdom (*sophia*) is 'free' not only because it is its own end, unlike the
practical knowledge that looks to an end beyond itself (see n. 16), but also because
it is the knowledge that befits free men. See Alexander's statement on this point,
17,5–10 below.

[35] 7,2–3. The source for this doctrine is *EN* 10.6–7, where Aristotle describes the
'pure' pleasures that accompany the life of theoretical activity.

[36] 7,5–7. It was pointed out in n. 29 that although *tekhnê* (art), as strictly defined,
is a form of knowledge directed to production, the term is sometimes elevated to the
status of *epistêmê* (scientific knowledge). In the present text, *tekhnê* has both these
senses; the 'art' referred to in l. 6 is probably astronomy, one of the mathematical
sciences (72,10 below), whereas the surveyor's 'art' of land measurement is utilitarian. On the origin of geometry, a science, from land measurement, and the
distinction between the two branches of knowledge, see Alexander *in Metaph.* 3,
198,35–199,6.

10   **981b25** What the difference is between art and scientific knowledge has been stated in the *Ethics*.

Because he has used the term 'art' and [spoken] of scientific knowledge as well, Aristotle sends us back to the *Ethics* for the difference between these terms; for in Book Zeta [6] of the *Nicomachean Ethics* he has explained their distinction [1139b14ff].[37] There he says there
15   are five [states] in virtue of which the soul possesses truth – truth in utterance (*logos*) and understanding (*sunesis*), since sense perception too is said to possess truth. These five states are art, practical wisdom, scientific knowledge, wisdom, and perceptive intuition (*nous*).[38] He says that art is 'a state capable of making, involving a true course of reasoning' [1140a10], and scientific knowledge 'a state capable of demonstrating' [1139b31]; by 'capable of demonstrating' [he means either] the ability to reason syllogistically from premises that are prior and immediate and better known than the
20   conclusion [*An. Post.* 71b22], or 'judgment about things that are universal and necessary' [*EN* 1140b31], or knowledge of the cause by reason of which the thing exists: 'That it is the cause of that thing, and that the thing cannot be other than it is' [*An. Post.*

---

[37] 7,2–26. In the famous passage from the *Nicomachean Ethics* to which Alexander here refers, Aristotle lists the so-called 'intellectual' (*dianoêtikai*) virtues, which he has previously distinguished from the 'moral' (*êthikai*) virtues (1138b31–1139a2) that are the subject of the preceding books of the *Ethics*. According to the psychology which is assumed in the *Ethics*, there are two 'parts' to the soul, one possessing reason, the other irrational (1139a4); the moral virtues perfect the irrational part, making it subservient to reason. Within the rational part, Aristotle further distinguishes a scientific (*epistêmonikon*) part, which has as its object 'the sort of things whose principles cannot be other than they are', and a calculative (*logistikon*) or deliberative (*bouleutikon*) part, the objects of which are contingent and variable (1139a6–12). The five intellectual virtues are 'the best states of each of these two parts' of the rational soul (1139a15): art and practical wisdom perfect the calculative part by directing productive activity and human moral actions respectively, while scientific knowledge, wisdom, and perceptive intuition are virtues, i.e. developed capacities, of the scientific part.

[38] 7,16, *nous*. This term, the *intellectus principiorum* of the medieval Aristotelians, has been variously translated: as 'intuitive reason' by Ross and as 'comprehension' in the Revised Oxford Translation of Aristotle (hereafter ROTA). The present translation, 'perceptive intuition', emphasizes the important point that the apprehension of truths by *nous is* an intuitive act – as distinct, that is, from apprehension through demonstration – but that the intuition results from an empirical inductive process based on sense perception (see n. 39). When Alexander uses *nous* in reference to the intellective power of the soul, I translate as 'intellect', except in those passages in which he discusses Anaxagoras, where I retain the traditional 'Mind'.
      Paul Wilpert has made a careful comparison of the definitions given here by Alexander with the text of the *Nicomachean Ethics* to which they are referred, and concludes that Alexander's fidelity to his source proves that he is not quoting from memory, but with the actual text of Aristotle before him; this fact, he argues, should give us confidence in the accuracy of Alexander's subsequent citations from the lost works of Aristotle ('Die Reste verlorener Aristotelesschriften bei Alexander von Aphrodisias', *Hermes* 75, 1940, 385–87).

71b11]. He says that practical wisdom is 'a true and reasoned state capable of acting in regard to the things that are good or bad for man' [*EN* 1140b5], the things that are also the object of deliberation; or 'The virtue of that part of the soul that forms opinions' [id. 1140b26]. Perceptive intuition, he says, is a power of the soul by 25 which we know the indemonstrable principles of things that can be demonstrated [id. 1141a7, 1143b1]; and wisdom, 'perceptive intuition combined with scientific knowledge . . . of the objects that are highest' by nature [1141a19].[39]

After Aristotle has referred us to these statements about the difference between art and scientific knowledge (for the former of these [consists] in making and acting, the latter in knowledge), his purpose in mentioning these distinctions follows; for this is both to

---

[39] 7,17–26. In this brief resumé, Alexander assumes that the reader possesses a thorough knowledge of Aristotelian doctrines set forth in the two *Analytics* and in the *Nicomachean Ethics*. Scientific knowledge of e.g. the shape of lunar eclipses looks for the cause (*aitia*), i.e. the explanation of the shape. It states this explanation by deriving the shape syllogistically from certain first principles, *arkhai*, which include both the axioms (see n. 62) and the principles proper to the particular science: definitions and assumptions (*An. Post.* 1.10); in the present example, the definition of lunar eclipse as the moon's loss of light due to the earth's shadow. Syllogism, as invented and described by Aristotle in the *Prior Analytics*, consists of two premises and a conclusion. Demonstrations are scientific syllogisms which are subject to further constraints, such as the requirement that the two premises be prior, immediate, and better known than the conclusion, as Aristotle explains in the *Posterior Analytics* 1, 2 and 3. The knowledge of the first principles themselves, whether of the axioms or of the principles proper to the particular sciences, cannot result from demonstration (*An. Post.* 1.3 and 2.19), but can be had only through a perceptive intuition (*nous*) (*EN* 6.6). Perceptive intuition is based on an empirical search for the causes of natural phenomena, an inductive process to which Aristotle refers in *An. Post.* 1.18; 1.31; 1.34; and 2.8. The *locus classicus* on this point is ch. 19 of Book 2 of the *Posterior Analytics*, which describes the process whereby universal concepts are formed out of repeated acts of sense perception (cf. *Metaph.* 1.1, and 4,22–5,9 above). At the end of this chapter, Aristotle indicates that universal *propositions*, the 'first principles', are similarly apprehended by a process of perceptive intuition (100b3).

There are three theoretical sciences that combine the disposition or developed capacity (*hexis*) for the intuitive understanding of first principles with the disposition to reason syllogistically to scientific knowledge: wisdom (the highest form of human knowledge), philosophy of nature and mathematics. The science of wisdom is the form of theoretical knowledge that Aristotle called 'first philosophy' or 'theology' (see below, 18,5ff and n. 77), but that later came to be known as 'metaphysics'. Wisdom, like the other theoretical sciences, deals with objects whose principles are necessary and immutable, whereas practical wisdom has for its object human actions, which are contingent and variable. It is the disposition or developed capacity of the deliberative part of the rational soul (see n. 37) which enables one to arrive, through deliberation, at the act of choice (*proairesis*): a right judgment, that is, about what ought to be done (*EN* 6,5). Finally, art is the disposition or developed capacity for knowing the right way in which to make things (*EN* 6,4). Like practical wisdom, it is a virtue of the deliberative part of the rational soul, but is directed to making (*poiêsis*) rather than to doing or acting (*praxis*): thus it looks to the production of an object extrinsic both to the agent and to his action, whereas practical wisdom terminates simply in the action which the agent performs.

8,1   postulate and to show that everyone supposes that knowledge in
       its highest and most proper sense, the knowledge we call 'wisdom'
       without qualification, has for its object the first causes and the first
       principles. It was to this end that he showed that art is superior to
       experience because of its knowledge of the cause, and that those
5   arts concerned with the knowledge of the cause of the things with
       which they deal are more estimable.

       981b27 The point of our present discussion is [that all men
       suppose that what is called wisdom deals with the first causes].

       By these words Aristotle himself states clearly both the purpose of
       what is being said and his reason for having said what he has; for
       this was to show that all men think the theoretical arts more
10   estimable than the practical, and consider wisdom capable of
       knowing the first principles. And this we did by showing that they
       always apply the name of wisdom to those especially who have
       more knowledge. For experience is wiser than sense perception
       because it is already rational knowledge of some sort (for the
       comprehension (*perilêpsis*) of the universal is rational); and art is
       wiser than experience in that art is already capable of knowing the
15   cause as well, since the recognition (*theôria*) of similarity comes
       about in virtue of the knowledge of the cause. 'The master-worker
       is wiser than the skilled worker' [981b31] means 'The master-
       worker is wiser than the skilled worker who makes [something]'.
       'And the theoretical arts are wiser than the productive' [981a1]
       because they [exist] not to serve a need but as a way of passing
       one's life and for the sake of knowledge itself.

CHAPTER 2

982a4 Since we are seeking this knowledge . . .

That is, since the inquiry in which we are engaged is a search for   8,20
the kind of knowledge just described, we must discern the sorts of
things with which the knowledge we are seeking deals. From what
Aristotle has already said, it is clear that it is knowledge about
principles and causes of some sort, and that the wise man is he who
knows these. Since, then, wisdom is, according to the common   25
notion about it, knowledge of the principles and causes, and there
are several kinds of cause, he first asks, as we might expect, of
what sort are the causes and what the principles the knowledge of
which is the wisdom we propose to discuss. He has already said, in
fact, 'All men suppose that what is called wisdom deals with the
first causes and principles' [981b28]; but since it is not clear[40] what   9,1
these first principles and causes are, he takes the proposition that
wisdom deals with principles and causes as conceded, and will now
inquire what sort of causes these are, and will show that they are
the first. Or else even in the previous text he did not take that
proposition as already conceded, but as one needing to be proved;[41]
of necessity, then, he mentions too the division of the causes, that   5
scl. causes are spoken of in four ways.[42] With good reason too he
brings in his account of those who said anything about causes before
him, so that if we should find that any of the things they said is
correct, we might follow it, but if not, that we might ourselves
inquire further.

From the present treatise we must therefore demand knowledge of the first principles and causes. These would be, as it

---

[40] 9,1. Reading *ou dêlon* for *eudêlon* (Brandis).

[41] 8,27–9,4. Citing this and related passages, Wilpert points out a characteristic
feature of Alexander's method as a commentator (op. cit., 370). When the text of
Aristotle admits of more than one interpretation, Alexander is careful to state the
possible interpretations while in most cases leaving it to the reader to decide which
is preferable. For further instances of this technique, see below 13,11–17; 21,11–28;
27,15–26; 47,1–15 (where Alexander sees a possible contradiction between two of
Aristotle's statements); 50,24–51,25; 99,7–101,3.

[42] 9,5. As Alexander notes at the very end of this chapter (19,17–18), Aristotle
first expounds the fourfold division of the causes (into material, formal, efficient,
and final) in *Physics* 1.3. With regard to the doctrine of the four causes, the distinctive
contribution of the *Metaphysics* is the demonstration, in Book 7, that the causes
other than the material are ultimately reducible to the formal cause. It is perhaps
with reference to this last point that Alexander says, in the text cited above, that
Aristotle's treatment of *eidos* (form) is in some way obscure.

10   were,[43] principles of being (*to on*),[44] in virtue of which exists each
of the things that are (*ta onta*)[45] of which we predicate (*katêgorein*)
being (*to einai*). Now the first substances (*ousia*),[46] those that are
substances in the most proper sense, are principles of this sort, for
(as Aristotle will show) they are the principles of substances, and
these latter are the principles of all other things.[47] It is therefore

---

[43] 9,10. Bonitz proposes to read *hêi on* for *hoion*, and this emendation is perhaps
correct in light of 11,7 below.

[44] 9,10. I translate both *to on* and *to einai* as 'being', transliterating each occurrence
of the former term as a guide to the reader. Kirwan rejects the traditional translation
of *to on* as 'being' in favour of 'that which is' or 'what is' (op. cit., 76); but this
concrete expression does not seem to me satisfactory in the contexts in which the
term occurs in Alexander; see Greek–English Index for a list of these.

[45] 9,10, *ta onta*. This term, of very frequent occurrence in the commentary, refers in
the first instance to substances, as Alexander remarks in a later text (117,25), and
in particular to material substances, 'the things constituted by nature'. But it comprehends intelligible beings as well: as Alexander says in his commentary on the *de
Sensu*, we have two modes of knowing, thinking and perceiving, because *ta onta* are
distinguished as intelligible and sensible (111,25–7; cf. *in Metaph.*, 265,37–40,
cited in n. 47). As *einai* means both 'to be' and 'to exist', so *ta onta* can be translated
either as 'the things that are' or 'that exist'; but I have adopted the former and
more neutral translation unless the context demands 'the things that exist'.

[46] 9,11, *ousia*. I retain the traditional translation, 'substance', in most occurrences
of this fundamental term, but adopt 'essence', 'reality', and 'substantial nature' as
variant renderings according to the context. See Greek–English Index for a complete
list, and for the types of *ousia* distinguished by Alexander.

[47] 9,8–12. This is difficult: how are *ousiai* the principles of *ousiai*? C.J. De Vogel
translates: '[Les substances premières et proprement dites] . . . (sc. les essences) sont
les principes des substances (sc. des choses qui "subsistent") . . .', and explains: '. . .
les *prôtai kai kuriôtatai ousiai* de nôtre commentateur . . . sont les "quiddités": les
formes qui sont les essences des choses naturelles. . . . Ensuite, ce sont les *formes*
qui, en effet, sont "les principes des choses subsistantes", lesquelles, d'après *Catég.*
5, sont souvent appelées "substances" ' ('La méthode d'Aristote en métaphysique
d'après *Métaphysique* A 1–2', *Aristote et les problèmes de méthode*, Louvain 1961,
151). But although Aristotle does use *ousia* of matter and form, the intrinsic principles of the composite, it seems most unlikely that Alexander would refer to the
forms or essences of natural things as 'first *ousiai*', those that are *ousiai* in the most
proper sense, for forms or essences do not subsist independently. A more natural
interpretation of our text is that by 'first *ousiai*' Alexander means principles extrinsic
to natural substances, i.e. the ungenerated and incorruptible *ousiai*, incorporeal and
immutable, that is, the divine intelligences which he distinguishes both from eternal
ousiai subject to motion and from *ousiai* subject to generation and destruction: *in
Metaph.* 4, 251,34–7; cf. 265,37–40: 'Being (*to on*) extends beyond natural things,
and there exist certain beings (*onta*) in addition to those that are natural; for the
incorporeal and immutable *ousia* is not natural'; also *in Metaph*, 2, 138,17–21.
Indeed, the more fundamental issue involved in the interpretation of our text is
Alexander's conception of the nature of 'first philosophy' or metaphysics. De Vogel
says that in light of her interpretation of the present text, Alexander describes the
metaphysics of Aristotle as essentially concerned with the knowledge of natural
forms, and that thus its method is one of logical analysis, not a speculative synthesis
(id., 152). But Pierluigi Donini thinks that this same text is one of those in which
Alexander seems to reduce the object of metaphysics to the first substance (see 18,10
below: 'god is the first principle and the cause of other things'), so that metaphysics
becomes theology (*Le scuole, l'anima, l'impero*, Torino 1982, 223). On this subject,
see further n. 77.

knowledge of these first substances that we must demand from the present treatise, and further of whatever contributes to knowledge of them. He even devotes the greater part of his discussion to these accessory questions, for it is impossible to acquire knowledge of the first principles in any other way than by having first established these other points and removed any obstacles beforehand.   15

982a6 If one were to take the suppositions we have about the wise man . . .

It is Aristotle's practice, in every inquiry, to use the common and natural conceptions of mankind as starting-points (*arkhai*) for what   20
he himself is proving; [thus] he confirms that knowledge and the desire (*orexis*) for it are natural to men from the fact too that we have been endowed by nature with these starting-points, for they are the common notions (*koinai ennoiai*).[48] Such too was his procedure in the lectures [entitled] *Physics* when he was investigating place (*topos*), and similarly time (*khronos*), and he has employed this method in dealing with almost all other problems.   25
This, then, is what he does now. For since he is inquiring about the nature of the causes with which wisdom is concerned, and asking what is the function of the wise man, and who in general the wise man is, he sets down the common and natural notions we have about wise men, so that by investigating the consequences of these we might take positions and draw conclusions in harmony with them.

The following are, as he says, the characteristics that the common conception attributes to the wise man and to wisdom. [1] To know   30
all things in a general and universal way, and to be able to deal with them comprehensively, and not in the way in which one who is wise in respect to a particular science or art deals with them; for men do not say that those who know in this way are[49] wise, but suppose them experts in [one] art and knowledgeable in that subject about which they speak with knowledge. Further, it is not even   10,1
possible for anyone to know all particular matters except in the way described; for this reason Aristotle adds, 'as far as possible' [982a9]. [2] Moreover, men call wise one who knows things that are out of the ordinary and difficult and not easily known, for they do not say that those who know commonplace and easy things are wise. This is why they do not say that sense perception is wisdom, nor call wise those who are using their senses [simply] inasmuch   5
as they are using them; for sense knowledge is easy and had by

48 9,23, *koinai ennoiai*. On this term, see n. 33.
49 9,33. Reading *einai* for *eti* (Ascl.).

Translation

everyone. [3] Again, they call wise one who is exact (*akribês*) and profound in relation to each of the objects of thought, and who is unerring. [4] Moreover, they say that 'the man who is more capable of teaching the causes' [982a13], i.e. who teaches by explaining the causes, is wise, rather than those who do not teach in this way. [5]

10 Among the sciences too, men call wisdom the one that pursues and chooses its objects for the sake of the knowledge itself appropriate to that science, but not because of some other things resulting from it; and clearly they give the name 'wise' in its turn to those who possess this kind of knowledge, i.e., who know things chosen on account of the knowledge itself, but not for the sake of some other

15 things resulting from it. (The statement that 'They say that he who is more exact and more capable of teaching the causes is wiser', should be understood as two points, not one, for these are certainly different from each other; and thus the characteristics set down are six in all.) [6] Again, men say that those who know superior and more authoritative[50] things are wiser than those who know inferior things, and that among the sciences wisdom is 'superior to' and more architectonic than 'the ancillary science' [982a16].[51]

20 Taking these characteristics, then, as the opinions held about wise men according to the suppositions [of mankind], Aristotle attempts to apply each characteristic to the man who knows the first and universal causes, thus showing [the truth of] the statement I quoted earlier [8,27], that everyone supposes that the knowledge we call 'wisdom' has for its object the first causes and the [first] principles; for the man who knows the first principles knows about all things both universally and to the highest degree and in a general way. For just as one who knows the principles of particular

11,1 things has a kind of universal knowledge of them, so too one who

---

[50] 10,17, *epistatikôtera*. Alexander may possibly be referring the adjective to *epistêmê*; in that case, the sense would be 'more scientific'. But the context suggests that he associates the term with *epistatês* (*ephistanai*).

[51] 10,16–19. As Ross points out, there is a difficulty in Aristotle's description of wisdom as the ruling or authoritative science; according to *EN* 1094b2, it is political science that answers to this description, whereas wisdom, a theoretical science, seems incapable of issuing commands or exercising authority (*Metaphysics* I, 121 ad 16). In his commentary on Book 3 (Beta), Alexander seems to be aware of this difficulty: 'For inasmuch as wisdom is the most authoritative and architectonic science, and as it is mistress of the other sciences, it must be knowledge of the end, for this is the good, and the other things are for its sake; for it is by looking to the end that they [scl. the other sciences] command the things that must be done. Therefore, the most authoritative and most perfect and best knowledge is knowledge of the best of causes, the sort of cause for the sake of which the other things [are or are done]. In this respect, then, wisdom will be thought to be knowledge of the end' (184,14–27). In effect, then, wisdom is authoritative not because it issues commands, but because the other sciences look to it for knowledge of what is to be commanded – an echo, perhaps, of *EN* 1145a9, where Aristotle says that *phronêsis* issues commands for the sake of *sophia*.

knows the principles of all things would have a kind of universal knowledge of all things.

982a21 Of these characteristics, that of knowing belongs to him who possesses in the highest degree the knowledge concerning all things.

[In this text] the words 'all things' are omitted before 'knowing',[52] for   5
[1] to know all things belongs to the man who possesses universal knowledge in the highest degree; for this was the assumption [in what preceded]. But the knowledge that is in the highest degree universal is knowledge about the things that are *qua* beings, for being (*to on*) is common to all things that are in existence (*huparxis*). But things that are in the highest degree universal are also the most difficult of the things that can be known to man because they are completely removed from the senses, and this was [2] the second   10
of the opinions set down as being held about the wise man; for of the things that are, the first and most simple are farthest from the senses. Aristotle adds 'to men' [982a24], to point out a contrast with nature; for by nature first and simple things are more knowable than sensible objects.[53]

Moreover, knowledge of the things that are first in the highest degree is [3] the most exact form of scientific knowledge; indeed, the more exact of the other sciences are those that involve the first principles – if, that is, sciences that involve fewer principles are   15
more exact.[54] But sciences that are closer to the [first] principles involve fewer principles, as Aristotle has said in the *Posterior Analytics* [1.27]; for it was for this reason that he said that demonstrations (*apodeixis*) that are such in the most proper sense are those proceeding from immediate and first premises (*protasis*), but that those that are proved through those of the first type are secondary. But if the sciences that are closer to the first principles are more exact because of their knowledge of the principles, it is clear that the most exact sciences would be those of the [first]   20
principles themselves, i.e. those in virtue of which the sciences

---

[52] 11,5. As quoted in the lemma at the head of this passage, the text reads *to men epistasthai* rather than *to men panta epistasthai*; but Alexander's commentary suggests that he was familiar with the latter reading.

[53] 11,12, *phusei*. LF has, 'for nature knows these things far better than it knows sensible objects', so that *phusei* in our text may be intended as a similar personification of nature. Elsewhere, however, Alexander gives the usual interpretation, e.g. *in Metaph.* 2, 142,9–10: 'Things that are knowable and first by their own nature are difficult for us to know'; cf. 5, 386,21–30, and (ps.-Alex.) 7, 465,31–466,2.

[54] 11,15ff. Alexander's lengthy commentary on this brief text of Aristotle (*Metaph.* 982a25–8) involves a digression from the main point, which is to show that characteristics attributed by common opinion to the wise man are found in one who knows the first causes and principles. That exposition is not resumed until 13,10ff.

proximate to them are also more exact than the others. In the
Posterior Analytics too it has been shown, as I said, that the sciences
that involve fewer principles and that are closer to the [first] principles are more exact than those that involve more principles and
are more remote (for those involving fewer and immediate premises
25   are more exact).[55] And here he makes this same point by bringing
in [the example of] arithmetic and geometry, which differ in that
geometry deals with things having position (for the point, the line,
12,1 and the other objects with which the geometrician deals have
position), whereas the unit and number are without position. This
is why geometricians make use of arithmetical proofs in addition
because they need these to establish their own proofs, but arithmeticians do not use geometrical proofs.

5   **982a25** The most exact of the sciences are those that deal most
       with first principles.

We should not suppose that this statement goes counter to what is
said in the introduction to the *Physics*. There, in saying from what
point we ought to begin, that is from things knowable by us, Aristotle says: 'For it is the whole that is more knowable by sense
10   perception, and the universal is a kind of whole' [184a24]. For what
is first is not the same as what is universal; at any rate, the first
cause imparting motion (*aition kinêtikon*)[56] to which he here refers[57]

---

[55] 11,13–24, with which cf. 12,21–5 below. Demonstration is scientific proof by
syllogism, and the premises of the syllogism must be immediate and first (see n.
39). In addition to the *koinai arkhai* (common principles) or axioms that are used
by all the sciences (see 13,2, and n. 62 below), each science needs *idiai arkhai*,
principles proper to its own genus that serve as the immediate and first premises of
its own demonstrations. There may, however, be a series of secondary syllogisms
leading back to a primary syllogism, i.e. one whose premises are immediate and
first in any particular science, hence 'fewer' than the premises of the secondary
syllogisms that are subsequent to the primary syllogism. Thus sciences whose own
proper principles depend on more ultimate and immediate premises are said to be
'under' the higher science from which they derive the principles proper to their own
genus or subject-matter, as optics and astronomy are subordinate to geometry,
and mechanics to solid geometry (*An. Post.* 75b16, 78b38).
[56] 12,11, *aition to kinêtikon*. Alexander's usual term for this cause is *aition poiêtikon*, which I translate as 'efficient cause'. Although *aition kinêtikon* has an equivalent meaning (33,9, *aitia kinêtikê te kai poiêtikê*; ps.-Alex. *in Metaph.* 6, 456,23–4,
aition kinêtikon êtoi poiêtikon), I translate it as 'cause imparting motion' to maintain
the verbal distinction between the terms.
[57] 12,11, *peri hou nun autôi legein prokeitai*, lit. 'about which he now intends to
speak'. Since Aristotle is not dealing with the efficient cause in this text of the
Metaphysics, *nun* (now) may be simply a general reference to the context: that
Aristotle has that cause in mind when he mentions 'first principles' at 982a26. But
since Alexander has just spoken of 'the first cause imparting motion', which can be
understood as a reference to the Prime Mover of *Physics* 8, or more proximately to
the eternal and separate substance that Aristotle identifies with god in *Metaphysics*
12.7, *nun* might possibly be taken as referring to *Metaphysics* as a whole. The

is indeed prior to everything else, but is not universal in the way
in which the genera (*genos*) are. But neither did he say, in the text
from the *Physics*, that what is called universal as genus is first in
relation to sense perception, but rather [that this latter is] what is
more common and an attribute (*sumbebêkos*)[58] of a number of
things, as he made clear by his examples.[59]

982a26 For those sciences involving fewer principles are more   15
exact.

For a thing that has fewer accidents (*ta sumbebêkota*) is harder to
know and requires greater exactness, and the knowledge of a thing
that has no accident at all is more difficult; for this reason it
requires even greater exactness because we are not aided in
arriving at the knowledge of the essence (*ousia*) of such things
from accidents, but [must obtain] this knowledge from the essence
alone.[60] The knowledge of these things is better because it makes   20
[us] know more. Again, demonstration in the proper sense proceeds
from premises that are prior; indeed, the other things are demonstrated when they have been proved by recourse to the kind
of premises whose certitude (*pistis*) has been established through
first premises. Demonstration from first premises is demonstration
from fewer premises, and this latter is a more exact form of
demonstration, so that demonstration from first premises too is
more exact, if the things proved by means of these premises are   25

implication of that interpretation is that Alexander thinks the object of metaphysics
to be the separated substance or substances, hence 'theology'. See n. 77 for a
discussion of this point.

   58 12,14. I translate *sumbebêkos* as 'attribute' in certain contexts, but usually
as 'accident', especially in the plural *ta sumbebêkota*, as in l. 16 below. On 'accident' see Kirwan, op. cit., 76–7, who criticizes this traditional translation of *sumbebêkos*.

   59 12,14. This explanation of the *katholou pros tên aisthêsin* is not relevant to
Aristotle's example of name and definition in the text from *Physics* (184b1), but may
be valid for his example of children addressing all men as 'father'. In this instance,
'what is more common' are the distinctive characteristics of the male, and these are
'attributes found in a number of things'.

   60 12,18–20. Translated literally, the text says: 'because [the knowledge] is not
aided in arriving at the knowledge of the essence . . . from accidents, but comes
about from the essence alone'. To avoid the ambiguity of the double *gnôsis*, I have
given the translation a personal reference. But what kind of knowledge is that which
Alexander here describes, and how is it a better kind of knowledge than that which
demonstrates the essence by means of essential or proper accidents? (See *in Metaph.*
5, 439,36.) And if there were a being whose reality consisted solely in its essence
(according to Alexander, the Platonic Ideas have certain essential properties in
common, but none that distinguish them: 94,11–20 below), would it be at all possible
for us to know it except through some kind of intuitive and direct apprehension for
which Alexander's noetic theory does not provide? This statement, then, must be
taken as a broad generalization.

in fact causes of the demonstration of things subsequent to them
as well.

13,1   One might raise the further question, how the knowledge of the
first principles and causes can be most difficult if we have greater
certitude with respect to them[61] than in the knowledge that comes
from demonstration. Or is this our situation in regard to principles
in the sense of axioms (*axiôma*), i.e. the principles of demonstration,
through which the other things are proved,[62] but not in regard to
the principles of being (*to on*)?[63] How then are these latter known?
Or are they too known through demonstrations? For [then] the
axioms are principles for proving the principles of being as well.

5   But since all demonstration proceeds from first principles, there
would [then] be some first principles even of the principles of being.
Or is there anything to prevent us from saying that there are some
first principles of the principles of being [considered] as objects of

[61] 13,1. Literally, 'if we are better off in respect to them', a reminiscence of Aristotle
Phys. 254a31.

[62] 13,2–3. The axioms, together with the principles proper to the particular
sciences (see n. 55), are the immediate and indemonstrable first principles which,
Aristotle says, must be apprehended if there is to be scientific knowledge through
demonstration (*An. Post*. 99b20, with which cf. id. 1.1). (Alexander's definition of
the axioms is given in n. 375.) An axiom in the strict sense – i.e. as distinct from
the first premises of the particular sciences – is not a premise used in demonstration
(although Alexander at times uses *axiôma* and *protasis* as equivalent terms, e.g. *in
Metaph*. 130,16), but a proposition that underlies all reasoning (*An. Post*. 72a17),
such as the principle of contradiction and the law of excluded middle: demonstration
is not from (*ex*) the axioms, as it is from premises, but rather through (*dia*) them
(id. 76b10), as Alexander says here. Although all the particular sciences make use
of the axioms, there is, properly speaking, no science of them (*Metaph*. 997a2–11),
since a science is demonstrative and the axioms are, by definition, indemonstrable
truths. But as Aristotle shows in Book 4 of the *Metaphysics*, metaphysics is itself in
some way a science of the axioms: it '... neither defines nor demonstrates them,
but commends them to common sense by showing the absurd consequences of their
denial' (Ross, *Metaphysics* I, 230). In his commentary on the *Prior Analytics*, Alexander speaks of 'the induction that helps [a person] to grasp the axioms, which is
used [as a means] to clarify what [an axiom] asserts but not to prove the universal
(for an axiom is intelligible of itself once it has been understood)'; and in his
commentary on *Metaph*. 1005b32, he illustrates how the axiom, 'Things equal to the
same things are equal to each other', can be thus defended. See further 130,15–18
and n. 375 below.

[63] 12,25–13,6. It was pointed out in n. 33 that Alexander includes the indemonstrable axioms of demonstration among the common and natural notions, so that
we are better off in their regard because they do not require demonstration,
but are comprehended intuitively by *nous*. In the cognitive order, these axioms, as
principles of demonstration, are in fact prior to the principles of being, those
principles the knowledge of which, as Alexander said above (9,7), we must demand
from the science of metaphysics, and which is knowledge *a posteriori*. But in the
ontological order, the principles of being are prior to everything else, because
each of the things of which we predicate being exists through them (9,10). The
present difficulty, then, involves a confusion between cognitive and ontological
principles, which Alexander elsewhere distinguishes (*in Metaph*. 3, 175,3–7 and
190,22).

demonstration?[64] But if demonstration proceeds from first principles, it would be possible to say that there are some [first principles of the principles of being]. But if demonstration is knowledge through a cause, there would [then] be a cause of these [principles of being] as well, and so first principles too. Or else it is not the case that all demonstration is through a cause.[65]

It is clear that those who know the causes are also [4] more capable of teaching, for (as Aristotle said previously) it is a characteristic proper to those who teach that they state the cause of what is being taught. Or he may rather be saying that the science that investigates the causes is more capable of teaching than one which is not of this sort (for teaching takes place through causes), on the ground that this science alone investigates causes; for these are causes in the proper sense. Or what he says is that the science that investigates the causes that are such in a higher degree is also more capable of teaching, since teaching takes place through causes; and this science which investigates the causes that are such in a higher degree is more capable of teaching.[66]

[5] Moreover, knowledge and understanding pursued for the sake of the objects of thought themselves and of the things known, and not for the sake of anything else, belongs most of all to the knowledge of the causes and principles, for these are the most knowable,[67]

[64] 13,6–8. Hayduck puts the interrogation mark after *tina legein einai* (l. 8), but this punctuation seems incompatible with the argument; I therefore punctuate after *prôta tina legein einai* (l. 7). *ê ouden . . . legein einai* (ll. 6–7) suggests a possible way in which to say that there are principles prior to the principles of being: if, scl., these latter are regarded as objects of demonstration. *all' ei . . . legein einai* (ll. 7–8) then says that since demonstration requires first principles, it becomes possible to assert that there are principles of the principles of being, on the hypothesis that these latter are demonstrated.

[65] 13,8–9. This is a further objection, resulting from the previous suggestion that it is possible to admit there are principles of the principles of being if these latter are regarded as objects of demonstration. Demonstration consists in showing the cause of the thing demonstrated; if it functions in the case of the principles of being, they therefore have a cause, hence principles, of their existence.

[66] 13,9–17. Aristotle's text reads *didaskalikê ge hê tôn aitiôn theôrêtikê mallon*; the reference of *mallon* (in a higher degree) is ambiguous, since it can be taken either with *didaskalikê* (teaching), as Alexander takes it in his first two interpretations, or with *tôn aitiôn* (the causes) *theôrêtikê*, as he takes it in his third interpretation, which is equivalent to saying that the science (*sophia*) that investigates first causes is more capable of teaching than the sciences that investigate secondary causes. Alexander's second interpretation might seem completely untenable, for *every* science, even the particular sciences that deal with secondary causes, investigates causes; but the final words, 'for these are causes in the proper sense', suggest that by '[a science] which is not of this sort', he means sciences which, unlike wisdom (*sophia*), do not investigate the highest order of causes.

[67] 13,19, *malista epistêta*. Alexander is here quoting Aristotle (*Metaph.* 982b2), and Ross has pointed out the difficulty in this statement if *epistêtos* (knowable) is taken in the sense of what is scientific, i.e. demonstrated, knowledge (*Metaphysics* I, 122 ad 982b2). This more technical sense of the term is found in Alexander's

20   given that it is through them that each of the other things that are
      knowable is capable of being known. So that if there are some forms
      of knowledge that are to be chosen on their own account, as was
      assumed [2,1–12], the science [that knows the causes and principles]
      would be such most of all.[68] 'For he who chooses to know for the
      sake of knowing will choose most readily that which is most truly
      knowledge' [981a32]. For to the man to whom knowing is in general
      something to be chosen for itself, that which is most knowable is
      what is most worthy of being chosen; and such are the first causes
25   and the principles, if indeed the knowledge of the other things too
      depends on the knowledge of them. For, as Aristotle himself said
      in the *Physics*, we think we know each thing when we know its
      principles and causes [184a12]. He shows that these causes are most
      knowable by adducing the fact that demonstrations proceed from
      first principles, and that the knowledge of things that can be known
      comes through demonstration; so that the first causes would also
      be responsible (*aitios*) for the fact that the other things that are
30   demonstrated and known can be known,[69] but not *vice versa*, for
      the latter are something posterior, and there is no demonstration
14,1 through what is posterior. Again, these causes are responsible for
      the fact that whatever is knowable can be known, if in fact the
      principles of the sciences too have them as their principles.
           Moreover, [6] the most authoritative science is that which is
      capable of knowing causes that are such in the most proper sense,
      and these are the things for the sake of which the other things
5   exist. For the science that understands for what end each of the
      things that come into being should be produced is in every instance
      more authoritative than the science that produces the thing and is
      ancillary, and this is obviously the case with an architectonic
      science. Having said, 'The science which knows for what end each
      thing must be done' [982b5], Aristotle shows what kind of cause is
      one for the sake of which each thing must be done, saying: 'This is
      the good'; for the final cause (*aition telikon*) is of this sort, as he
10   also said at the beginning of the *Nicomachean Ethics*: 'Every art
      and every inquiry, and similarly every action and choice, is thought
      to aim at some good' [1094a1]. The cause of all the things that are
      is also of this sort, for all things that come into being by nature

---

commentary (e.g. 164,20; 181,26–31; 217,21–2), but *epistêtos* is also used in the
general sense of 'knowable' (e.g. 165,5; 245,2).

    [68] 13,20–1. Reading *hôste ei eisi . . . malista an eiê* (Bonitz after S).

    [69] 13,27–30. Aristotle does not in fact mention demonstration, saying only that
'By reason of [the first causes and principles], and from them, all other things are
known' (*Metaph.* 982b2–3). Alexander seems to be involved in the same ambiguity
about first principles as that pointed out in n. 63. The first principles which are the
concern of metaphysics are the source of being for other things, and hence of their
intelligibility, but they are not principles of demonstration.

come to be and exist for its sake, and tend towards it in accordance
with the desire that is innate (*sumphutos*) to them, so that the
science capable of knowing a good of this sort would be the most
authoritative. Wishing to make clear how the first cause is cause   15
of the things that are, that scl. it is an end, and that the science
capable of knowing this kind of cause is more architectonic than
those that produce the things that are for its sake, he made the
statement that 'The science that knows to what end each thing
must be done is more authoritative than the ancillary science'. The
reasoning is this: if among arts and sciences generally the one that
knows that for the sake of which, i.e. the end, is more architectonic   15,1
than one that produces something, [then] the science that knows
the end of all things and that for the sake of which all things exist
and come into being would be most authoritative and first. But
wisdom, which investigates the first cause, is a science of this kind;
for all the things that are aim at the good, that good supreme
among all goods, and the good is the first cause.   5

To the things that have been shown Aristotle adds a summary
of what has been said, pointing out that from all the characteristics
that belong to wise men, wisdom has been shown to be the science
that investigates the first principles and causes. For the good and
that for the sake of which all things are and come into being, that
which the science under consideration investigates, is one of the
causes, for the cause as end is of this sort; 'For this must be a   10
science that investigates the first principles and causes' [982b9]. As
a result therefore of all that has been said, wisdom becomes the
science that investigates the first principles and causes. He adds,
'Indeed, the good, i.e. that for the sake of which, is one of the causes',
since h̨ said earlier that, according to the common conceptions,
wisdom must be an authoritative, not ancillary, science, and also
that the more authoritative science is one which knows that for the   15
sake of which something must be done; and this is the good. Having
said, then, that the more authoritative science is one which knows
that for the sake of which each thing is, which is the good, he shows
by this addition that the science which knows the first principles
also knows the good, and for this reason is authoritative.

982b11 That it is not a productive science is clear from the   20
earliest philosophers.

That philosophy or wisdom is a theoretical rather than a productive
or practical science Aristotle also shows from the fact that originally
the first philosophers came to investigate and discover the causes
because each of them wondered how things are as they are; but to
wonder is the mark of those who are ignorant. If then men wondered   25

because they were ignorant, and came to philosophize because they
wondered, they therefore came to philosophize because they were
ignorant. They came to philosophize, then, for the sake of that
which would put an end to their ignorance, and it was knowledge,
not action, that would accomplish this; it was therefore for the sake
30   of knowledge, not action, that they came to philosophize. For if it
was because of their ignorance that they came to the investigation
of things, this was obviously out of a desire for knowledge, since
the cure for ignorance is not productive activity but knowledge.

Aristotle regularly calls the same science both 'wisdom' and 'first
philosophy'. For philosophy in its most perfect form began in wonder
16,1   and went on to investigation; then, having found the objects of its
investigation, its attitude towards them is such that it wonders that
they can be other than they are, as he will subsequently say. He
says that men at first came to investigate and philosophize because
they wondered at the apparent strangeness of ordinary things
5   around them: for example (as the case might be) why amber attracts
chaff-like things and the magnet iron,[70] or what the rainbow is, or
about the composition of the clouds in general, or where claps of
thunder come from, or how flashes of lightning occur. Then,
advancing little by little, they came to be puzzled by more important
matters too, to wonder about these, and to philosophize. (And for
this reason Aristotle adds the word 'some'.[71]) [As examples,] he
10   mentions the phenomena of the moon, its eclipses and waxings and
wanings, and similarly the eclipses and the risings and settings of
the sun. Now a man who is puzzled and wonders comes to do so
because he supposes he is ignorant. 'Even the lover of myth,' Aristotle adds, 'is in a sense a lover of wisdom' [982b18], for he is eager
to learn the things that, because of his ignorance, he thinks wonders
('for myths are composed of things wondrous' and contrary to expec-
15   tation); and those who are eager to learn because they wonder at
things are lovers of wisdom (*philosophoi*).

That men originally came to philosophize for the sake of knowledge rather than for some need or action Aristotle also establishes
from history; for it was after the necessities and the things that
make for comfort of life had been provided that men came to investi-
20   gate the things that pertain to philosophy and to speculate about
17,1   matters of this sort. But if they began philosophical investigation

---

[70] 16,5. Alexander (?) devotes an entire question to the problem of why the magnet
attracts iron, reviewing various theories and giving his own explanation (*Qq.* 2.23;
72,10–73,30 = Diels-Kranz, *Die Fragmente der Vorsokratiker* (hereafter *DK*) I,
306,9–25). Simplicius also reports Alexander's theory on this point (*in Phys.* 7.2;
1055,24–7).

[71] 16,9. This remark is obscure, because the word 'some' (*tinôn*) does not appear
in our text of *Metaphysics*. Perhaps Alexander read *peri tinôn tôn meizonôn* (about
some more important matters) at 982b15.

when all necessary things and those that make for comfort already existed, they were obviously not investigating to discover any of the necessities that contribute to a pleasant life. But surely [this is the end] of all the productive sciences, for they seek and produce either things necessary and useful, or those that make for a pleasant life. ([In the present text,] he means by 'knowledge' (*phronêsis*) the 5 sort of theoretical wisdom we are describing.)

He compares this kind of theoretical knowledge to free men, those who exist for themselves and not for others, as do slaves. (For in the *Politics*, Aristotle said that a slave is one who, although a man, belongs to another [1254a14]; and such is the man who, because of native incapacity, does not see clearly the things that must be done, but [merely] carries out the orders of another.) Such knowledge, indeed, since it alone among the sciences is free, 'exists solely for 10 its own sake' [982b27]. An indication that it is chosen simply for itself is the fact that even though it provides nothing answering any need, but on the contrary even hinders useful pursuits, it works so great a charm on those who have engaged in it that they wish to do nothing else, but regard anything that distracts them from this activity as a serious annoyance. Hence Aristotle says that the 15 possession[72] of this knowledge might reasonably be thought divine rather than human, for in many matters men are slaves because of their needs, and are forced to perform many actions for the sake of these. For since they are [creatures] of this sort, they make health a good, and prosperity, and each of the other goods of this kind, and as a result are fully occupied in the pursuit of them. But the divine (*to theion*)[73] is free of all need. What he says here is consistent with 20 his statement in the *Nicomachean Ethics*, where he says: 'We must not follow those who advise us, being men, to think of human things, and, being mortal, of mortal things' [1177b31]; for his present words also have this sense.[74] Therefore, he says, if what the poets say about the divine were true (*alêthês*) – that it is jealous of those who are pre-eminent (and for this reason they say too that all who excel and are above their fellow men are unfortunate) – it would be most 18,1 jealous of those [who have acquired wisdom], for such men truly

---

[72] 17,16. Reading *ktêsin* (see *Metaph.* 982b29) for *gnôsin*, to avoid the meaningless expression, 'the knowledge of this knowledge'.

[73] 17,19, *to theion*. Ross translates 'the divine power', and 'the divine nature' or 'divinity' are also possible translations, but the more neutral 'the divine' is consistent with Alexander's use of the term in other places, e.g. *in An. Pr.* 5,26 (*to theion* is without passion); *in Top.* 192,29 (*to theion* is desirable); *DA* 32,13 (likeness to *to theion*); *de Fato* 164,9; 201,3; 207,2 (Sharples 41, 81, 87).

[74] 17,22, *toiauta gar kai tauta*. Alternatively *tauta*, which I translate as 'his present words', might be a backward reference to health, prosperity, etc., so that the sense would be: 'for the particular goods such as those mentioned are human and mortal goods'.

possess something that transcends mortal nature. But 'the divine cannot be jealous' [983a12] (for as the divine Plato says, 'jealousy is excluded from the divine choir' [*Phaedr.* 247A]); it is rather that 'Bards tell many a lie', and this is one of them. Nor should any [of
5	the particular sciences] be thought more estimable than one of this sort. For the knowledge that is most divine is for this reason most estimable, and knowledge of the sort [we are describing] is most divine in that it most resembles the activity of divine beings[75] (for it is reasonable [to suppose] that the divine acts, and no activity is worthy of gods except one of this sort). But [this science] is also [divine] because it is knowledge of the first causes and principles,
10	and god[76] is the first principle and cause of the other things. By these considerations Aristotle shows that the present treatise is rightly called 'theology'.[77] He says that all the other sciences are

[75] 18,7–8. The subsequent reference to the gods shows that *tôn theiôn* is not simply the ambiguous neuter plural (of divine things), and this point is confirmed by the fact that the inspiration for Alexander's statement here is obviously *EN* 10.8 (1178b10–22), where Aristotle is speaking of the gods. On the *energeia* (activity) proper to the gods, see the text quoted in n. 12, and cf. Alexander (?), *Ethical Questions* 20: 'It is absurd to say that the activities of the gods are directed to anything useful for them, they who have no need of anything of this sort, but are outside all need and all passion' (141,2–4).

[76] 18,9, *ho theos*. When this substantive is preceded by the definite article, it is sometimes capitalized, but see Joseph Owens, *The Doctrine of Being in the Aristotelian Metaphysics*, 3rd ed., Toronto 1978, 171, n. 47. Other occurrences of *ho theos* in Alexander are *in An. Pr.* 6,8; 385,2; *in Top.* 144,10; 190,12; 304,18–19; 440,23–4; and in Alexander's (?) *Qq.* 2.19, there is a reference to *ho prôtos theos* (63,20). On the doctrine that god is the first principle and cause, cf. ps.-Alex. *in Metaph.* 7: '[Aristotle] pursues the discovery of the first substance, I mean the greatly revered and much-desired god and father of all things; for he asks what it is that moves matter to its reception of forms, and shows that this is the first form, that precisely which must be called "substance". But if the form in particular things is what moves matter and imposes order on it, it is clear that there exists some form that moves and orders things here below and makes them to be as they are, and this form is the god much celebrated in song' (538,29–35). The *alt. rec.* adds a further reason for saying that the science of metaphysics is divine knowledge: 'Therefore, we should not think that [any other science] is more estimable than the science that is the very first; for this latter is most divine and most estimable in two ways, both because god knows it and because through it, he says, it is possible to know god. For this reason he says that [the science] which god knows is divine among the sciences; and god knows this science as containing in itself the principles of the things that are' (18). These last two texts are clearly far removed from the doctrine of Aristotle; it is a question, whether they represent the mind of Alexander (see n. 77).

[77] 18,11, *theologikê*, lit. 'relating to god', or 'theological'. With this text cf. *in Metaph.* 3: ' "The science we are seeking" . . . is wisdom and the theological science . . . Aristotle also calls it "first wisdom", because it speculates about things that are first and most estimable. For this same reason it is also theological, for it deals with the cause and form that, according to Aristotle, is a completely immaterial substance, which he also calls "first god" and "intellect" . . .' (171,5–10). Texts such as these led Philip Merlan to argue that Alexander identified Aristotle's *to on hêi on*, 'being *qua* being', with the first substance or god, so that, for him, metaphysics becomes theology ('Metaphysik: Name und Gegenstand', *Journal of Hellenic Studies* 77, 1957, 87–92; reprinted in his *Kleine Schriften*, Hildesheim 1976, 189–94). Merlan's thesis

more necessary (*anankaios*) than it (for this one is not even necessary at all), but that none is better; for this science is better than all the others, if indeed it is also more estimable.

Next he describes the method for acquiring this knowledge; for this is to wonder about things that are the opposite (*enantios*) of those about which men originally wondered and thus arrived at knowledge of them. For prior to their knowing they wondered that things could be as they are, but once they had come to know they wondered that things can fail to be as they are. [As examples of] 'wonders' [983a14] he mentions the toys, exhibited by the creators of [such] marvels, that seem to move by their own power,[78] and 'the solstices', which bring winter and summer. 'For it seems wonderful to all that there is something which cannot be measured by even the smallest unit' [983a16]. He is referring to the diagonal; because people imagine that there is a smallest unit in the case of lines too, as there is in the case of numbers, it seems wonderful that all lines cannot be measured by a smallest unit or be commensurable with one another by virtue of their having a common unit of measurement (*metron*). But this is not so, because all numbers are measured by a unit (*monas*) but all lines are not measured by any one thing, since there is no smallest line. For it is because of this that all lines are not commensurable either, since commensurable magnitudes

15

20

19,1

---

has been criticized in detail by Charles Genequand ('L'objet de la métaphysique selon Alexandre d'Aphrodisias', *Museum Helveticum* 36, 1979, 48–57), but Donini does not find this refutation completely convincing: '. . . l'edificio sistematico dell'aristotelismo tende in Alessandro ad assestarsi sotto il primato della teologia, sia vista questa come una parte speciale della metafisica, o sia identificata con la metafisica' (op. cit., 223, and see n. 47). Gérard Verbeke, while admitting that Alexander makes first philosophy theology, thinks that this latter is a universal discipline: '. . . the commentary of Alexander . . . supports the interpretation of Merlan: being *qua* being does not directly refer to sensible substance; it immediately designates supersensible substance; therefore, it is the proper object of theology, which nevertheless is a universal discipline. Hence physical beings are indirectly included in metaphysical research inasmuch as the highest substance is the source of all being, unity, and truth' ('Aristotle's Metaphysics viewed by the Ancient Greek commentators', in Dominic O'Meara (ed.), *Studies in Aristotle*, Washington D.C. 1981, 107–27).

[78] 18,17–18. *tôn thaumatôn tautomata*, *Metaph.* 983a14. On the meaning of *automata* in Aristotle's text, see Walter Spoerri, 'Inkommensurabilität, Automaten und philosophisches Staunen im Alpha der "Metaphysik" ', *Aristoteles Werk und Wirkung* I, Berlin 1985, 239–72. He concludes that Ross's translation, 'self-moving marionettes', is meaningless, because the word 'marionette' suggests figures moved by the hand of the exhibitor, whereas *automata* means (as Alexander explains) figures that seem to move automatically '. . . ohne direkten menschlichen Eingriff' (246). The *alt. rec.* confirms this interpretation: 'Toys such as certain inanimate figures that seem to move themselves' (18). Thus the translation of Alexander's *thaumatopoiôn* is difficult, since 'puppeteer' would again suggest one who manipulates the figures. On *automata* in Aristotle, see also Anthony Preus, 'Michael of Ephesus on Aristotle *IA* and *MA*', *Proceedings of the World Congress on Aristotle* II, Athens 1981, 25–8; and Martha Nussbaum, *Aristotle's De Motu Animalium*, Princeton 1978, 347 (ad 701b2).

(*megethos*) are those that can be measured by the same unit of
measurement. Nevertheless, people end in the contrary and better
5   state when from being ignorant, and because of their ignorance
wondering at things that are true, which they think cannot be as
they are, they change to a state of knowledge; for those who acquire
knowledge of things wonder that any of them can be other than it
is. In saying, 'according to the proverb', [983a18], he might perhaps
mean the one that says, 'Second thoughts are better'.

10   'We have stated, then, what is the nature of the science for which
we are searching': that it is theoretical, not practical, and that it is
knowledge of the first causes and principles; 'and what is the goal
our search and our whole investigation must reach' [983a21]: that
from wondering, through ignorance, at things which are true we
must change to wondering, through knowledge, at things which are
the opposite of these truths – [to wonder, that is,] that it is possible
for things to be in any other way, and not in the way that knowledge
shows them to be. Since he has made it clear, by way of an introduction to this inquiry, that wisdom is theoretical knowledge of the
things that are first, it is reasonable that Aristotle begins by
making the division of the causes, just as in the lectures [entitled]
Physics, dividing them into four. His treatment of the other causes
15   is clear, but what he says about form (*eidos*) has a certain
obscurity.[79]

---

[79] 19,19. This remark is itself obscure, if Alexander is referring, as the context
seems to indicate, to Book 1, for in this Book Aristotle does not expound his own
doctrine of the four causes, but reports and criticizes their treatment by the philosophers who preceded him – although one might well agree that if Alexander has in
mind the critique of the Ideas, which Aristotle takes to be formal causes, that chapter
is certainly not without its obscurities. But Alexander might also be thinking of the
entire *Metaphysics*, and in that case his remark about Aristotle's account of *eidos*
(form) could have special reference to the dense and difficult argument of Book 7,
on which see n. 42.

CHAPTER 3

983a24 We must obviously acquire knowledge of the original causes, for we say that we know each thing only when we think that we recognize its first cause.

'The original causes' stands for 'the first causes'. That scientific   19,25
knowledge in the case of things having principles and causes depends on knowledge of the first principles and causes he also said at the beginning of the lectures [entitled] *Physics* [184a10]; but he showed it too in the *Posterior Analytics* [1.2], and now he speaks in a similar way. For if someone knows things not from their first causes but from causes that are proximate to these things, ones that have different first causes, he would not know the causes themselves that are proximate to the object of his study – if, that is, one knows something having principles and causes when he knows the principles of that thing; but the man whose knowledge proceeds initially from things that are not known could not properly be said to know. Hence Aristotle rightly says that know-ing depends on knowledge of the first causes, thus establishing   20,1
that the status of the other sciences too, as forms of scientific knowl-edge, comes to them from the wisdom that investigates the first causes.

983a27 We say that one of these causes is the substance or essence.

Aristotle speaks of 'the substance' with reference to the form, and   5
he rightly said that the substance of each thing is its form, since it is in virtue of its form that each thing is what it is. For this reason definitions (*horismos*) too are formulated by reference to the form of the things defined, for he speaks of the definition or the formula (*logos*)[80] as 'essence' (*ti ên einai*).[81] 'For the "why" is finally reduced

---

[80] 20,8. Although Alexander, following Aristotle, frequently uses *logos* in the sense of 'definition', I have reserved the latter term to translate *horismos*, and give *logos* in such contexts as 'formula' or 'definitory formula' (*logos horistikos*, 204,23; 429,8; *alibi*).

[81] 20,8. Ps.-Alexander, however, distinguishes *to ti ên einai* from *logos* or *horismos*: essence designates the thing itself and its nature, conceived as a single entity, that which is signified by the name, e.g. 'man'; whereas definition is a kind of unfolding of the thing through an enumeration of the parts of which it is composed (*in Metaph.* 7, 471,18–22).

to the formula' [983a28],[82] i.e. to the definition, and this is the
10   formal cause (*aitia kata to eidos*); for he says that the 'why'[83] is
finally reduced to this formula. [He says] 'finally' because, as a
result of having been given the definition, we no longer keep on
asking 'why', obviously in the belief that we have now learned the
sort of cause that was the object of our inquiry. For if we are asking
why fire heats, once we have learned that to be fire is to be what
15   is primarily hot and capable of heating, we no longer ask why fire
heats, in the belief that we have learned what we were seeking.
[But] when someone asks in turn why snow pierces the eye, if he
were to hear, 'Because it is white', he does not yet cease to concern
himself about the 'why', for he still demands to know why white
pierces the eye; but one who continues to ask 'why' after the answer
to some question has been given has not yet heard the cause. But
20   once he has learned that this is what it is to be white (for the
formula or definition of white is 'that which pierces the eye'),[84] he
no longer seeks the cause of white's piercing the eye, for after an
answer of this sort there no longer remains [any necessity] for
asking why the thing [acts] in this way. Quite properly, therefore,
21,1 Aristotle says that the substance or essence of each thing is one of
the causes; and to show that this is a cause, he adds: 'For the "why"
is finally reduced to the formula.' He says 'finally' because there
might also be certain other answers to the question 'why' that do
5   not yet contain the formula or definition; for this reason answers[85]
of this kind are incapable of teaching the formal cause, nor does
the one asking this question yet terminate his inquiry. For if he
continues to ask 'why', it cannot be said that the cause has been
given, for the question 'why' is an inquiry after the cause. Consequently, when we are asking 'why', and have heard something that

---

[82] 20,8, *anagetai gar to dia ti eis ton logon eskhaton*, *Metaph*. 983a28. Is *eskhaton*
an adjective (final) modifying *logon*, or an adverb (finally) modifying *anagetai*? In
his commentary, Ross adopts the former explanation (*Metaphysics* I, 127 ad 27–9),
but in the second edition of his translation he translates, 'For the "why" is reducible
finally to the definition'. For a discussion of the problem, see Giovanni Reale, *The
Concept of First Philosophy and the Unity of the Metaphysics of Aristotle*, English
translation by J. Catan, Albany N.Y. 1980, 48–9, n. 52. Reale correctly cites the
present text of Alexander as evidence that the latter interpreted *eskhaton* adverbi-
ally; note, however, that from 21,11 on Alexander understands *eskhaton* as 'that
which is last'. See further n. 86.

[83] 20,10, *to dia ti*, lit., 'the [question], "For what reason?"', a translation that
brings out more clearly the notion of cause contained in the formula than does the
simple 'why?'

[84] 20,20. Plato's definition of 'white' (*Tim*. 67E), where *diakritikon* is more accurately translated, 'dilutes the visual ray'.

[85] 21,5. *Apodidosthai* is to give an answer; but when the question put is 'why?' it
has the accessory notion of giving an explanation; *sic* e.g. 28,6; 31,10; 36,30. In
certain contexts, *apodosis* might therefore be translated as 'explanation', but I give
it simply as 'answer' or 'answer given'.

[enables us to] cease asking 'why' because of it, this is a cause; but
we cease asking 'why' when we have heard the definition and the   10
form; this too, therefore, is a cause.

After saying that the 'why' is reduced to the last definition,[86]
Aristotle makes clear, by what he says next, how what is 'last'
(*eskhaton*) is also 'first' (*prôton*) and a cause, for what is stated last
in giving the answer [to a question] is first in nature and a cause;
for this reason he adds, 'The first "why" is a cause and a principle'
[983a29]. For the final answer given in answer to the question 'why'   15
is a cause in the proper sense; but what is a cause in this way is
first among the [other] causes of this kind;[87] therefore, the final
answer given in answer to the question 'why' is the first cause
among the [other] causes of this kind. And if this last statement
were to be taken in conjunction with the [earlier] statement that
the definition is the final answer given to the question 'why', the
conclusion would be that the definition is first among the formal
causes. Therefore, the essence and the definition are the first cause,   20
i.e. the form, for each thing has its essence in virtue of its form.[88]
Or in saying, 'The first "why" is a cause and a principle', Aristotle
means, 'The first "why" ', i.e. the substance or essence, 'is cause and
principle and first', since the final answer given to the question
'why' is a first cause. Or he is saying that a cause and principle of   25
the things given as answers before it [i.e. the first cause] is among
those [contained] in the answer to the question 'why', since this
latter is the final answer given; for the final answer given to the
question 'why' is a first cause and principle. He did not say, however,
that the final answer given to the question ['why'] is first in nature,
but, without having [first] made this point, he states its sequel:
'The first "why" is a cause and a principle', and thus makes [the   30
sense of] the text obscure. For it is for this reason that the 'why' is
first, because scl. the final answer given to the question 'why' is in

---

[86] 21,11. At this point, Alexander gives a different interpretation to Aristotle's
text, taking *eskhaton* not as an adverb (finally), but as an adjective modifying
horismon (definition) (=Aristotle's *logon*). In the subsequent discussion, he suggests
three solutions to the difficulty that what is *eskhaton* (last) is also said to be *prôton*
(first); but his own conclusion is that Aristotle has omitted a step in the argument,
a lacuna that he supplies (21,28–31).

[87] 21,16. That is, of other formal causes, the point made explicitly at l. 20. Presumably, causes of the kind referred to in 21,3 are those of a more superficial kind.
Alexander seems to envision a series of answers to the question 'why', each of them
containing some reference to the form and all of them leading back to the ultimate
answer, that which states the form explicitly by way of definition. Thus the form is
'first' in the ontological order, but 'last' in the order of explanation. For a commentary
on these lines, see Owens, op. cit., 177.

[88] 21,21. On the relation between *eidos* and *to einai*, see further 64,30–1; 96,17–19;
135,18–24 below; Book 5, 357,25–9.

nature the first cause and principle.[89] But that the last answer to the question 'why' reveals the first cause is already evident from the fact that the question 'why' demands a principle [as an answer];

35   but the answer after which [one] no longer asks 'why' would be the principle in the proper sense, and the principle is what is first.

22,1   **983a29** We say that another of the causes is the matter and the substrate.

The term 'substrate' (*to hupokeimenon*) has greater extension than the term 'matter' (*hulê*), for the substrate in the divine [bodies] is not matter.[90]

983a31 We say that a fourth cause is the one opposed to this
5   latter,[91] that for the sake of which and the good; for this is the end of all coming-to-be and movement.

Having mentioned the efficient cause (*aition poiêtikon*), the one whence [comes] the origin of movement (*kinêsis*),[92] Aristotle says that the final cause is opposed to the efficient, in that the efficient cause exists before [the process of change], but the final cause comes
10   into being last. He makes this point clear by adding, 'for this is the end of all coming-to-be and movement', for if the efficient cause is a beginning and the final cause an end, they are plausibly [said to be] opposed. Now the end is a cause of the efficient cause, being last in generation (*genesis*)[93] but first in nature and in reason; for it is after we have first apprehended the end by reason that we begin the action because of it. Moreover, even in things that come into being by nature the end is a goal (*skopos*), and the goal exists before

---

[89] 21,32. Omitting *en têi . . . apodosei*, bracketed by Hayduck after Bonitz.

[90] 22,2. In his commentary on Book 2, Alexander again says that although the body whose motion is circular is a 'natural' body, its substrate is not matter (169,18–19); and in his commentary on Book 5 he says that the forms in the divine bodies are not *enula*, 'enmattered' (375,37–376,1). But according to Aristotle, such bodies do have *hulê topikê*, matter enabling them to change place (*Metaph.* 1042b5); and ps.-Alexander makes this point in the commentary on Book 12: 'All things that are sensible and corruptible, and all that are sensible but not corruptible, have matter, but a different matter. For the matter . . . of things that are ungenerated . . . is capable of change only with respect to movement' (673,27–31).

[91] 22,4. i.e. to the efficient cause. The text of *Metaphysics* in which Aristotle refers to the efficient cause (983a30) is not given as a lemma, although Alexander mentions this text in the commentary that follows.

[92] 22,8, *kinêsis*. Ross, and other more recent translators, give this term as 'change' as well as 'motion, movement'; but I adopt the latter, reserving 'change' for *metabolê*.

[93] 22,12. I translate *genesis* either as 'generation' or as 'coming-to-be', since there are contexts in which one or other of these terms seems more suitable. Similarly, I give *gignesthai* either as 'to come to be' or 'into being', or as 'to become', again according to the context.

[generation begins]. But that the good is the cause as end, and that   15
a principle of this sort is the end of all coming-to-be and movement,
he made clear (as I said before) at the beginning of the *Ethics* too,
saying: 'Every art and inquiry [is thought to aim at] some good'
[1094a1]. But if all things desire their appropriate end as a good,
that which is the sovereign end and which all the things in movement desire would be *the* good and the most excellent of all the
things that are. And this he himself made clear in the *Ethics* when   20
he said, 'And for this reason people have rightly asserted that the
good is that which all things desire' [1094a2].

Aristotle has now made the division of the causes, and intends
to investigate what sort of cause it is that the wise man in particular
should know. [But] since the causes [are spoken of] in various ways,
it is reasonable that he first reviews the opinions (*doxa*) of the   23,1
others who preceded him [to learn] to what sort of cause or causes
they had recourse. This procedure, he says, will also be advan-
tageous [in enabling] us to confirm the causes of which we have
spoken. For either we shall discover another type of causes as well, if
it is obvious that what was said about the causes by the early [philo-
sophers] does not fall under the division, or, if the causes of which   5
they spoke do not exceed the causes we have enumerated, we shall
then have greater confidence in the division as being sound.

983b6 Most of the early philosophers, then, [thought that only
the principles belonging to the class of matter are the principles
of all things].

Aristotle has himself clearly stated the reason why he now reports
what was said by the other [philosophers]. He mentions the ancients   10
not because they thought these [material] principles are the principles [only] of natural substances (for that inquiry would no longer
seem appropriate to the present subject-matter), but because they
thought them [the principles of] all the things that are, among
which the matters now under consideration are also [included].[94]
For they did make these principles of which he is speaking [the
principles] of natural things; but because they thought that only
these [material] things exist and that there is nothing beyond them,
they were seeking the same principles both for natural things and   15
for all the things that are. That they assumed only the material

[94] 23,11–13. This obscure statement seems to refer to Aristotle's remark (*Metaph.*
983a33) that the doctrine of the four causes has been dealt with adequately in the
Physics. Applying this statement specifically to the materialists, Alexander says
that an inquiry into the principles they invoked 'would not be appropriate to the
present subject-matter', i.e. metaphysics, were it not for the fact that the materialists
made these the principles not only of material substances but of all reality, and this
latter is indeed the subject-matter of metaphysics.

cause (*aitia kata tên hulên*) he makes clear by pointing out that they said that the cause and principle of the things that are is 'that from which something first comes to be and into which it is finally resolved, while the substance remains but changes its modifications'

20 [983b8]. But a thing of this sort is matter, which preserves its own reality (*ousia*) incorrupt (*aphthartos*) and ungenerated (*agennêtos*) in whatever things it might be [found], while the change (*metabolê*) it undergoes in its modifications (*pathê*) takes place in the generation of the things that come to be out of it.[95] (The statement that 'They thought that only the principles belonging to the class of matter [are the principles of all things]' means 'They thought that the only principles are those that belong to this class of principles that is related to matter'.) 'And for this reason they think that nothing is either generated or destroyed, on the ground that a nature of this sort is always preserved' [983b12]. The consequence,

24,1 for those who make matter a kind of body in actuality (*energeiai*) and not, as Aristotle says, potentially (*dunamei*), is that nothing whatever is either generated or destroyed (*phtheiresthai*) in an unqualified sense, but that generation so called is alteration (*alloiôsis*), as he showed in his treatise *On Generation* [1.4]. For [they say] that matter exists in actuality and is forever permanently

5 the same, since they assume that the principle is incorruptible and unchangeable in its substantial nature (*ousia*), and that it alters the modifications of the substances coming to be out of it; for alteration is change with respect to a modification.

Aristotle also records who [those philosophers] were who assumed only the material cause (*hê hulikê aitia*), according to whom what is called 'generation' in the proper sense is not preserved, [naming them] in sequence.[96] He says that Thales was the first of these (for

---

[95] 23,20–21. Reading *en têi ... genesei* for *en tois ... genesin* (Bonitz). This statement might seem to imply that the material principle of the early philosophers was in fact Aristotle's own 'material cause'; but as Ross points out, Aristotle himself does not credit the early philosophers with having recognized that cause in his sense of entirely formless matter (*Metaphysics* I, 128 ad 7). Alexander probably means only that the early philosophers did not understand the implications of their own theory. On *eidos* in this text, see Ilsetraut Hadot, 'Recherches sur les fragments du commentaire de Simplicius sur la Métaphysique d'Aristote', *Simplicius: sa vie, son oeuvre, sa survie*, Berlin 1987, 226.

[96] 24,8ff. A useful study of Alexander's treatment of the early Greek philosophers has been made by Winnie Frohn-Villeneuve: *Alexander of Aphrodisias as a Source for the Presocratics*, (unpublished) dissertation, University of Laval, Québec. Chapter II discusses every passage in Alexander's works in which he may be supplying new information on the Presocratics, and Appendix A lists all passages in which Alexander refers to the individual philosophers. Her general conclusion on the value of Alexander's testimony: '... [Alexander's] main preoccupation was to explain Aristotle ... It is evident that [his] main purpose is not to discuss the Presocratics but to clarify Aristotle's text. Alexander would not have seen any need for finding and consulting the Presocratics' texts directly' (262).

of those who are mentioned, this man seems to have been the
originator of natural philosophy (*hê phusikê philosophia*), and sets   10
forth his opinion clearly. By his example with reference to Socrates
he shows, in a way that can be understood, how generation is not
preserved according to those for whom the substrate is completely
actualized, preserving forever its proper substantial nature (*ousia*)
in whatever things it is [found]; for each of the things that come to
be out of it *is* the substrate in a certain state. 'For there must be
some nature, either one or more than one, from which the other   15
things come to be while it itself is preserved' [983b17] – this he
says [in reference both to those] according to whom there is one
substrate and matter, which, since it is something in actuality,
already exists independently; [and also to those] for whom the principles are more than one, as Aristotle also makes clear by what he
says next. But the principles are not the same even for those
according to whom they are more than one;[97] hence he says, 'But
they do not all agree about the number and kind of this sort of
principle; but Thales, the originator of this kind of philosophy, [says   20
the principle is water]' [983b18]. [By] 'this kind of philosophy' [he
means] the one that [treats of] nature in a theoretical way; for
[Thales] is the most ancient of the natural philosophers (*phusikoi*)
who are mentioned. Aristotle [says] that according to Thales water
is the principle, and adds a clear explanation of why [he made it
such]: because the nutriment of all things is moist, and each thing
has its being from its nutriment; and because the seeds of all things,
from which they have their generation, are naturally moist; and   25
because heat itself comes to be out of the moist. For the associates
of Thales held that heat and fire are generated from the exhalation
[arising] from the moist, and that in fact they are nourished by the
moist and [thus] both exist and are preserved; for this is [what
Aristotle means by] 'and are kept alive by it' [983b24]. Consequently the moist was, in their view, a principle and element
(*stoikheion*) even of heat, if indeed the latter is nourished by it and   25,1
comes to be out of it; for that from which the things that come to
be are generated is in fact their principle, so that water is the
principle even of fire if this latter is generated from it, and fire is
generated from water because it is nourished by it. 'Water is the

---

[97] 24,18. This remark is puzzling, because the Milesian monists who are the subject
here all postulated a single material principle, although naming this variously as
water, fire, etc.; and Aristotle, for his part, intends to distinguish this group from
the materialistic pluralists, whom he mentions only later. A reader has suggested
to me that *ou ta auta* in Alexander's text may mean that the result, for those who
posited more than one principle, was no different than that reached by those who
posited only one: that, scl., all these principles exist actually, and not only potentially, before generation begins. But the succeeding *dio* and quotation seem to run
counter to that interpretation.

principle of the nature of moist things' [983b27] means that water
is principle and nature and cause of the being of the things that
5   are moist. But if the moist is a principle of other things such as
even seeds, and water is a principle of moist things, [then] water
would also be a principle of things dependent on the moist. [He
says,] 'There are those who [include] in their account even the
ancient [poets]',[98] as if some people trace this opinion about water
back to the very earliest thinkers and to those who were the first
to say something about the gods; and he states how [they make this
10   connection]. He must be speaking about Homer and Hesiod, the
first mythologists (*theologoi*).[99]

983b32 For what is oldest is most honourable, and that by
which men swear is the most honourable thing.

What Aristotle wishes to prove is that those who assume that what
the gods swear by is water are assuming, in much the same way
as Thales, that water is a principle of the things that are. This we
15   learn through the following syllogism: it is cear that what is most
honourable and oldest is also a principle; but that by which men
swear is the most honourable, for when we swear an oath we invoke
what we consider most honourable; therefore, that by which men
swear is the oldest and a principle. But this was water; for according
to the mythologists, the river Styx [signified] water. The syllogism
in the text would seem to be in the second figure, containing two
20   affirmative premises, because he does not say, 'what is most honourable is oldest', but, 'what is oldest is most honourable'; and this
latter seems equivalent to 'The oldest is most honourable'.[100] If the
premise is stated thus, the syllogism is in the second figure, the term
26,1 'most honourable' being predicated affirmatively in both premises –
and such a syllogism does not conclude.[101] But in fact this is not

---

[98] 25,7. This quotation differs slightly from the text of *Metaph.* 983b27–8, which
reads: *eisi de tines hoi kai tous pampalaious kai polu, ktl.*, 'there are some who think
that even the very ancient (thinkers), those [who lived] long before the present
generation . . .' *Historousin* [include] in their account, which in the translation
appears as part of the quotation, is Alexander's own word.

[99] 25,10. 'Mythologists' is Ross' apt translation of *theologoi*, whom Alexander
describes, in his commentary on Book 3, as those who use myths in confirmation of
lies (219,6–9); cf. *in Meteor.* 66,13, where he explains that Aristotle uses the term
of those who make pronouncements about the gods.

[100] 25,21. Reading *tôi to presbutaton timiôtaton* for *tôi timiôtaton presbutaton*
(Bonitz).

[101] 25,21–26,1. According to this explanation, the presumably faulty syllogism
would be: What is oldest is most honourable; but that by which men swear is most
honourable; (no conclusion). Alexander's proposed revision of the syllogism is to
rewrite it in the first figure, thus: What is most honourable is oldest [and a principle];
but that by which men swear [i.e. water] is most honourable; therefore, that by
which men swear, [water,] is oldest [and a principle]. The bracketed additions are

the case: the argument is in the first figure, and the term 'most honourable' is predicated of 'that by which men swear', but is the subject of 'oldest'. He states [the argument] in this way on the ground that [the two terms] 'oldest' and 'principle' are convertible with reference to 'most honourable', and the statement is equivalent 5 to 'For what is most honourable is oldest'. He makes it clear that his statement is equivalent to this latter by adding, 'that by which men swear is the most honourable', thus ensuring that the term ['that by which men swear' would be referred] to 'the most honourable'.

983b33 Whether this opinion [about water] is ancient [is perhaps not clear].

He says this because it is not clear whether the first mythologists 10 held this opinion or not; for they did not say this outright, although some people attempt to prove the fact by a syllogism. But if they came to this conclusion by using [a syllogism] in the second figure with two affirmative premises, as seems to be the case with the argument stated, the matter is even less clear.

984a2 Thales at least is said to have expressed this opinion about the first cause. 15

The statement 'is said to have expressed this opinion' is reasonable, for no writing of his can be produced from which one can be certain that he said these things in this way.

---

necessary if the syllogism is to conclude to that which is to be proved, that scl. water is a principle. Note that Alexander's own syllogism, as reported in Hayduck's text (25,15–16), does not follow the above model: as a first premise it has *both* terms, 'most honourable' and 'oldest', as subject of still another term, 'principle', one not found in Aristotle's text; while in the conclusion, 'oldest' appears as the equivalent of 'principle'. (His final statement, 26,3–5, seems to be an attempt to justify this inclusion of 'principle' in the argument.) Since Alexander is explicitly criticizing the formal validity of the syllogism used to prove that water is the principle, the version of the argument given in the *alt. rec.* may be closer to his intent: 'Those who [attempt to] show that water is the principle of all things that are generated argue from the fact that water is that by which the gods swear, thus: that by which [the gods] swear is something honourable; but what is honourable is older. The conclusion [is], Therefore, that by which the gods swear is older. Then the additional minor premise: Water is that by which the gods swear, and the drawing of the [final] conclusion, [Therefore], water is what is oldest.' To complete the argument, a still further conclusion is needed: What is oldest is the principle of all things that are generated.

984a3 No one would think Hippo worthy of being included
20   among these men because of the triviality of his thought.

They report that Hippo assumed that the moist in an unqualified
sense is a principle without [making] any distinctions, not stating
clearly whether it is water, as Thales, or air, as Anaximenes and
Diogenes.[102] For this reason Aristotle also rejects his opinion on the
ground that it is superficial and makes nothing clear. Or he does
not reject Hippo's opinion on the ground that it is confused (for he
25   does not say, 'because of the triviality of his opinion'), but [dimisses
him] on the ground that he ought not to be numbered among the
philosophers because of the triviality of his thought; for it is for
27,1 this reason that he says, 'among these men', speaking of the philosophers. He might also say this about him because Hippo was an
atheist; for the inscription on his tomb ran thus:

> This is the monument of Hippo, whom fate
> Made equal to the immortal gods after his death.

5   Next Aristotle speaks of those who said that air is a principle,
positing this instead of water; these were Anaximenes of Miletus
and Diogenes of Apollonia. He says that Hippasus of Metapontium
and Heraclitus of Ephesus said that fire is the principle of all things.

984a8 Empedocles [says] that [the principle is] the four
10   elements, adding earth as a fourth to those already named.

For some of those who preceded Empedocles had assumed fire,
others water, still others air; to these three, then, he added earth
as a fourth.

984a9 For these, he says, always remain and do not come to
be except by becoming more or fewer, being aggregated into
one and segregated out of one.

15   Aristotle states how [they come to be by becoming] more or fewer.
For their commingling (*mixis*) and coming together into one thing,
brought about by friendship [*philia*], produced the change towards
fewness and unity, whereas their segregation and separation,

---

[102] 26,21–23 = DK I, 385, fr. 6. Ross notes that the other ancient sources who
mention Hippo say that his principle was specifically water rather than the vague
'moist' reported here by Alexander (*Metaphysics* I, 139 ad 3); and the *alt. rec.* says,
'For he too thought [the principle] water, as did Thales' (26). The *alt. rec.* also
explains the supposed atheism of Hippo as his refusal to make god the *dêmiourgos*
of the things that are; but according to ps.-Alexander, he was called 'the atheist'
'. . . because he asserted that there is nothing beyond sensible things' (*in Metaph.*
7, 462,29–31 = DK I, 386, fr. 9).

brought about by strife [*neikos*], made them many out of the one;
but he says this with the implication that the elements are able to
preserve their proper nature in a change of this sort. Or he does
not say this about the aggregation and segregation brought about   20
by friendship and strife, but about the generation and destruction
of the elements that [only] seem [to be such], for each of them
seems to come into being when a certain plurality of them has been
brought together at the same time; for whenever the parts of fire
in a particular mixture are greater in number [than those of the
other elements], it seems that the generation of fire is taking place,
but whenever the parts of fire are less, there seems to be the destruction of fire. Or the statement means that [the elements] themselves
do not come to be, but that a greater or lesser number of the things
that are comes to be out of their segregation and aggregation.[103]   25

984a11 Anaxagoras of Clazomenae was older than Empedocles, but inferior[104] to him in [the merit of] his works.

Aristotle says that Anaxagoras was earlier than Empedocles in his
works and inferior to him in his opinion about natural things. He   28,1
does not express complete preference for Anaxagoras' opinion as
being more intelligent than that of Empedocles and superior to it,
but thinks it inferior and less sophisticated. In other places, in fact,
he expresses a preference for Empedocles over Anaxagoras because
the former accounts for the same [phenomena] by assuming that
the principles are limited (*peperasmenos*) [in number];[105] for it is
better to make the principles limited rather than infinite (*apeiros*)   5
if one would be able to explain the same things by means of the

---

[103] 27,15–25. Of the three interpretations offered here, only the first two merit
serious consideration; see Ross, *Metaphysics* I, 131 ad 10, for a discussion of how
they differ. Ross believes that the first interpretation agrees better with fr. 17 of
Empedocles, which (he says) Aristotle is evidently paraphrasing.

[104] 27,26–7. The lemma correctly reproduces Aristotle's text: *Anaxagoras . . . têi
men hêlikiai proteros ôn toutou, tois de ergois husteros*, which Ross translates, 'Anaxagoras, though older than Empedocles, was later in his philosophical activity'. In
the commentary, Alexander understands *tois ergois* with both *proteros*, so that the
phrase means 'in his literary activity', and with *husteros* (28,1), where the phrase
has the sense of 'in the merit of his works', as I have translated the lemma, an
interpretation that Ross thinks probably correct (*Metaphysics* I, 132 ad 12). (David
Furley accepts Alexander's statement that Anaxagoras wrote before Empedocles:
The Greek Cosmologists I, Cambridge 1987, 72, n. 10.) Note, however, that later in
this commentary Alexander gives a different interpretation of the text: *husteros*
means either 'later in time' or 'more modern' (69,1–3). Pierre Aubenque comments
briefly on this text and its implications: *Le problème de l'être chez Aristote*, Paris
1966, 82.

[105] 28,4. See e.g. *Phys.* 188a17; 189a15; *de Gen.* 314a13. The following statement
(28,6–7) perhaps refers to *Metaph.* 989a30 (Alexander 68,6ff), but especially to
Anaxagoras' introduction of *nous* as a cause, *Metaph.* 984b15 (Alexander 32,9ff).

limited principles. There are of course texts in which Aristotle
even shows a preference for the opinion of Anaxagoras over that
of Empedocles. Here, however, it seems likely that he says that
Anaxagoras is 'inferior in the merit of his works' because of the
infinity of his elements; for after saying [that he is inferior] he adds,
10   'He says the principles are infinite'. Later on, however, he shows
that Anaxagoras's opinion agrees with that of Plato [989a30], who
came after him. For after explaining what Anaxagoras intended,
and [showing] that by what he says he might be calling the One
and the indefinite (*to aoriston*) 'principles', Aristotle adds: 'But he
intends something similar to what the later thinkers say, and to
what is now more clearly seen to be the case' [989b19]. 'For almost
all the things that are uniform, in the manner of water and fire'
15   [984a13] and each of the four bodies, seem to be generated by
aggregation and destroyed [by segregation]; for it is by the coming
together of a greater number of the elements that are similar that
each thing comes to be [as] this thing. It was in this way, he says,
that Anaxagoras thought that these uniform things (*homoiomerês*),[106] which are infinite in number and eternal, are generated
and destroyed: generated by the coming together of a greater
number of the elements that are similar, and destroyed by their
segregation. He says, '*almost* all the things that are uniform', for
20   Anaxagoras did not put all of them among the principles; he did
not, at any rate, say that water, fire, earth, and air are 'elements'
but 'compounds' (*sunkrima*) although they are uniform, as can be
learned from the clear evidence [of the senses].

984a16 From these, one might think that the only cause [is
the one called material].

[He means] from these causes that have been spoken of, for he
adduced [only] the material and corporeal principles. And yet he
29,1   referred to both Empedocles and Anaxagoras, who posited efficient
causes as well; but he mentioned these men also in making clear
what material causes they too employed in contrast to those [philos-
ophers] who preceded them, although he criticized them on the
ground that they used the efficient cause to the extent of talking

---

[106] 28,14, *homoiomerês*. In the *de Mixtione*, Alexander defines uniform things as
'things whose parts bear the same name as the whole' (235,5; translation of Robert
Todd, *Alexander of Aphrodisias on Stoic Physics*, Leiden 1976, 165); cf. Aristotle *de
Part. Anim.* 647b17. A number of translators give the term in its transliterated
form, but this itself requires an explanation, at least for readers not familiar with
Greek. 'Uniform', proposed by Peck (Aristotle, *Parts of Animals*, in the Loeb edition
(London 1937; revised 1945), 28, seems preferable to Ross's 'things that are made of
parts like themselves'.

about it, but did not include it [among the causes] in the generation of those things that they generate from the elements.[107]

984a18 But as men advanced in this way, [the very facts   5
pointed out the way].

He states why it was that men came to investigate the efficient cause after the material; for it was because there must be some cause [to account for] the change of the substrate into the things that come to be, for certainly nothing makes itself change without [there being] some cause outside it.

984a27 Now those who from the very beginning [engaged in this kind of inquiry . . . were not displeased with themselves].

He is again speaking of those who employed only the material cause   10
and principle. But it seems that he adds the words 'from the very beginning' to make it clear that he means the associates of Thales and Anaximenes, since Anaxagoras and Empedocles at least among those he has mentioned appear to have said something about the efficient cause as well, as Aristotle himself will note as he continues. 'They were not at all displeased with themselves': that is to say, they paid no attention to the absurdity of their statements, nor did   15
they find fault with what they said because it was not well said, nor did they look for any other cause beyond the material cause in the realization that even the cause of which they spoke was inadequate.

984a29 But some at least of those who say [the substrate] is one, as though defeated by this search, assert that the One is motionless.

Aristotle is speaking of Xenophanes and Melissus and Parmenides,   20
for these men declared that the universe (*to pan*) is one.[108] He says
they were defeated by this search because, once they had assumed   30,1
that the universe is one and began to inquire how it is possible for
this One to change from itself [to something else], they could no

---

[107] 28,24–29,4. The material causes of Empedocles and Anaxagoras are presumably in contrast to those of their predecessors because they are multiple, rather than the single principle of the Milesian monists. As for the rest of this laboured statement, the point is simply that Aristotle, although saying that the philosophers he has mentioned were concerned only with the material cause, has included Empedocles and Anaxagoras in this group, despite their having some notion of the efficient cause. Alexander says 'mentioned', but the texts to which he refers come later: *Metaph.* 985a18, 988b6.

[108] 30,1. Omitting *to*, bracketed by Hayduck.

longer keep it one unless they were to do away with things that
5   are obvious [to perception]; and they did eliminate from the things
that are those that are almost the most evident, movement and[109]
change, because, if these exist, being (*to on*) would no longer remain
one for them. After saying, 'they assert that the One is motionless',
he adds, 'and nature as a whole as well', for in their view nature
as a whole is the One. And to point out more clearly the absurdity
of their assertion that nature as a whole is motionless, he adds
[that it is] motionless not only with respect to generation and
destruction, but also with respect to all the other changes. (Gener-
10   ation and destruction are indeed changes, even though not movements – but some things are in motion [to produce them].)

984b1 None of those who asserted that the universe is one
succeeded in seeing a cause of this sort . . .

'A cause of this sort' is the efficient cause, for according to them
31,1   nothing whatever comes into being at all. Or Aristotle says this not
only about those who posited that the universe is one and motionless, but also about those who posited one substrate and one matter,
for they too made the universe one. Perhaps [we could infer] from
the present text that shortly before too, when he said, 'from these,
one might think that there is only one cause' [984a16], he was
5   speaking about those who assume that the element is one.

984b3 . . . except perhaps [Parmenides].

In the first book of his *On the Natural Philosophers*, Theophrastus
says this about Parmenides and his doctrine.

Parmenides of Elea, son of Pyres, the successor to this man (he is
speaking, in fact, of Xenophanes) took both ways; for he both declares
10   that the universe is eternal and also attempts to explain the coming-
into-being of the things that are, although he does not regard these
two things in the same light. But according to truth, he supposes that
the universe is one and ungenerated and shaped like a sphere, but in
accordance with the opinion of the majority of men [he attempts] to
explain the coming-into-being of perceptible things, making the principles two, fire and earth, the one as matter, the other as cause and
agent.[110]

[109] 30,4. Omitting *gar*, bracketed by Hayduck.
[110] 31,8–14 = Diels, *Doxographi Graeci* (editio quarta; reprinted Berlin, 1976),
482, fr. 6. See also his Prolegomena, 113; the text he there cites, in which Simplicius
quotes Alexander's account of Parmenides from his commentary on the *Physics*, is
38,18–28 in the CAG edition of Simplicius. On Theophrastus' *Peri phuseôs historia*,
from which the present passage in Alexander is taken, see O. Regenbogen,
'Theophrastos' in Pauly-Wissowa, *Real-Encyclopädie*, Suppl. 7, 1950, 1535–9; and

For this reason Aristotle says, 'except perhaps Parmenides', and [he   15
excludes him only] to the extent that he posited two causes, but not
inasmuch as he said that being is one.

984b5 But those who make the elements more than one are of
course better able to state [a second cause].

Obviously, as an efficient cause, too, in addition to the material
cause. Aristotle might not be speaking about those who directly
assumed an efficient cause too (these are Anaxagoras and Empedocles), but of those who say that the causes are more than one.   20
For it was possible for them to make one of these underlying causes
active, the other passive, as he said about Parmenides too. For one
who calls the principles hot and cold, or fire and earth, as does
Parmenides,[111] is speaking of heat and fire as an active cause.
For they assume that fire has a nature that enables it to impart
movement, but that water and earth and things of this sort have a
passive nature. (He might be speaking of air, or of the things that   25
are a mixture of these [two], water and earth.)

984b8 After these men and causes of this sort [men were again
forced to investigate the next kind of cause].

'These men' are the very ancient philosophers, and 'causes of this
sort' are the material ones. Aristotle might also mean, 'And after   32,1
those who located the efficient cause too among the material principles', because they realized that these latter principles are not
adequate to generate the nature of the things that are; for these
things participate (*metekhein*) in order and are seen to come into
being according to a certain sequence, but none of those [material
principles] could provide an explanation of such order. Nor was it
reasonable to make spontaneity (*to automaton*) responsible for this   5
order, and therefore they were seeking the cause of this sort of
generation, as if things themselves and the truth (*alêtheia*) in them
were showing them the way and forcibly leading them on. Now the
principle of generation that follows the material cause is the

more fully, Peter Steinmetz, 'Theophrasts Physik und ihr Verhältnis zu den
Phusikón doxai', in *Theophrastos von Eresos*, Bad Homburg 1964, 334–51, especially
on the variations of the title under which this work is reported.
    [111] 31,23. Ross thinks Alexander wrong in referring 'those who make the elements
more than one' to Parmenides, because of the opposition between this description
and that of 'those who asserted that the universe is one' (*Metaph.* 984b1); he believes
the reference is to Empedocles (*Metaphysics* I, 135 ad 5). In naming Parmenides'
two causes fire and earth, Alexander is anticipating Aristotle's remark at 986b34;
but, as Ross points out, the second cause is, for Parmenides, not earth but night (id.,
134).

efficient cause; and indeed, when Anaxagoras said that Mind (*nous*)
is the principle of the generation of the things that are, he came to
10 be admired, as if he alone were speaking rationally while the others
were talking at random because they spoke without reference to
this sort of cause. Aristotle adds, 'as in animals' [984b15]; for in
those animals that possess intellect (*nous*), this [faculty] is principle
and cause of the things that come to be in the right way through
their agency. Hence it seems, he says, that Anaxagoras was clearly
15 the first to arrive at a cause of this sort, although his fellow-citizen
Hermotimus might be thought to have mentioned it before him.
These men therefore posited, together with the efficient cause, the
principle [responsible for] the fact that things come to be in the
right and orderly way, and [made it] the cause of the things that
are (for Mind [is a cause] of this sort), and [said] that a movement
of this kind, one that leads to a good [end], is from the cause,
obviously the efficient cause. For they made a principle the cause
[responsible for the fact that things] not only come into being and
20 move, but do so in the right way; for Mind [is a cause] of this sort.[112]

---

[112] 32,16–21. Alexander takes Aristotle's reference to order, goodness, and beauty
to mean that Anaxagoras had in mind not only the efficient but also the final cause;
but Ross denies that Anaxagoras sought or envisioned a final cause: he explained
the order in things by a pre-existent reason that ordered them (*Metaphysics* I, 135
ad 8–11).

CHAPTER 4

Nevertheless, Aristotle says, one might suspect that before [Anaxagoras and Empedocles] Hesiod too had been inspired in this way, and anyone else who included love (erôs) or desire (epithumia) among the principles, as Parmenides also seems to say; and he cites the verses in which [Parmenides and Hesiod] say this. For love and 32,25 the desire for the beautiful (to kalon) would be the principle of 33,1 movement according to those who speak in this way. Hence these men put the cause of the things that are good among the principles; but whereas Anaxagoras [thought of] the good (to agathon) as efficient cause, [Parmenides and Hesiod,] when they make love and appetite responsible [for movement], might perhaps be speaking of the good as final cause, for the object of appetite (to orektikon) is of this sort. Or the object of appetite [might be] the final cause and love the efficient, if love produces its effects in response to desire. 5

984b29 [The words of Parmenides and Hesiod imply] that among the things that are there must be [a cause that will move things and bring them together].

Aristotle means those who spoke about love as a principle, inasmuch as they showed good sense [in doing so]; for they made love a principle because they realized that there must exist, among the things that are, some moving and efficient cause. There will be occasion later on, he says, to investigate who first touched on this sort of cause, whether it was Anaxagoras (as seems likely), or 10 Hermotimus before him, or even before Hermotimus the associates of Hesiod.

984b32 But since the contraries of the things that are good [were also obviously present in nature . . . another thinker introduced friendship and strife].

Aristotle has spoken about those [philosophers] who included among the principles the one that produces the good and the right [generation of things] – for intellect is [a principle] of this sort, since it has this role in those animals that possess it. [Now] he 15 states in turn what it was that motivated Empedocles to include among the efficient principles the principle too that produces evil things (ta kaka). For since evil things too exist among the things that are, Empedocles included among the causes not only the prin-

57

ciple of good things, which is friendship, but also the principle of evil things, which is strife. For if one were to extract the thought
20 from what he says, and not merely pay attention to [the literal sense of] his verses, he would find that so far as the latter are concerned, Empedocles postulated friendship and strife as principles, the former as the principle which produces good things, the latter as that which produces evil things. (Aristotle says that he 'lisps' because he did not speak clearly, for those who lisp babble in this way.) But if the cause of good things were to be good and that of evil things evil, Empedocles would be making good and evil
25 his principles, friendship the good, strife evil. (Since Aristotle has said this about the good, he leaves it to us to supply [the complementary statement] about evil.)

He says, then, that these men, Empedocles and Anaxagoras, as
34,1 well as Hermotimus, and Hesiod and Parmenides among the poets, made mention of an efficient cause in addition to the material. And these causes, he says, are the same as those we spoke about in our treatise *On Nature*, and do not fall outside them; however, [these men did not speak] clearly but vaguely, and made only limited use
5 of the efficient cause. And to show that they did so, he adds, 'It is obvious that they made almost no use of these causes, or used them in only a limited way' [985a17]. But he does credit Empedocles with having been the first both to divide the efficient cause and to employ the four bodies as material principles and elements; he says, however, that Empedocles did not give equal status to these principles, but set three of them, as being a single nature, in opposition
10 to fire, as is clear, he says, from his verses. He reminds us that Anaxagoras and Empedocles did not make use of the efficient cause, [thus] pointing out that he was correct in saying shortly before,
35,1 'From these, one might think that the only cause is the one called material' [984b16]. He says that Anaxagoras employed Mind as a *deus ex machina*, just as in tragedies the gods are dragged in by a stage device [to resolve] an impossible situation, a point which Aristotle himself has explained.[113] He says the same about Anaxagoras as did Plato too in the *Phaedo* [98Bff].

5 **985a21** Empedocles indeed makes greater use [of this cause].

He says that Empedocles made greater use of the efficient causes than did Anaxagoras, but that not even he employed them sufficiently nor maintained consistency. For he ought to have made

---

[113] 35,3. Aristotle does not in fact offer such an explanation in the present text of *Metaphysics* (985a18–20). Alexander may perhaps be referring to *Poetics* 1454a37–b2.

friendship the cause of aggregation and strife the cause of segregation in all cases; nevertheless, he did not do so, but often his
friendship segregates and his strife aggregates, and Aristotle states   10
in what circumstances [this happens]. For whenever [the
universe][114] has been dissolved by strife out of its unity into the
elements and is divided and separated, then the parts of the
elements that had until that time been intermixed with one another
(for it was thus that all things were one) are aggregated and brought
together into the same thing, the like parts of fire into fire and the
like parts of air into air, so that the parts of air are with one another   15
and those of fire in similar fashion. In the same way too the parts
of each of the other elements [are brought together], for it is thus
that the division of the one into its elements [takes place]. And in
this way strife is not, for Empedocles, the cause of separation any
more than of aggregation. Friendship in turn, on the contrary,
whenever it aggregates the same bodies and elements and brings
them together into one thing, first separates and cleaves and segregates them. For what friendship produces is certainly not [a state   20
in which the elements] are [homogeneous] wholes, each of them
being something by itself, for by contiguity with one another they
could be [united] in one thing under the influence of strife as well;
but [under the influence of friendship] they are blended together
with one another in a mixture.[115] For *this* is the effect that friendship produces, and not that of [mere] contiguity [of the parts] with
one another, an effect that could come about under the influence of
strife as well.

Next Aristotle reports the opinions of Leucippus and Demo-   25
critus[116] about the elements; this he sets forth clearly and [explains]

---

[114] 35,11. The subject of *diistêtai* could conceivably be [*ta moria*], but Alexander is
obviously paraphrasing *Metaph.* 985a25, *hotan eis ta stoikheia diistêtai to pan.*

[115] 35,19–22. The statement is confusing because *allêla* is used in two different
senses. In l. 21, Alexander means by 'one another' that all the parts of the *same*
element, e.g. fire, could be united into a homogeneous whole (*holoklêron*), and hence
be one thing; this is the effect that, as he has explained above, is produced by strife,
not by friendship. In l. 22, however, 'one another' refers to the *different* elements
brought together by friendship into the unity that is that of the universe or the One.
The *alt. rec.* brings out this point clearly: 'For [Empedocles] says that friendship is
the cause of aggregation, and strife the cause of segregation, but we see that the
opposite is often the case: that friendship, scl., is the cause of segregation, for it
segregates the [different] kinds [of elements] from matter, and produces the sphere
[i.e. the universe or the One]; and that, on the other hand, strife aggregates the
elements, for it brings together into one thing the fire that exists here and there in
a dispersed state in the sphere, and imposes the forms on matter and adapts them
to it' (34).

[116] 35,24. Alexander speaks favourably of Democritus in the *de Mixtione*, calling
him 'a lover of truth and a philosopher' (214,25; translation of Todd, *Alexander . . .,*
111); but in his commentary on the *Meteorologica* he says that Aristotle does not
bother to refute a certain opinion of Democritus, 'perhaps because of its superficiality'
(116,10–11).

both how it differs from that of the other [philosophers] and what
aspects of doctrine it has in common with theirs. They said that the
body of the atoms is full because it is solid and not mixed with the
36,1   void (*to kenon*). They named the full (*to plêres*) 'being' and the void
'not-being', [but] since in their view both the full and the void alike
were in existence, they said that the full does not exist any more
than the void. But he says that these men too posited only the
material principle, for thus their principles are the atoms and the
5   void. From these principles, according to them, the generation of
the other things too [comes about] in virtue of the differences of the
shape (*skhêma*) and order and position [of the atoms]; and they
called shape 'rhythm', order 'mutual contact', and position 'turning'.
Like the earlier philosophers, [the atomists] too thought the modifications of the material cause sufficient [to explain] the generation
of the things that are, but they said nothing about an efficient
cause, just as those who generate the other things by the rarefaction
10   and condensation of matter, except that these latter used two differences, rarefaction and condensation, to generate the things that
come to be out of matter, but [the atomists] employed the three
differences mentioned above: shape, order, and position.

Some manuscripts contain this reading: 'And these men too
proceed in the same way *as do the mathematicians*'.[117] If this were
the reading, Aristotle would be speaking about Plato, because as
15   Plato, in [attempting] to make bodies come into being from mathematical objects, generates the different bodies in accordance with
the different [shapes] of the triangles and their number [*Tim.*
54Aff], so [the atomists] also used the different shapes of the
primary bodies to generate the things [made] out of these latter.

985b19 But the question of movement, whence [it originates]
20   or how it belongs to the things that are, these thinkers too, like
the others, carelessly dismissed.

He is speaking of Leucippus and Democritus, for they say that the
atoms are in motion because they strike on and knock against one
another. But they do not say from what source natural things have
the beginning of their movement;[118] for the movement [produced]
25   by things striking one another is forced (*biaios*), but forced movement is subsequent to natural movement. Nor do they even say

[117] 36,13. A reference to *Metaph.* 985b12, where the modern text reads *arkhas
tithemenoi tôn pathêmatôn*, 'they made [the rare and the dense] principles of the
modifications'.

[118] 36,21–3. These lines are quoted, with a brief commentary, by W.K.C. Guthrie,
A History of Greek Philosophy, II, Cambridge 1965, 400–1; and by Furley, op. cit.,
149. See also Guthrie's quotation of 36,25–7, op. cit., 505.

what is the source of heaviness (*barutês*) in the atoms; for they say
that the partless particles conceived [as being] in the atoms, which
are their parts, are weightless, but how could weight (*baros*) come
to be from the combination of things without weight?[119] (Aristotle
has spoken about these matters at greater length in the third book
of *On the Heaven* [300b8ff].) He says, 'Like the others', because
neither had any of those [earlier philosophers] given an explanation   30
of the cause of movement, the one that is in natural bodies – at
least none of the other natural philosophers said anything about   37,1
movement, as he remarked in the *Physics* when he dealt with
movement [8.1]. [In saying,] 'With reference therefore to these two
causes' [985b20], he is speaking of the material and efficient causes.

---

[119] 36,21–37,2. For a careful evaluation of the reliability of Alexander's testimony
on the doctrine of the atomists, already judged mistaken by David Furley (*Two
Studies in the Greek Atomists*, Princeton 1967, 98–9), see D. O'Brien, 'Alexander:
the "parts" of atoms', *Theories of Weight in the Ancient World, I. Democritus, Weight
and Size*, Leiden 1981, 211–22. O'Brien concludes that '. . . [the] authority [of Alexander's argument], from an historical point of view, is obviously nil' (222). He includes
a translation of the present text of Alexander, as well as of passages from Alexander's
lost commentary on the *de Caelo* as reported by Simplicius.

CHAPTER 5

985b23 Along with these men and even before them . . .

37,5   **985b26** Since of these principles numbers are by nature first
. . .[120]

With reference to the Pythagoreans, Aristotle says that some of them were born before Democritus and Leucippus, others were contemporaries of these men. Or he says, 'Along with these men and before them', in reference not only to Democritus and Leucippus but to all the natural philosophers who have been mentioned
10   earlier; for the Pythagoreans were older than some of these but flourished at the same time as the others. Or [he means] rather that Pythagoras himself[121] came shortly before Democritus and Leucippus, but that many of those who heard him flourished at the same time as these men. He says that the Pythagoreans, having been brought up in the study of mathematics, made mathematical principles the principles of the things that are. But numbers are the principles of mathematics, and according to the Pythagoreans
15   numbers are by nature first because the other [mathematical objects result] from addition (*prosthesis*); for extended things take on the additional [property] of position, as Aristotle has already mentioned.[122]

> **985b26** But since of these principles numbers are by nature first [that the elements of numbers are the elements of all things, 985a11].

Having said that the Pythagoreans, because they had been brought up in the study of mathematics, thought that mathematical prin-

[120] 37,4–5. The lemma combines portions of two texts from *Metaphysics* that do not belong together (985b23, 985b26), and the second of these is repeated as the lemma introducing the next section of the commentary (17–18 below). The first text has *heôs* after *pro toutôn*; *heôs* is not found in Aristotle's text, and makes little sense in this combination. It may be a variant for *pro*: 'along with these men and until them'. As Alexander quotes the text in the commentary (7–8), *heôs* is omitted.

[121] 37,10. References to Pythagoras himself are infrequent in the commentary, the doctrine reported being referred to 'the Pythagoreans' or 'those about Pythagoras'. Thus the following text from ps.-Alexander *in Metaph.* 14 is of some interest: 'Pythagoras and Plato, even though they differ with regard to matter, are nevertheless in agreement about form, for both of them sing the praises of the One' (797,10–12).

[122] 37,15. This is probably an inexact reference to *Metaph.* 982a26, where Aristotle speaks of *prosthesis*, 'addition', to describe a science that involves principles beyond first principles. His example is geometry in comparison with arithmetic: numbers, the object of arithmetic, are 'first' as being the simplest mathematical objects; plane and solid exist only by addition to numbers.

ciples are the principles of all the things that are, Aristotle next
states what reasoning they used to arrive at this conclusion. (There   20
would be better correspondence between [the parts of] the text if
'for' were substituted for 'but'.) For numbers are by nature first
among the things that are (for they are from abstraction (*aphairesis*)), and [the Pythagoreans] imagined they could see in numbers
many resemblances (*homoiôma*) to the things that are and that
come into being, and [this] in numbers more than in the simple
bodies; and they saw that the ratios (*logos*) and modifications of the   38,1
musical scales (*harmonia*)[123] are in numbers. Since [then] all the
other things have a resemblance to numbers,[124] and numbers are
first of the whole of nature, i.e. of all the things that are and that
are constituted according to nature, they made the principles of
numbers the principles of all the things that are.[125] They thought   5
that resemblances to the things that are and that come into being
are in numbers rather than in those bodies we call 'elements', such
as earth and the others that Aristotle also mentions [985b28];[126] for
this reason they reduced the things that are to numbers, and said
that these, not the [four] bodies, are the elements of things.

What resemblances they said there are in numbers to the
things that are and that come into being Aristotle showed [in his
treatise *On the Pythagoreans*].[127] For since they assumed that re-

---

[123] 38,1, *harmonia*. This term means, in general, a 'fitting together', and in music,
'tuning'. It must be translated in different ways according to the context; in addition
to its technical sense of 'scale' or 'octave', it has the more general sense of 'concordance' or 'concordant interval' that occurs frequently in the translation. It does *not*
mean 'harmony' in our sense of this term (cf. *sumphônia*, 89,4, and n. 273), but that
translation is used, in deference to the tradition, when there is reference to the
Pythagorean doctrine of 'the harmony of the spheres'; see J.A. Philip, *Pythagoras
and Early Pythagoreanism*, Toronto 1966, 123 and 128, n. 1; Walter Burkert, *Lore
and Science in Ancient Pythagoreanism*, English translation by E. Minar, Harvard
1972, 390; and Hans Schavernoch, *Die Harmonie der Sphären*, Freiburg 1981, esp.
41–7. On the meaning and role of *harmonia* in Greek musical theory, see R.P.
Winnington-Ingram, *Mode in Ancient Greek Music*, Cambridge 1936; repr.
Amsterdam 1968), esp. 56–61; Burkert, op. cit., 369–71; Jacques Chailley, *La
musique grecque antique*, Paris 1979, 23–58; and Andrew Barker, *The Harmoniai:
Greek Musical Writings* I, Cambridge 1984, 163–8.

[124] 38,2–3. Do the Pythagoreans wish to stress that numbers resemble things, or
things numbers? The propositions are of course convertible, but Aristotle's statement
(*Metaph.* 985b27), which Alexander reports accurately at 37,22, is that the resemblances to things are found in numbers. Here, however, Alexander says that the
resemblances to numbers are in things.

[125] 38,5. Supplying *pantôn tôn ontôn arkhas* for the lacuna (Brandis); cf. LF 38
ad 7.

[126] 38,7. The text reads: *hoion gês kai tôn allôn epênenke*, which seems grammatically impossible. I therefore read: *hoion gên kai ta alla ‹ha› epênenke*.

[127] 38,8–41,15 = Ross, *Fragmenta Selecta*, 138–41; Ross, *Select Fragments*, 141–5;
ROTA II, 2443–5. Alexander's sources for the information in this passage are
discussed by Wilpert, op. cit., 371–6.

10   quital[128] or equality is a property of justice, and found that this was
in numbers, they therefore said that justice is the first equal-times-
equal [i.e. square] number; for they thought that what is first in
every [class] of things that have the same formula is most [truly]
that which it is said to be. But some [Pythagoreans] said that this
15   number is 4, since, as the first square number, it is divided into
equals and is itself equal (for it is twice 2), while others said that
it is the number 9, which is the first square number produced from
an odd number (3) multiplied by itself. They said, again, that the
number 7 is opportunity (*kairos*), for natural things seem to have
their seasons of completion, both of birth and of maturity, according
to [periods of] seven, as in the case of man. For a man is born seven
months [after conception], and cuts his teeth after the same number
20   of months, and reaches puberty at about the end of the second
period of seven years, and grows a beard at about the end of the
third. The sun too, since it is itself thought to be (he says)[129] the
cause of the seasons,[130] they say is situated [in the place] where the
number 7 is, which they call 'due season' (*kairos*); for they say that
the sun occupies the seventh place [from the periphery] among the
ten bodies that move around the centre, or hearth. For the sun,
39,1 they say, moves after the sphere of the fixed stars and after the five
spheres of the planets; after it is the moon, eighth, and the earth,
ninth, and after earth the counter-earth.[131]

Now since the number 7 neither generates any of the numbers
in the dekad[132] nor is generated by any of them, they called it
5   'Athene'. For 2 generates 4, 3 generates both 9 and 6, 4 generates
8, and 5 generates 10, and 4, 6, 8, 9 and 10 are generated; but 7
neither generates any number nor is generated from any; so too

---

[128] 38,10–11, *to antipeponthos*. See Aristotle, *EN* 1132b21: 'Some think that
requital is without qualification just, as the Pythagoreans said; for they defined
justice without qualification as requital to another.' Guthrie notes that '*to antipeponthos* was in use as a mathematical term meaning "reciprocally proportionate"'
(op. cit. I, 303, n. 2).

[129] 38,21, *phêsi*. Bonitz proposed to change this unexpected insertion to *phusei* (by
nature); but Wilpert argues that *phêsi*, and *edeiknue* (used to prove) at 40,18, are
convincing evidence that Alexander is quoting directly from Aristotle's lost treatise
on the Pythagoreans (op. cit., 374). Guthrie thinks the subject of *phêsi* might possibly
be Pythagoras, but that it is more probably Aristotle. In his translation, Ross
understands Pythagoras as the subject of *edeiknue* (40,18), and the imperfect
supports this assumption.

[130] 38,21, *tôn kairôn*, 'the seasons'. Hayduck adopts this reading from Asclepius,
although the MSS and Bonitz have *karpôn*, 'crops'.

[131] 38,23–39,3. The meaning of *hestia*, 'hearth', becomes clearer at 40,31–2.
According to the present text and 40,27–41,1, the Pythagoreans numbered the heavenly bodies or spheres from the outermost inwards; but in a later passage (74,12–16),
Alexander counts from the centre outwards. On this point see J.E. Raven, *Pythagoreans and Eleatics*, Amsterdam 1966, 169–71, and Burkert, op. cit., 40, n. 64.

[132] 39,3, *hê dekas*, i.e. the numbers 1 to 10. The term is translated thus by Julia
Annas, *Aristotle's Metaphysics, Books M and N*, Oxford 1976, 223.

Athene was motherless and forever a virgin. They called the
number 5 'marriage' because marriage is the union of male and
female, and according to them male is the odd and female the even,   10
and 5 is the first number generated from the first even number, 2,
and the first odd number, 3; for as I said, the odd is, in their view,
male, and the even female. The number 1[133] they called 'mind' and
'substance, for he[134] spoke of soul as 'mind'. Because mind is stable
and everywhere alike and sovereign, they called it 'unit' or 'one';   15
but they also [gave these names to] substance because substance is
primary. The number 2 they called 'opinion' because it can move
in both directions, but they also referred to it as 'movement' and
'addition'.[135]

Selecting such resemblances as these between things and
numbers, they assumed that numbers are the principles of things,
saying that all the things that are are composed of numbers. But
seeing that the concordant intervals (*harmonia*) too are composed   20
according to particular numbers,[136] they said that numbers are the
principles of these concordances as well; for the octave is in the
ratio 2:1, the fifth in the ratio 3:2, the fourth in the ratio 4:3. They
also said that the whole celestial system (*ouranos*) is composed
according to a kind of musical scale (for this is what Aristotle is
pointing out when he says, 'And the whole heaven is a number'
[986a2]), because it is [made up] of numbers both numerically and
musically. For the bodies moving around the centre have the inter-   25
vals [separating them] in a [mathematical] proportion, and some of
them move more rapidly, others more slowly, and in their motion
they produce a sound – the slower bodies a deep note, the faster
bodies a high note. Because these notes are in proportion to the
intervals separating the bodies, they make the sound resulting from   40,1

---

[133] 39,13, *to hen*. Ross translates 'the One', as he also renders *to hen* in his translation of *Metaph*. 986a19: '. . . the One proceeds from both of these [scl. the even and
the odd], . . . and number from the One.' (The former version is retained in ROTA,
which however changes 'the One' to 'the 1' in the latter.) But Alexander's equation
of *to hen* with *monas*, 'unit', both here and in his subsequent references to *Metaph*.
986a19 (41,29–30 and 47,10–12 below), shows that he understands *to hen* as the
number 1.

[134] 39,14, *eipe*. Ross prints this singular in his edition of the *Fragmenta Selecta*,
but translates, 'Reason, which was the name *they* gave to soul' (italics added),
thus reading *eipon* with Asclepius. Guthrie translates, 'For soul he [presumably
Pythagoras] classified with mind' (op. cit., I, 304). Burkert also reads *eipe*, but thinks
that Aristotle is the subject, and that Alexander is correcting Aristotle's *psukhê kai
nous*, *Metaph*. 985b30 (op. cit., 467, n. 4).

[135] 39,16–17. 'It' in the translation is purposely ambiguous. *Metablêtên*, feminine,
would seem to refer to *doxan* (opinion), with the meaning, 'Opinion can fluctuate
both ways'; but the subsequent *autên*, a clear reference to *ta duo* (two), may indicate
that both feminines are such by attraction. 2 is called 'addition' (*epithesis*) because
it results from the addition of 1 to 1.

[136] 39,19–20. Reading *kat' arithmous tinas* for *kat' arithmon tina* (Ascl.).

them harmonious; and since [the Pythagoreans] said that number is the principle of this harmony, they naturally made number the principle both of the heavens and of the universe.[137] For they thought[138] that the distance of the sun from the earth is, let us say, twice that of the moon from the earth, that of Venus three times,

5   that of Mercury four times, and that there is a certain numerical ratio for each of the other [heavenly bodies], and that the movement of the heavens is harmonious; and that the bodies travelling the greatest distance move most rapidly, those travelling the shortest distance most slowly, and that the intermediate bodies move in proportion to the size of their orbit.[139]

On the basis, then, of these resemblances to numbers in the

10 things that are, [the Pythagoreans] supposed that the things that are are composed of numbers and are [in fact] numbers of some sort. And since they thought that numbers are prior to nature as a whole and to the things that exist by nature (for none of the things that are could either be or be known at all without number, whereas numbers can be known without reference to the other things), they

15 made the elements and principles of numbers the principles of all the things that are. These principles were, as we have said, even and odd; and of these they thought the odd limited, the even unlimited; the principle of numbers they thought to be the unit, since it is composed of the even and the odd. For [they said] that the unit is at the same time even-odd, something that [Pythagoras][139a] used to prove from the fact that it is capable of generating

20 both the even and the odd number; for added to an even number it generates an odd, and added to an odd number it generates an even. 'And whatever agreements they could find in numbers' or in concordant combinations 'to the attributes and parts of the heavens' [986a3], these they straightway took as obvious, attempting to prove [from them] that the heavens are composed of numbers in the manner of a musical concordance. But if any of the celestial

25 phenomena seemed not to conform to the implications of numerical theory, they themselves supplied such missing elements and tried

---

[137] 39,22–40,11. This passage is translated by Guthrie, op. cit., I, 296. On Alexander's account of 'the harmony of the spheres', which contrasts with that given by Plato, see Burkert, op. cit., 336.

[138] 40,3–9. In his translation of the fragment, Ross makes these lines part of the doctrine of the Pythagoreans, presumably as reported by Aristotle. But Guthrie considers them an attempt by Alexander to offer an illustration of the Pythagorean theory as he understood it (op. cit., I, 301); and Burkert believes that Alexander is here supplementing Aristotle's account. 'If Aristotle had credited the Pythagoreans with an unambiguously described scale, Alexander would not have used a fictitious example' (op. cit., 354).

[139] 39,27–40,1. Guthrie translates, and comments on, this passage (op. cit., I, 288). See also Philip, op. cit., 129, n. 3.

[139a] 40,18, *edeiknue*. See n. 129.

to fill in the gaps, to insure that their whole treatment would be consistent throughout. From the outset, at any rate, they considered 10 the perfect number, but seeing that, in what appears to the eye, the moving spheres are nine in number – seven spheres of the planets, an eighth that of the fixed stars, a ninth that of earth (for they thought, in fact, that earth too moves in a circle around the stationary 'hearth', which, according to them, is fire) – they themselves added, in their theory, a counter-earth as well, which they assumed to move in a direction opposite to that of the earth, and for this reason to be invisible to those on earth.

Aristotle discusses these matters both in his treatise *On the Heaven* and, with greater precision, in his [collection of] the doctrines of the Pythagoreans. As he has already said, they made the arrangement of the celestial bodies harmonious by supposing that the ten moving bodies which make up the universe (*kosmos*) are separated from one another by concordant intervals, and that they move [at a velocity] proportionate to the distances separating them, some of them more rapidly, others more slowly. [And they supposed] that the bodies moving more slowly produce deeper notes, those moving more rapidly higher notes, and that because these notes are produced in harmonious proportions, there results from them a harmonious sound, which however we do not hear because we have been familiar with it from childhood. Aristotle also discussed this theory in his treatise *On the Heaven* [2.13], where he showed that it is not true. As for the fact that the even is, in their view, the unlimited and the odd the limited, and that these are principles of the unit (for the unit, being from these, is even-odd) and moreover of all number, if indeed the units are in turn the principles of numbers; and that the whole heaven, i.e. all the things that are in the heavens, which is to say [all] the things that exist, are number – this he says here too, but he has spoken of the subject more fully in those other places.

986a13 But the reason for our entering on this inquiry [is that we might learn from these philosophers too what they think the principles are].

Aristotle reminds us of the utility of the foregoing account for the present inquiry, for it is useful to see to which of the causes the Pythagoreans too reduced their principles. It is certainly obvious from their own statements, he says, that for them number was a principle of the things that are such as matter is, since they generated all the other things from the combination of numbers. But the words, 'as modifications and states' [986a17], might indicate that for [the Pythagoreans] numbers are responsible for generating both

the modifications and the states, since it is in virtue of the differences in numbers that both the modifications and the states come
25 to be in the things composed out of numbers. For the modifications
and states of numbers, e.g. [the ratios] 2:1, 4:3, and 3:2, are causes
of the modifications and states in the things that are.[140] Or, as
Aspasius[141] [explains], number is matter, the even is modification,
and the odd is state. Or the even number is matter and modification,
the odd number state. What Aristotle adds to this statement is,
however, clear: that according to [the Pythagoreans], the odd
30 number is limited, the even number unlimited, and the 1 is from
both of these; for this reason the unit is both even and odd. [He
says] too that number is generated from the 1, composed as it is
out of odd and even, and [explains] how; for this is as we have
already stated [40,11ff].

But he reports that certain Pythagoreans assumed the principles
to be ten oppositions, since in their view ten is also the first perfect
number; these opposites they arranged according to columns of a
35 sort into which they fitted too the things that are; and he lists what
these oppositions are. For they are limit and unlimited, odd and
42,1 even, one and plurality, right and left, male and female, resting
and moving, straight and curved, light and darkness, good and
evil, square and oblong. He reports that Alcmaeon of Croton also
expressed the same view about the principles as these [Pythago-
5 reans,] for he too attempted to reduce each of the things that are to
some form of opposition, in the belief that the oppositions are principles. But he differed from the Pythagoreans because the latter,
by making the oppositions ten [pairs], articulated them with precision,
whereas Alcmaeon called any chance opposition a principle without setting any limits, and in this way every opposition would be a
principle for him. The assertion that the principles of the things
that are are opposites is therefore common to the Pythagoreans
10 who held this theory and to Alcmaeon, but [to have stated] how many
and what these principles are is peculiar to the Pythagoreans.

Aristotle further reports that [the Pythagoreans][142] called number

[140] 41,21–28. Ross thinks that none of the interpretations suggested by Alexander
really explains how numbers can be principles as being 'modifications and states'. His
own explanation is that Aristotle's *pathê te kai hexeis* is a hint that the Pythagoreans
'thought of numbers as in some sense formal as well as material causes' (*Metaphysics*
I, 147 ad 17).

[141] 41,27. On Aspasius, see Paul Moraux, *Der Aristotelismus bei den Griechen* II,
Berlin 1984, 226ff; and H.B. Gottschalk, 'Aristotelian philosophy in the Roman
world', *Aufstieg und Niedergang der römischen Welt* 36.2, Berlin 1987, 1156–8. The
present text is analyzed by Moraux, 246–7. Philip calls Aspasius' interpretation
'impossible' (op. cit., 97, n. 4).

[142] 42,12, *elegon*. The subject seems to be the Pythagoreans of whom Aristotle first
spoke (*Metaph.* 986a15–17), and to whom he reverts at 986b4–7; it is this latter text
to which Alexander now refers.

a principle and cause as matter [is a cause] – not as if any of them expressed this view unequivocally (for he himself says that none of them spoke clearly about these matters), but as a conclusion that follows from their explicit statements; for they do assert that all the things that are are composed and constituted out of the numbers existing in them. It is reasonable for him to apply the term 'to   15 have been fabricated' (*peplasthai*) to this kind of generation, for generation of this sort resembles a fiction (*plasma*) because it has no rational basis whatever.

986b8 [From this we can sufficiently understand the thought] of those ancient philosophers who said that the elements of nature are more than one.

He is referring to the elements of the things that come into being   20 naturally. By 'more than one' he either means the material elements, or he is saying that 'the elements' are more than one instead of 'the causes', for, as he reported, some [ancient philosophers] spoke of the efficient cause in addition to matter. After his account of these [pluralists], he again mentions those thinkers who posited that being (*to on*) is one – not one principle, as some of the natural philosophers [said], but in the sense that the universe is one entity (*phusis*). Among these were Xenophanes, Melissus, and   25 Parmenides,[143] but he says that an account [of their doctrine] is of little value for the investigation into principles and causes. For they did not posit the One as principle or cause in the way in which those who spoke of water or fire or air [as cause], then generated the other things from its movement; but [the Eleatics] said that being is one and immobile. Aristotle does, however, report in addition how Melissus and Parmenides differed with respect to the One, for although both declared that the universe is one, they did   43,1 not express themselves about it in the same way, 'either in the excellence of their statement or in what is in conformity with nature' [986b12]. [He says,] 'in what is in conformity with nature', because one of them looked on nature as matter, the other as form; and, 'in the excellence of their statement', because one of them spoke better, the other less well, and one of them more reasonably, the other less so. For Parmenides, he says, was looking to the form   5

---

[143] 42,24–5. In his commentary on Book 4, Alexander expands somewhat on Aristotle's reference to Xenophanes (108,11–14); in his commentary on the *Prior Analytics* he gives a critique of Parmenides' argument (357,1–10); and in his commentary on the *Topics* he ascribes this argument to both Melissus and Parmenides, referring to Aristotle's criticism in the *Physics* (567,16–25). See Winnie Frohn-Villeneuve, 'Space, time, and change: Alexander's interpretation of Melissus', *Mélanges d'études anciennes offerts à M. Lebel*, Québec 1979, 173–86; the author includes the Alexander-fragments contained in Simplicius.

and the definitory formula when he declared that being is one, and for this reason limited as well (for the effect of the definitory formula or form is to limit that in which it is present); but Melissus leaned towards matter, and therefore assumed that being is also unlimited, for infinity belongs to matter.[144]

10   **986b17** But this much at least is appropriate to our present inquiry.

He says that it is not appropriate to his discussion of the causes to set forth the other aspects of the doctrine of those who say that the
44,1   universe is one, for those who speak in this way do not posit the One as either principle or cause. But the account even of these men is useful, he says, to the extent that one of them, looking to the matter, said that being is unlimited, while the other, looking to the form, said that it is limited; so that even if these men do not speak
5   of any cause, nevertheless the things of which they do in fact speak and towards which they were tending[145] are among the causes that have been enumerated.

He criticizes Xenophanes on the ground that, although he was the first to embrace this opinion (for Parmenides, he says, was his pupil), he did not even grasp the nature of either of these [causes], therefore neither form nor matter, but, 'gazing on the whole world', simply proclaimed that 'the One is god' [936b24]. (The term
10   'reducing to one' (*henisas*, 986b21) is equivalent to saying that Xenophanes was the first to say that being is one.) But Aristotle praises Parmenides on the ground that he stated the thesis that being is one in a more rational way than Xenophanes and Melissus, for he employed a kind of syllogistic argument to prove this assertion, whereas they expressed themselves in rather crude fashion. The argument which he employed is this: he assumed that what is over and beyond being is not being, just as what is over and beyond white is not white, and that not-being is nothing; and
15   on the basis of these assumptions he thought that it followed of necessity that being is one. Such, then, is the plausible character of his argument; but Aristotle has discussed these matters in greater detail in the first book of the lectures [entitled] *Physics* [186a22ff], a passage to which here too he refers us. [The argument

---

[144] 43,9. The *alt. rec.* adds this pertinent comment: '[Melissus] was not correct in assuming that the One is infinite, for there is no knowledge of the infinite.'

[145] 44,5, *kath' ha kinêthentes*. The sense of this is not clear. The meaning might be 'what motivated them', a sense of *kineisthai* found at 32,23 and 33,15; but *kata* suggests the meaning adopted in the translation.

is false,] for being is homonymous (*homônumos*),[146] and even if it be taken as signifying one nature, one could not prove even in this way that being is numerically one. Again, the conclusion of the argument is that what is over and beyond being is nothing,   45,1 certainly not that it is one or not-one;[147] and the converse of this proposition is not that being is one, but that the One is being.

Aristotle also reports the two-fold opinion of Parmenides, who, being forced to follow [sensible] phenomena as well [as reason], said that being is one according to reason and truth, but more than one according to sense perception. In accordance with this latter   5 opinion, he said that the universe is generated, and assumed two principles, fire and earth, of it and of the things that exist in this way.[148] He called fire being, earth not-being as well as the cold, so that it was not only Democritus and Leucippus who located being and not-being among the principles. But perhaps Parmenides called the cold not-being inasmuch as cold [resembles] a material cause more [than does fire], and matter seems to be a kind of not-being.

987a2 And from the wise men who have now sat with us in   10 this council [we have got this much].

'Those who have sat with us' means those who have investigated and pondered the matters about which we are speaking. Or, 'the wise men who have sat with us in this council', are those of whom we have spoken; for he would be saying that those whom he has already mentioned have sat in council with us and been present, as it were, at this discussion. [In saying,] 'from the first philosophers', he reminds us that of the ancient philosophers of whom   15

---

[146] 44,17. I have adopted 'homonymous' and 'synonymous', the transliterated forms of *homônumos* and *sunônumos*, rather than translating these terms as 'equivocal' and 'univocal', because of difficulties created by these latter at various points in Alexander's commentary. See the discussion of J.L. Ackrill, *Aristotle's Categories and De Interpretatione*, Oxford 1963, 71, and that of C.J.F. Williams, *Aristotle's De Generatione et Corruptione*, Oxford 1982, 113. Readers will be familiar with Aristotle's explanation of the terms at the beginning of *Categories*, summarized thus by Ackrill: 'Roughly, two things are homonymous if the same name applies to both but not in the same sense, synonymous if the same name applies to both in the same sense.' But as Alexander will use the terms later, especially in the critique of the Ideas, 'synonymous' emphasizes the fact that two things share the same nature or essence.

[147] 45,1. Hayduck's text, *ou mên hen ê mê on*, yields no satisfactory sense. I therefore adopt the reading of the *alt. rec.*: *ou mên hen ê oukh hen* (44,17). After repeating the converse of the proposition, LF continues: 'For the one is opposed to not-one, and being to not-being; therefore, if not-being [adopting Hayduck's *mê on* for *mêden*] is nothing [i.e. is not-one, an etymological reduction of *mêden* to *mê hen*, not-one], the one is being.'

[148] 45,6, *tôn houtôs ontôn*. This is obscure; 'in this way' might refer back to *tên aisthêsin* (l. 4), hence mean 'as perceptible', or more immediately to *genêtos* (l. 5), hence mean 'as generated'. The translation adopts the latter alternative.

he has spoken, the more ancient, i.e. the first, made their principle corporeal and material, as Thales water, Hippasus and Heraclitus fire, and the things similar to these; for (as he has said) Anaximenes and Diogenes posited air as a principle. Anaximander too would belong to this group, positing as he did an intermediate nature, an opinion that Aristotle mentions in the treatise *On Generation*

20   [328b35, 332a20]. Both Leucippus and Democritus are to be included among these, for they too posited that the principles are material. 'And some of them posited one [material principle], others more than one' [987a5]. Some posited one principle, as Thales, Anaximenes, and Heraclitus, others more than one, as those associated with Leucippus and Democritus; for according to all these men, and Parmenides as well, the material principles are more than one.

25   'But from some who posit both this cause and in addition the cause that is the source of movement' [987a7] – 'this cause' is the material one. He says that those who posited, in addition to the material cause, the cause that is the source of movement were Anaxagoras

46,1 and whoever [else] put Mind among the principles as an efficient principle; and also Empedocles, who, adding friendship and strife to the four elements, which for him were matter, used them as principles. Hence Aristotle says that one man posited one efficient principle, with reference to Anaxagoras, but the other two; for this was Empedocles.

5   **987a9** Down to the Italians, then, and apart from them, philosophers have spoken rather moderately.[149]

He calls the Pythagoreans 'Italians', for it was in Italy, at Tarentum,[150] that Pythagoras established their school. After saying, 'Down to the Italians', he adds, 'and apart from them', so that we

10   might not include them too among the opinions that have been mentioned, since it is possible to understand 'down to' someone as if the one of whom 'down to'[151] [is said] were being numbered among those before him. Aristotle would not, however, be saying 'down to' in a chronological sense, for Empedocles was not prior to Pythagoras, yet Aristotle mentions his opinion as being among [the

---

[149] 46,5. The lemma has *metrióteron*, 'rather moderately'; but Alexander himself seems to have read *monakhóteron*, 'too monistically' (46,23), for which he reports as a variant *morukhóteron*, 'more obscurely', the reading of the modern text of *Metaphysics*. At 46,16 we find *malakóteron*, 'too loosely'; but as Brandis remarks, Alexander's exegesis of the text at this point suggests that *monakhóteron* is the correct reading here as at 23 below. On *morukhóteron*, apparently a *hapax legomenon*, and Alexander's interpretation of it, see Ross, *Metaphysics* I, 155 ad 10.

[150] 46,7, *en Taranti*. Pythagoras founded his school at Croton, but it was re-established at Tarentum in the fourth century.

[151] 46,11. Reading *mekhri hou* for *mekhri ou* (Hayduck).

opinions] of those who were 'down to the Italians'. But 'down to'
refers to the numerical order [in which he lists] the opinions of those
whose opinions he recounts; for he mentioned first the opinions of
those [others], then mentions in this way that of the Pythagoreans. 15
He says that down to the doctrine of the Pythagoreans most [philos-
ophers] had spoken too loosely about cause, i.e. had used only one
cause (the material), except for the two men, Anaxagoras and Empedocles; for they took the efficient cause too in addition to the
material, one of them, Anaxagoras, saying it was one, but the other
dividing it into two; for this was Empedocles. This Aristotle makes 20
clear by saying, 'Except that, as we said, they have in fact used two
causes, and the second of these, the source of movement, some of
them made one, others two' [987a11], a statement that would lack
the [qualification], '[Only] some of them [used two causes]'.[152]
Instead of '[Philosophers have spoken] too *monistically* (*monakhô-
teron*)', some manuscripts read *morukhôteron*, a term that some
explain by saying, 'more obscurely', others, 'more imprecisely'. The
word is not familiar; nor is it consistent with what Aristotle has 25
stated previously to say that the philosophers down to the Pythagoreans had spoken more obscurely about the principles, since there
is a greater possibility of finding things said by the Pythagoreans
that are stated more obscurely. And had he wished to say 'more
imprecisely', he would have used that very word, as he does in other
places.[153] Later on, of course, he says about all who had spoken
about the principles before him, 'but all of them talk vaguely' 47,1
[988a23].

He says that the Pythagoreans too spoke of two principles, as did
the others, for 'they spoke in the same way' [987a14] probably has
this meaning. But shortly before, he said that they too made use
only of the material cause [986b6]; how then can he now say *two*
causes? Either he is not speaking of two kinds of cause, but is 5
saying that the Pythagoreans made the material principles two, as
did the others, for in positing earth and fire they too made the
material principles two; or he means that it was their doctrine, or
even a consequence of what they said, that the unlimited number
(this was the even) was matter for them, and form the limited
number, which was the odd[154] – and in what follows, he does in fact 10

---

[152] 46,22–3, *hôi leipoi an . . . autôn.* The sense of this remark is uncertain. The
interpretative translation suggests that Alexander means that Aristotle has
neglected to say that *only* some, i.e. two, philosophers had mentioned two causes.

[153] 46,28–9. Aristotle uses the adverb *malakôs* (comparative) of demonstration
that is less than convincing (*Metaph.* 1025b13), and of arguments that may be
lacking in cogency (*Rhet.* 1396b1). Alexander uses it again, see 50,7 below.

[154] 47,5–10. Since Aristotle does not refer, in the present summary, to any philosophers who spoke of two *material* causes, Alexander's first interpretation can scarcely
be correct; see Ross, *Metaphysics* I, 156 ad 13. But his second interpretation of 'spoke

say this about them. But how are the principles still two according
to the Pythagoreans if indeed, as Aristotle says, their principles
were the limited and the unlimited and the 1?[155] For thus they are
three. Or [rather], the 1 was not outside the remaining two,[156] for
he said earlier that they called the unit 'even-odd' [986a19]. But if
it is even-odd it is both limited and unlimited, and according to
them the even is unlimited and the odd limited; for in their view
15   odd and even are principles of the unit first of all. And those
Pythagoreans who put the ten oppositions among the principles
would also have been employing two principles, for they reduced
these oppositions to good and evil, calling one of the columns 'good',
the other 'evil'.

Aristotle says that the doctrine of [the Pythagoreans] differs from
20   that of the other [philosophers], inasmuch as the others, although
making use of the unlimited and the limited in their principle,
made them something else, i.e. a body, which had the unlimited
and the limited as an accident (for some of them said that water
is unlimited, others air, others a kind of intermediate nature, as
Anaximander). But [the Pythagoreans] say that the unlimited itself
and the limited itself are the substrate; for they made the even
25   number, which by its nature is unlimited (for to be even is,
48,1   according to them, to be unlimited), and the odd number, which is
a limited nature, the substrate of the things that are. For they said
that the unlimited is not an accident of that of which it is predicated
(they predicated it of the unlimited number), but its substance. For
according to them, the even number is unlimited not by being so
5   great but by being of this sort, for whatever is even is, according
to them, unlimited inasmuch as it is even. Similarly, [they said]
that the One is substance in and of itself, but that to be one does
not belong to something else which exists. But because these [i.e.
the limited and the unlimited] are the underlying [realities], they
said that number is the substance of all things,[157] on the ground
that all the things that exist are constituted out of numbers; for
just as fire is the substance of all things for those for whom it is

in the same way', scl. as those who posited two *different* causes, seems valid, although
he himself appears to reject this interpretation (l. 5). The Pythagoreans spoke of two
causes, as did other pluralists before them, but made these causes material and
formal rather than material and efficient.

[155] 47,11–12. Alexander seems to have read *kai to hen* at *Metaph.* 987a16; these
words are bracketed by both Ross and Jaeger.

[156] 47,12. Reading *exô tôn loipôn duo* (LF) for *exô toutôn*.

[157] 48,7. Alexander omits a step in the argument. Odd and even are the principles
directly of the unit (see 47,15 above: 'Odd and even are the principles of the unit
first of all'). Numbers are composed out of the unit, and numbers in turn are the
principles out of which other things are constituted.

the substrate, so number is the substance of all things for those for whom number is the substrate.

Aristotle says that [the Pythagoreans] were the first to attempt to answer the question, what each of the things that exist is, and to define (*horizesthai*), but that they treated this matter too simply and without sufficient examination or attention; and in addition he explains the theory they held about definitions. For they said that the first subject of which is predicated the definition they gave is what is expressed by the definition, and that it contains the substance of the thing, the substance expressed by the definition. If, for instance, they happened to call friendship 'equality', and for this reason supposed that the formula of friendship is 'equal-times equal', they said that the first number of which this definition is predicated is friendship, doing the same as one who would think that double and 2 are the same because 2 is the first number of which double is predicated. In censuring this theory, Aristotle adds: 'But surely to be double and to be 2 are not the same; if they are, one thing will be many, a consequence which actually resulted for them' [987a25]. For one thing did become many for them; for just as 2 becomes many for one who says that 2 and double are the same (for it becomes all the things to which the formula of double applies), so each of the things [they defined] became many for the Pythagoreans because they stated the matter thus. For if they maintain that the first number to which 'equal-times-equal' applies is friendship, then equal-times-equal does [in fact] become their definition of friendship;[158] but, given that this is the definition of friendship, all the numbers to which this definition applies will be friendship, and thus one thing will be many. For they believed that the first number of which this formula is predicated is the substance of the thing [defined], but such is not the outcome; for anything to which the definition of a thing might be applied is the thing to which the definition belongs, and [the definition and the thing defined] are convertible. But there are many square numbers; and in fact 4, 9, and 16, although they are different numbers, will [all] be friendship; but in this way friendship, although it is one thing, becomes many, since equal-times-equal is predicated truly of many things because they have the same formula as that which [the Pythagoreans] assigned to friendship. And the same conclusion results for them in the case of the other things [they define]. – Or the statement,

[158] 48,26–49,1. The first equal-times-equal number is, of course, 4; but since Alexander later mentions 4 only among the various numbers that fit this definition (49,7), one wonders if he is here thinking of friendship as being in fact identified with 2, i.e. the double. There seems to be special force to his statement that 'Equal-times-equal does in fact become their definition of friendship'; he may be pointing out, that is, that for the Pythagoreans the essential nature of friendship is found in equality itself, not in a particular equal number.

['But surely to be double and to be 2 are not the same; if they are, one thing will be many'] means this. If the first things of which the formula is predicated truly are identical with those which the formula expresses, but there are many formulae that apply to the one thing that is first (for [the Pythagoreans] called the same number, as chance might have it, [both] 'opportunity' and 'Athene'), then the same number will be both many things and one, since
5   there are many different formulae that apply to it.[159]

987a27 From the earlier philosophers, then, and from the others [we can learn this much].

That is, 'and from all the other philosophers [who came] after those earlier ones'.

---

[159] 49,11–15. Ross notes that since Aristotle has said only that the *first* number for which a definition is valid is identified with the thing defined, the second of Alexander's two interpretations of the text must be the correct one (*Metaphysics* I, 157 ad 27).

CHAPTER 6

Next Aristotle sets forth the doctrine of Plato, who, he says, followed
the Pythagoreans in many respects but also took certain positions
that are peculiar to him; one of these distinctive features was that
concerning the Ideas. And he tells the source which led Plato to   49,20
posit Ideas, and reports that from Cratylus, a Heraclitean, whose
associate he was, he took [the belief] that all sensible things are in
flux and never stand still, and that Plato continued to maintain this
opinion as true. Socrates, however, occupied himself with ethical
questions and in seeking the universal (for in dealing with beauty   50,1
or anything else, he would ask in general what the beautiful is, not
looking to this particular beautiful thing), and was always trying
to define the thing under discussion. Aristotle says of Socrates that
he paid no attention to natural things; but how is it that he says
that Socrates was the first to concern himself with definitions if in   5
fact, as he said before [48,10], the Pythagoreans too, who were older
than Socrates, attempted to do the same? Perhaps [it is] because,
as he said [there], they defined loosely and unscientifically. –
Having taken over from Socrates, then, the inquiry concerning
definitions and the universal, Plato supposed that definitions are of
things of another sort – that they are of natures and not of any
particular sensible thing, not even of the universal above sensibles,   10
because sensibles and all the things in them, and among these
latter even the universal, are always in flux and changing and
never remain attached to the same nature. [And he held] that for
this reason it is also impossible for the common and universal
definition (for definitions are of this sort) to be of any sensible thing,
because these sensibles cannot even be defined because they do not
even remain the same things.[160] And these natures that are apart
from sensible things, and to which definitions belong, he called   15
'Ideas', from which, he said, sensible things too both are and are
named.

---

[160] 50,14. Reading *tôi mê menein ta auta* (Ascl.) for *tôi mêde einai tauta*; the adopted
reading seems better to reflect Aristotle's *aei ge metaballontôn* (987b7). If Hayduck's
reading is retained, the sense is: 'because these sensibles do not even exist', a genuine
enough Platonic notion but one not yet introduced by Aristotle. Cf. ll. 16 and 21
below.

987b9 For most of the things synonymous with the Forms exist
by participation in them.[161]

20   Aristotle has said, 'All sensible things are apart from the Forms
and are named after them' [987b8], a point he explains by saying
that most sensible things have their being through participation
(*methexis*). Then, explaining what 'most of them' are, he adds, 'of
things synonymous with the Forms', which would be the equivalent
of saying, '[of things synonymous] with the Forms that are synonymous with them'; for the things that are synonymous with the
Forms are of this sort.[162] He says this because the Platonists[163] did
51,1 not say there are Ideas of all sensible things, for they did not posit
that there are Ideas of those things among the relatives (*ta pros ti*)
that exist by relation (*skhesis*),[164] nor of any of the things that are
contrary to nature, nor in general of evil things. Or he might be
saying 'the many'[165] instead of 'the sensibles', so that the meaning
would be that the many sensible things exist by participation in
5   those Forms with which they are synonymous; for men are by
participation in 'man', and horses by participation in 'horse'. Thus
the statement would mean that the sensible things synonymous
with the Forms have their being through participation, scl. in the
Forms. One could also understand the text in this way: 'For the
many things exist by participation in the Forms, but these many
are those that are synonymous with one another', for the things
that are many and synonymous with one another have their being

---

[161] 50,17. *Metaph.* 987b9–10. Ross, *kata methexin gar einai ta polla tôn sunônumôn*
[*tois eidesi*]; Jaeger, *kata methexin gar einai ta* [*polla tôn sunônumôn*] *homônuma
tois eidesin*. The text quoted in the lemma contains both phrases bracketed by the
respective editors. See n. 162.

[162] 50,23. Aristotle says simply, 'of things synonymous with the Forms', but in
giving his alternative version of this, Alexander adds: 'with the Forms that are
synonymous with them', an addition he then attempts to explain in ll. 23–4, where
'are of this sort' means that the synonymity is on both sides: things are named after
the Forms that have the same name as things named after them. On *sunônumos*,
see n. 166.

[163] Although Alexander frequently uses the collective term 'the Pythagoreans', the
term *hoi Platônikoi*, 'the Platonists', does not occur in the genuine books of the
commentary on *Metaphysics*, and only once in ps.-Alexander (783,21). At 70,6 he
speaks of *hoi peri Platôna*, but the usual format is simply 'they say' or 'said'. I supply
'the Platonists' in such cases, omitting the usual square brackets because of the
frequency with which the term must be used here and below in the commentary on
ch. 9.

[164] 51,1, *tôn kata skhesin*. Alexander seems to be distinguishing the genus of
relatives (*ta pros ti*) from one of its species (*ta kata skhesin*); these latter are perhaps
things whose whole being consists in their relation to another. According to this
text, only the latter type of relatives would lack Ideas.

[165] 51,3. In his first interpretation of *ta polla*, *Metaph.* 987b9, Alexander understands it to mean 'most' (50,20ff), although, for the Platonists, *all* things synonymous
with the Forms exist by participation in them. In Alexander's two subsequent
interpretations, *ta polla* means 'the many things' or 'the multiplicity of things'.

by participation in one Idea. For not all things participate in one   10
Idea, but only as many as are of the same kind (*homoeidês*) and
synonymous. For Aristotle would not say, in reporting the opinion
of Plato, that sensible things are synonymous with the Ideas, since
Plato said that the Ideas are [only] homonymous (*homônumôs*) with
the things that come to be by reference to them [*Parm.* 133D].[166]
Or [perhaps] even Plato would not hold that the Ideas are [merely]
homonymous with the things referred to them, but are synonymous
[with them]; for in the places where he uses the term 'homonymous',
he might be using it in a somewhat common sense as equivalent to   15
'synonymous'. For if the things that are referred to the Idea are not
made like it in formula and form, in what other respect could they
be [made like it]? For nothing else belongs to the Ideas, nor do they
have any accidents. But things that are like [something else] in
form are synonymous with it, for if man-himself is the kind of Form
that is simple, clearly the thing made like it would be so likened
in virtue of its form; but surely the definitions even of enmattered   20
(*enulos*) things are by reference to their form. Hence, if it is in
virtue of their form that individual men are like the Idea [of man],
itself nothing but form, their definition too would be the same as
that of the Idea because, even if it is [only] the Forms that can be
defined, and not these [sensible] things, nevertheless at least the
definitions of the Forms are applied to these [sensible] things as
well; for 'rational mortal animal'[167] is predicated even of perceptible
men, although it is not the definition of them in the primary sense.   25

987b10 But Plato changed only the name 'participation'.   52,1

That is, he altered the name; for what the Pythagoreans called
'imitation' Plato, changing the name, termed 'participation'. But
neither any of the Pythagoreans nor Plato explained what this
participation is or how it comes about, but left for joint investigation   5
the question, how and in what way it occurs – although this point
does seem to be clarified by Plato in the *Parmenides* [130Eff]. The
Pythagoreans might be speaking with reference to imitation of the
first numbers, which, they said, are in the primary sense the things
predicated of them, whereas the other numbers are such [only by
imitation of the first].

[166] 51,12–13. On the translation of *humônumos* and *sunônumos*, see n. 146. It was
there pointed out that *sunônumos*, when used in reference to the theory of the Ideas,
emphasizes the fact that such things have not only a name but also a nature in
common with the Ideas in which they participate. See 51,10–11, *homoeidê te kai . . .
sunônuma*, 'things of the same kind and synonymous'.

[167] 51,23. As variant forms of the definition of man we find 'rational animal' (*in
Metaph.* 4, 299,3); 'two-footed animal' (id. 277,8.24); 'two-footed land animal' (id.
276,37 and *in Top.* 43,16); 'animal capable of choice and deliberation' (id. 434,10–11).

987b14 Again, in addition to sensible things and the Forms [he says there are the objects of mathematics].

10   Aristotle also reports this point, that Plato made mathematical objects natures or substances of some sort intermediate between the Ideas and sensible things. For according to him they were between [these two] because they differ from sensible things in that they are eternal and utterly unchangeable, and from the Ideas inasmuch as the Ideas are something numerically one, but math-
15   ematical objects reveal their likeness [to one another]¹⁶⁸ in the many things, i.e. in sensible particulars, existing as they do in these. For these mathematical objects do not subsist independently, but by thought (*epinoia*); for after the matter and the motion have been separated (*khōrizesthai*) from enmattered things, the things according to which and with which mathematical objects have their subsistence, these objects are left, revealing that likeness [to one another they possess] in enmattered things that are both many and different according to their accidental material attributes.¹⁶⁹ Or this
20   may indeed be the truth of the matter, but Plato certainly did not speak in this way, seeing that he made these objects natures and independent and eternal substances. But Aristotle might be saying, 'There are many alike' [987b17], with reference to mathematical objects, on the ground that none of them is numerically one; for the mathematical objects triangles and squares and each of the others are numerically many, just as sensible things too, although they preserve their likeness to one another in virtue of their definition,
25   whereas each of the Ideas is numerically one.

987b18 Since the Forms are the causes [of all other things, he thought that their elements are the elements of all things].

Plato thought, says Aristotle, that the Forms, i.e. the Ideas, are
53,1   principles and causes of the being of all the other things, since the

¹⁶⁸ 52,11–15. The triangles that are the objects of geometrical study are not the Idea, triangle-itself or triangularity, which is unique. But though multiple, neither are they the approximately triangular objects found in sensible things; as Alexander goes on to say, the process of abstraction strips away the differences with which these mathematical objects exist in sensibles, so that they reveal a common likeness or unity at the intelligible level.

¹⁶⁹ 52,15–19. On the process whereby the intellect 'separates' the intelligible form from its encumbering matter, see Alexander's *DA*, 83,2–86,5 *passim*; and Paul Moraux, *Alexandre d'Aphrodisie, exégète de la noétique d'Aristote*, Liège 1942, 7–25, where Moraux translates, and comments on, a number of pertinent texts. See also Heinz Happ on *khorizein* in Alexander, *Hyle*, Berlin 1971, 617–18. In his notes, the author cites a number of texts from ps.-Alexander *in Metaph*. On Alexander as originator of what became the standard interpretation of Aristotle, see Ian Mueller, 'Aristotle's doctrine of abstraction in some Aristotelian commentators and Neoplatonists', *Aristotle Transformed*, London and Ithaca N.Y. 1989.

other things are by participation in them. But the principles of the
Ideas themselves he made in turn principles of all things: the great
and the small, which are a kind of dyad (*duas*) that is, he says,
indefinite (*aoristos*), he called principles of the Ideas as matter and
substrate, and the One [principle] as substance and form. Next he
states in what sense Plato said this: 'For from them, by participation   5
in the One, come the Forms, [i.e.] the numbers'.[170] 'From them', i.e.
from the great and the small, as they unite and are given a form
by the One through participation, i.e. by participating (*metalam-*
banein) in it, come the Forms, i.e. the Ideas, which are themselves
also numbers, for the Platonists call the Ideas 'ideal (*eidêtikos*)
numbers'. Having said 'the Forms', Aristotle adds 'the numbers',   10
for the Forms as numbers are the Ideas, since there are also other
forms,[171] just as there are of course [other] numbers too.

987b22 [Plato agreed with the Pythagoreans] at least in this,
that the One is not called one while being something else.

For Aristotle has said that the Pythagoreans did not make some
other nature the substrate of the numbers, but said that the   15
numbers themselves are substances, and in particular that they did
not predicate the One of something that is other [than it], but
assumed that the One is a kind of substance that has its being in
being one [47,23–48,10]. He reports this also about Plato, that in
much the same way as [the Pythagoreans] he said the One is substance, not something that is other [than one] in its substrate, and
then takes on the property of being one. On this point, then, he   20
says that Plato agreed with the Pythagoreans, and [also] in making
numbers the principles and causes of the things that are, although
not in the same way; for the Pythagoreans made them principles
as existing in the things and as matter (on the ground of course
that all existing things are composed out of numbers), but Plato
placed numbers outside the things of which they are the causes, for
[he regarded them] as models (*paradeigma*). Aristotle says, 'In the
same way', not in the sense that Plato spoke of numbers as causes   25
of being (*ousia*) in the same way as the Pythagoreans, but in the

[170] 53,5–6. *Metaph.* 987b22 presents a textual problem: Ross, [*ta eidê*] *einai tous*
arithmous; Jaeger, *ta eidê einai* [*tous arithmous*]. Alexander's text contains both
bracketed terms. See n. 171.
[171] 53,10–11. As indicated in n. 170, Ross brackets *ta eidê* in this text; he explains,
'Alexander ... think[s] that *tous arithmous* is added in apposition to *ta eidê* to
indicate that it is the Platonic idea-numbers and not *eidê* in some other sense, i.e.
species such as Aristotle himself believes in, that are meant' (*Metaphysics* I, 171–2).
A more natural interpretation, however, is that Alexander is contrasting the forms
in sensible things with the Platonic Forms that are numbers, as he contrasts ideal
numbers with the numbers used for counting.

sense that he too called numbers causes of the things that are, just as they did.[172]

54,1   **987b25 But that Plato posited a dyad rather than treating the unlimited as one, but made the unlimited out of great and small, is a distinctive feature of his theory.**

After stating the points in which Plato's theory agreed with that of the Pythagoreans, Aristotle adds in turn those too in which he differed from them. The Pythagoreans made the unlimited one and
5   a kind of single nature, and in their view this unlimited was material substrate (this is the even number, for the even is specifically (*tôi eidei*) one since it is what is divided into equal parts). But Plato made [the unlimited] a dyad, calling it the substrate and the unlimited, inasmuch as of itself it has no form; for [he called it] great and small and excess (*huperokhê*) and defect (*elleipsis*), [thinking] that the nature of the unlimited is in these, which were
10   for him the material cause. But the great is not specifically the same as the small, nor excess [specifically] the same as defect, for they are contraries, and so not one. (Aristotle says, '*but* [he made] the unlimited [out of great and small', rather than '*for* [he made] the unlimited', etc. [987b26]. [But] according to Plato, the unlimited comes from great and small, for this is what is consistent with the text.[173] Again, Plato left numbers outside sensible things, not making them the substrate as matter of the things that are, nor
15   was it in this way that he posited them as causes of things; but the Pythagoreans said that things and beings are composed out of numbers, and the consequence of this was for them to say that the things that are are numbers. Plato also differs from the Pythagoreans in that he located mathematical objects between sensible things and the Ideas, but they did not do so at all.

[172] 53,24–7. Although Alexander may appear to cavil, the distinction is, for him, a real one. Since the Pythagorean numbers were immanent in sensible things they are, from an Aristotelian viewpoint, intrinsic causes, hence causes of the being of things. But Plato's numbers, as described here, are extrinsic causes, hence not directly causes of the being of sensible things (see 54, 13–17 below) – although Alexander will argue later that they are either immanent in things or else not causes at all.

[173] 54,11–23. If the translation of this obscure piece of textual paraphrase is correct, Alexander means that Aristotle's text requires *gar* (for) rather than *de* (but), because 'He made the unlimited out of great and small' corresponds to the previous statement that 'Plato posited a dyad', etc.

987b29 The fact that Plato, unlike the Pythagoreans, put the   20
One and numbers apart from things, and his introduction of the
Forms, came about because of his investigation of definitions.

Having stated the points of disagreement between Plato and the
Pythagoreans, Aristotle now gives the reason why Plato did not
make numbers principles of the things that are in the same way as
the Pythagoreans, but separated them too from sensible things and   25
posited the Ideas as substances and natures of another kind apart
from sensible substances. This was, he says, because of his critical
inquiry into definitions (*logoi*) and because of dialectic, of which the   55,1
earlier philosophers were still without experience. Having begun
to speculate about the consequences [of this study], and having
become habituated, from dialectic, to the use of both division (*diairesis*) and definitions (for both of these are the province of the dialectician), Plato came through these to the idea of separating certain
things from sensible objects, and of supposing that there are certain   5
other natures apart from sensible things. Now there is the division
that divides genera and species (*eidos*), which are not sensible, and
the one that resolves sensible things into the elements and the
principles, which are not sensible.[174] For no sensible thing is identical with that in virtue of which being a thing of this sort belongs
to it; for neither is the product of art identical with art, nor the
natural thing with nature. So that, [Plato reasoned,] if the numbers   10
too, and similarly the Ideas, are responsible for the fact that sensible
things are of such or such a kind, they would be separated from
these sensibles.[175] But neither are definitions of sensible things, for
they are not of particulars but of universals. Through dialectical
considerations of this sort, Plato therefore became accustomed to
speculation about intelligible things. He too said that the One is a
kind of independent substance and nature, just as [the Pythago-
reans]; but they generated things from the One and the other
numbers, whereas Plato did not.   15

[174] 55,7, *stoikheia*. Not the elements of the early philosophers (earth, etc.), which
are sensible (see 72,2–4), but the Aristotelian intrinsic principles, matter and form.
For this sense of *stoikheion*, see 96,33–7; and for the distinction between *arkhê*
(principle) and *stoikheion*, see Aristotle *Metaph.* 1070a22. In his commentary on this
text, ps.-Alexander says that *arkhê* is a more universal term than *stoikheion*: every
element is a principle, but not *vice versa* (681,2–3). For other texts in which Alexander equates the two terms, see Subject Index s.v. element.

[175] 55,11, *eiê an kekhôrismena autôn*. The neuter may be explained by the diverse
genders of *arithmoi* and *ideai*, or as an instance of Alexander's occasionally loose
use of a neuter plural in reference to antecedents of other genders; see e.g. 99,9;
100,17–18; 113,4; 123,7; 133,4.

987b33 But the fact that Plato made the other nature [besides the One] a dyad was because he thought it easy to generate the numbers, except those that are first, out of the dyad as out of a matrix.

20   Both Plato[176] and the Pythagoreans assumed that numbers are the principles of the things that are, because it seemed to them that what is prior and incomposite is a principle, and that planes are prior to bodies (for things that are simpler [than another] and that are not destroyed along with it are by nature prior [to it], and that lines are prior to planes by the same reasoning, and that points (*stigmê*), which the mathematicians call *sêmeia* but [Plato and the
25   Pythagoreans] called units, are prior to lines, being totally incomposite and having nothing prior to them; but the units are numbers; therefore, numbers are first among the things that are. And since
56,1   the Forms and the Ideas are, according to Plato,[177] prior to the things that exist by reference to them and have their being from them (that these Forms exist he tried to prove in a number of ways), he called the Forms numbers. For if that which is one in kind (*monoeidês*) is prior to the things that are from it,[178] but nothing is prior to number, the Forms are numbers. For this reason he said
5   that the principles of number are also principles of the Forms, and that the One [is principle] of all things.

Again, the Forms are the principles of the other things, and the principles of number are principles of the Ideas, since the Ideas are numbers; and Plato said that the principles of number are the unit

[176] 55,20–57,28 = Ross, *Fragmenta Selecta*, 114–15; Ross, *Select Fragments*, 117–19. Simplicius also records Alexander's excerpt from the *de Bono*, *in Phys.* 3.4, 454,2–455,11 = Ross, *Fragmenta Selecta*, 115–16. Konrad Gaiser prints 55,20–56,35 as 22B of his *Testimonia* (*Platons ungeschriebene Lehre*, 2. Aufl., Stuttgart 1968, 478–80, translates the earlier portion of the text (49), and refers to it at several plces in his text. (Gaiser's Testimonium 22B is reproduced, with a French translation, by Marie-Dominique Richard, *L'enseignement oral de Platon*, Paris 1986), 254–7.) The reliability of Alexander's excerpt from, or paraphrase of, the *de Bono* has been established by Paul Wilpert, op. cit., 376–8, and, more exhaustively, in *Zwei aristotelische Frühschriften über die Ideenlehre*, Regensburg 1949, 121–221. On the point of authenticity, Richard declares: 'Tout nous porterait . . . à conclure à l'authenticité du témoigne d'Alexandre si H. Cherniss ne l'avait jugé sujet à caution' (op. cit., 92), and goes on to examine the objections raised by Cherniss. For commentary on various parts of the fragment, see Julius Stenzl, *Zahl und Gestalt bei Platon und Aristoteles*, 3. Aufl., Bad Homburg 1959, 170–4; Hans Krämer, *Arete bei Platon und Aristoteles*, Heidelberg 1959, 249–60; Hermann Schmitz, *Die Ideenlehre des Aristoteles* II, Bonn 1985, 265–70; Richard, op. cit., 180–4 (with translations of the Alexander-fragments from Simplicius mentioned above). The last three sources contain copious references to the secondary literature on the *de Bono*.

[177] 56,1. Plato is not named until the very end of this lengthy text (l. 34), but I have supplied his name throughout. The same situation obtains in the continuation of the excerpt from the *de Bono*, 57,4–34 below.

[178] 56,3. Reading *par' autou* for *pros autou* (Bonitz).

and the dyad. For since there are in numbers both the One and
that which is apart from the One, which is many and few, he made
the first thing that is in numbers apart from the One the principle   10
both of the many and the few. But the dyad is the first thing apart
from the One, containing within itself both manyness and fewness;
for the double is many and the half is few, and these are in the
dyad; and the dyad is contrary to the One, if indeed the One is
indivisible but the dyad divided.

Again, thinking he was proving that the equal and the unequal
are the principles of all things, both of those that exist independently and of their opposites (for he tried to reduce all things to   15
these as their simplest elements), Plato assigned the equal to the
unit and the unequal to excess and defect; for inequality involves
two things, a great and a small, which are respectively excessive
and defective. For this reason he also called it the 'indefinite'
(*aoristos*) dyad, because neither of the two, neither that which
exceeds nor that which is exceeded, is, of itself, limited (*hôrismenos*),
but indefinite and unlimited. But he said that when the indefinite   20
dyad has been limited by the One, it becomes the numerical dyad;
for this kind of dyad is one in form.

Again, the dyad is the first number. Its principles are that which
exceeds and that which is exceeded, since the double and the half
are first found in the dyad; for the double and the half are respectively excessive and defective, but that which exceeds and that which   25
is exceeded are no longer double nor half, so that these are elements
of the double.[179] And since that which exceeds and that which is
exceeded become double and half when they have been limited (for
they are no longer indefinite, just as the triple and the third or the
quadruple and the fourth are not indefinite, nor any of the other
things whose excess has already been limited), and [since] it is the
nature of the One that produces this limitation (for each thing is   30
one inasmuch as it is this particular thing and limited), the One
and the great and the small would be the elements of the dyad that
is in numbers. But the dyad is certainly the first number; therefore,
the One and the great and the small are elements of the dyad. And
it was for reasons such as these that Plato made the One and the
dyad principles of numbers and of all the things that are, as Aris-   35
totle says in his treatise *On the Good*.

[179] 56,25–6. The *numerical* dyad is the number 2, which is the double of 1, and is
made up of 1's, the half of two. In this case, therefore, the ultimate principles, excess
and defect, are limited, 'for they are no longer indefinite', as Alexander goes on to
say. But in the *ideal* dyad, which unites with the One to produce the numbers other
than prime, 'the excessive and defective are not necessarily double or half', as Ross
translates l. 25, thus interpreting Alexander's *ouketi*, 'no longer': that is, they are
unlimited, hence principles not only of the ideal dyad but of the double, the latter
a limited quantity. See Krämer, op. cit., 254.

57,1 And here he says that it is also for this reason that Plato 'made the other nature [besides the One] a dyad because he thought it was easy to generate the numbers, except those that are first, out of the dyad as out of a matrix' [987b34].[180] This is because it seemed to him that the dyad divides everything to which it is applied; for

5 this reason he also called it 'duplicative'. For by making into two each thing to which it is applied it somehow divides that thing, not allowing it to remain what it was; and this division is the genesis of numbers. Just as matrices[181] and moulds make similar to themselves all the things inserted into them, so the dyad too, as if it were a kind of matrix, becomes generative of the numbers after it, making each thing to which it is applied two, or doubling it. For

10 when it is applied to 1 it makes 2 (for twice 1 is 2); when applied to 2 it makes 4 (for twice 2 is 4); when applied to 3 it makes 6 (for twice 3 is 6); and so in the other cases.

By, 'except the numbers that are first', Aristotle means, 'except the odd numbers'.[182] For the generation of the odd numbers no longer takes place in this way, for their generation is not by doub-

15 ling or division into two. Here, then, he means by 'first numbers' all the odd numbers without exception, for it is customary [to regard these as] prior to even numbers. But those numbers are called 'first simply' that are measured only by the unit, as 3, 5, and 7 (although 2 would also be of this sort), whereas those numbers are 'first by reference to one another' that have 1 as their only common factor

[180] 56,35–57,3. After this brief reference to the text of *Metaphysics* that introduced his quotation from the *de Bono* (987b33), Alexander returns to the latter. Ross prints 57,3–11 and 24–8 as part of the quotation, but Annas notes that these lines may be part of Alexander's own comment (op. cit., 45, n. 54). Wilpert believes they are from the *de Bono* (*Zwei* . . ., 208ff), but Gaiser expresses doubt (op. cit., 363, n. 92). For commentary on these later portions of the fragment, see Stenzl, op. cit., 51–3; Schmitz, op. cit., II, 235–41 *passim*, especially 235, n. 347; Annas, op. cit., 45–60.

[181] 57,6. The meaning of *ekmageion* in Aristotle's text (988a1) is disputed. In the second edition of his translation of *Metaphysics*, Ross translates, 'as out of some plastic material', a version retained in ROTA; in his commentary, he says the word is Platonic, citing *Theaet.* 191C, 196A, and *Tim.* 50C. Schmitz, however, cites *Laws* 801D7 as evidence that Aristotle had in mind a matrix or stamp, as Alexander interprets (op. cit., II, 235).

[182] 57,12ff. The meaning of Aristotle's *exô tôn prôtôn* has been much debated. Schmitz asserts, "'ausser den ersten" kann gemäss griechischer Ausdrucksweise anstandslos nur im Sinne von "ausser den Primzahlen" verstanden werden' (op. cit., II, 234); but that view is disputed by Ross (*Metaphysics* I, 173–6), who believes that the suggested emendation, *exô tôn perittôn*, 'except the odd numbers', gives the sense that is needed, but that there is nothing in the MS tradition or the Greek commentators to support it – despite Alexander's exegesis in the present text. (Annas favours the emendation to *perittôn*, op. cit. 50 and n. 62.) Although Ross, in the second edition of his translation of *Metaphysics*, translates, 'except [the numbers] that are prime', retained in ROTA, I have thought it best to adopt the more neutral, 'except those that are first', especially since 'prime' would make Alexander's interpretation of this text even more difficult. See n. 183.

(*metron*), although, taken independently, they are measured by some [other] number as well. 8 and 9 are related to each other in   20
this way, for their only common factor is 1, yet each of them has also [another] number as a factor: 8 has 2 and 4, 9 has 3. Here, however, Aristotle must be calling 'first' all the odd numbers, as being prior to even numbers, for none of them is generated by the dyad in the way described above. For the odd numbers are produced   25
by the addition of a unit to each of the even numbers, but the unit is not the One as a principle (for this latter One confers a form and is not material); but just as the great and the small were 2 when limited by the One, so each of them is also said to be a unit when limited by the One.[183]

[By,] 'Except for the numbers that are first', he means those that are simply first; but these were the ones measured by the unit   30
alone, as 3, 5, 7. He says that these alone are not generated by the dyad, because all the other numbers except the first are generated when a number is added to a number[184] (hence, since they are generated from two numbers, they would be from a dyad); but the numbers that are simply first, because they do not come to be in this way, would also not be said to be generated by the dyad.[185]

988a1 And yet it is the contrary that results; the matter cannot   58,1
be reasonably explained in this way.

Aristotle has said that according to Plato, the indefinite dyad is a principle as matter, and further that the dyad seems to be for him a material principle. After adding that the dyad is of course unlimited by its own nature and generative of plurality, he criticizes the opinion on the ground that the statement does not correspond   5
to things either as they are perceived or as they come into being.[186]
For after making the dyad a principle as matter, the Platonists use

[183] 57,12–27. Alexander's first interpretation, according to which the *prôtoi arithmoi* are prime numbers, is difficult to comprehend in itself, and seems impossible as an explanation of Aristotle's text, which speaks not of the number 2 but of the indefinite dyad (Ross, *Metaphysics* I, 173 ad 34). See Annas, op. cit., 46–7, on how Alexander may be in error.

[184] 57,31–2. Reading *arithmou ep' arithmôi genomenou* (A) for *arithmoi ep' arithmou genomenoi*.

[185] 57,27–34. Bonitz suspects the authenticity of these lines ('Dubito num ab Alexandro scripta sint') and certainly the confused statement is even more puzzling than the one that precedes.

[186] 58,4–12, *aitiatai, ktl.* Aristotle's own criticism seems to be simply that, according to Plato, a single union of form and matter would produce a plurality of different numbers. In the first part of his commentary, however, Alexander takes the objection as directed at the Platonists' supposed material cause, the indefinite dyad, which both unites and divides. Since the function of their formal cause, the One, is only to unify, the dyad is responsible for all even numbers both by uniting and by dividing them.

it to generate many things, for they assume it is the same dyad that generates plurality and all the even numbers – some it generates by combining, others by dividing into two; but their formal principle
10   is a unifying principle because every form is something one, since it is finite and limited in its being. Each of the numbers is in fact something one, for the One itself is something that unifies, but the indefinite dyad is what divides [things] into two. But surely this is not the case with the things that come into being, which [according to the Platonists] are made like [the Forms] and have their being by reference to them; but rather the opposite [is true]. For matter, I mean matter that is numerically one, can receive and generate
15   only one particular form, for it is impossible for there to be more than one form at the same time in matter that is numerically one, so that the same piece of wood would be at once bed and table and chair; but one portion of matter has only one particular form in actuality. The form, of course, although it is numerically one, produces many forms, for art, which is one particular form, and the artisan, who is numerically one particular person, are capable of producing many things and even different ones – at any rate the
20   carpenter's art and the man possessing it, the same man and numerically one, make both a bed and a chair and a table. The same is true in the case of the male and female: the female, who provides matter for the thing generated, 'is impregnated by one copulation, whereas the male impregnates many females' [988a5].

988a7 Plato, then, declared himself thus on the matters we are investigating.

25   It is the principles and the causes of the things that are that we are investigating, and Plato has made the foregoing statements about the principles. 'It is evident, from what has been said, that he used only two causes' [988a8]. Of the four causes that Aristotle himself listed, Plato, he says, used only two, the material and the formal. For the Forms and the Ideas are, in his view, causes capable
30   of supplying the form, as in fact the One in turn is the cause of form for the Forms and Ideas themselves; for among the Ideas the dyad has the role (*logos*) of matter.
59,1   Some manuscripts have this reading: 'For the Forms are the causes of the essence for the other things, and, for those who know, the One [is the cause of the essence] even for matter'.[187] [Read thus,]

---

[187] 58,31–59,8. These lines present a number of difficulties, which Paul Moraux has discussed in his detailed analysis of the text ('Eine Korrektur des Mittelplatonikers Eudoros zum Text der Metaphysik des Aristoteles', *Beiträge zur alten Geschichte und deren Nachleben*, Berlin 1969, vol. II, 492–504). Bonitz and others proposed to emend the variant quotation from Aristotle (59,1–2), reading *eidesi* (for the forms) for *eidosi* (for those who know) (cf. *Metaph.* 988a10–11), but *eidesi* is not consistent

the text must be informing even[188] those who do not know Plato's doctrine about the principles that the One and the underlying matter are principles, and that the One is cause of the essence for the Idea too. The first reading, however, is better; this makes it   5 clear that the Forms are cause of the essence for the other things, and the One for the Forms. Aspasius relates that the former[189] is the more ancient reading, but that it was later changed by Eudorus and Euharmostus.[190]

---

with Alexander's subsequent commentary. A more serious problem is the statement that the One is the cause of essence 'even for matter'; as Moraux points out, this seems to imply a contrast between *tois allois* (for the others), those ignorant of this esoteric doctrine, and *tois eidosi*, the initiates, so that the import of the whole sentence would be: 'The Ideas are causes of the essence in the view of those who do not know, but in the view of those who know, it is the One that is cause, even for matter' (496). Some interpreters have therefore seen the alteration of Aristotle's text by the Platonist Eudorus as an attempt to introduce a monistic system, '. . . in dem das Eine die einzige Ursache des ganzen Seienden, einschliesslich der Materie, ist . . .' (497). But in his commentary on the variant reading, Alexander finds nothing in the altered text that goes counter to the orthodox interpretation of Platonism presented in the text of Aristotle on which he is commenting (*Metaph.* 988a14), according to which Plato used *two* causes, the One and matter. Moraux's resolution of the difficulty is to take the critical words, *kai têi hulêi*, as standing outside the variant reading that Alexander reports; he reconstructs the text that Alexander read: *phaneron . . . hoti duoin aitiain monon kekhrêtai, têi te tou ti esti (ta gar eidê tou ti estin aitia tois allois, tois de eidosi to hen) kai têi hulêi*, 'it is clear that [Plato] used only two causes, the essence (for the Forms are causes of the essence for the other things, [and], for those who know, the One), and matter.' Thus the words *kai têi hulêi* '. . . sind nichts anderes als eine Variante für die Worte *kai kata tên hulên* der Vulgata' (499). (*Eidosi*, the word that distorts the meaning of *to hen*, was a scribal error for the *eidesi* in Aristotle's original text (500).) If this interpretation is sound, Eudorus did not attempt to falsify the text of Aristotle, nor to interpret Aristotle's account of Plato according to the Pythagoreanizing tendencies of middle Platonism (503; see further 501–2).

[188] 59,2, *eti*. According to Moraux, this word has the rare sense of 'also', 'even'. He suggests that the correct reading might be *epi*, in the sense: 'für (oder gegen) die jenigen, die Platons Prinzipienlehre nicht kennen und die Idee als die einzige Ursache des *ti esti* betrachten' (op. cit., 498, n. 18).

[189] 59,7, *ekeinês*. It seems natural to take this word as referring to 'the better reading', that which corresponds to the text of *Metaphysics* (*eidesi* for *eidosi*). But Moraux points out that a surprising consequence of his analysis of this passage is that the reading *eidosi* is actually the older reading, and that the alteration which, according to Aspasius, Eudorus made in the text was to restore the *eidesi* of Aristotle's original text.

[190] 59,7–8. One of Moraux's conclusions is that the 'Euharmostus' named in Alexander's text is purely fictional (493–4 and 503). On Eudorus, see Heinrich Dörrie, 'Der Platoniker Eudoros von Alexandreia', *Hermes* 79, 1944, 25–38; reprinted in his *Platonica Minora*, München 1976, 297–309; John Dillon, *The Middle Platonists*, London and Ithaca N.Y. 1977, 115–35; Paul Moraux, 'Eudoros von Alexandrien', *Der Aristotelismus . . .* II, 509–27. With specific reference to the Eudorus-text in Alexander, Dörrie argued, in an Appendix to the original version of his article, for the adoption of Bonitz's proposed emendation, *eidesin* (for the Forms) for *eidosin* (for those who know), but this Appendix is omitted from the reprint because Dörrie was convinced by Moraux's analysis; see Moraux, *Der Aristotelismus . . .* II, 249 and 511, n. 6. Dillon, on the other hand, seems to find a Platonizing tendency in Eudorus'

988a11 [It is evident] what the underlying matter is of which [the Forms are predicated].

10   After saying that Plato used two causes, and having mentioned the formal cause and shown how it is a cause, Aristotle adds the second cause, saying it is the material one; for he states what 'the underlying matter is' of which the Forms are predicated both among sensible things and among the Ideas. 'For the Forms', he says, 'are causes of the essence for the other things, and the One the cause
15   of the essence for the Forms' [988a10]. Speaking also about the matter that is given a form by the causes named above, he mentions the matter that is found in both [the Ideas and sensible things], saying, 'of which the forms are predicated, some in the case of sensible things, others in the case of the Forms' [988a12].[191] This is equivalent to saying, '[the matter] of which the forms are predicated, both those in sensible things and those in the Forms', i.e. the Ideas; for there is said to be, both in the Ideas and in sensible
20   things, some underlying matter of which the forms are predicated, namely the matter that is given a form. For that this matter is a dyad, but what sort of dyad it is, he makes clear through the added words, ['the great and the small' [988a13];] for it is not the limited dyad, the one in numbers, but the indefinite dyad, for the great and the small are a dyad of this sort. – The text is also written in this way: '[the underlying matter] of which the Forms are predicated in the case of sensible things, and the One in the case of the Forms'.
25   And this statement would mean the matter of which the Forms are

---

emendation of Aristotle's text (op. cit., 128, n. 1); and Gianmaria Calvetti, who offers his own interpretation of the passage ('Eudoro di Alessandria: medioplatonismo e neopitagorismo nel I secolo A.C.', *Rivista di Filosofia Neoscolastica* 69, 1977, 3–19), does not accept Moraux's conclusions. Linda Napolitano accepts Calvetti's belief that, on the basis of Alexander's testimony, Eudorus intended, by his emendation of Aristotle's text, to subordinate matter to the One. She does not refer to Moraux's critique of that interpretation, but admits that Alexander's text presents difficulties of exegesis ('Il platonismo di Eudoro: Tradizione protoaccademica e medio-platonismo Allesandrino', *Museum Patavinum* 3, 1985, 47 and n. 47). But in the judgment of H.B. Gottschalk, '[Moraux's] findings supersede all previous discussions . . .' (op. cit., 1112, n. 170).

[191] 59,16–17. The text of *Metaph.* 998a12, as quoted by Alexander, reads: *kath' hês ta eidê ta men epi tôn aisthêtôn ta de epi tois eidesi legetai*, although at 23 below he quotes, as a variant reading, the text as printed by Jaeger: *kath' hês ta eidê men epi tôn aisthêtôn to d' hen en tois eidesi legetai*. Despite Alexander's attempt to explain the first reading, the ambiguity of *ta eidê . . . epi tois eidesi legetai* remains: how is it possible to say that the Forms are predicated of the Forms? The difficulty is mitigated by understanding the first occurrence of *ta eidê* as generic: 'forms' in the widest sense, as they are found in both sensibles and intelligibles, so that forms in this sense, conferred on intelligible matter by the One, *produce* 'the Forms'. That Alexander may have this interpretation in mind is seen from his addition at 18–19: 'the Forms, i.e. the Ideas'. On this understanding, it is possible to say that the ideal form, that conferred by the One, 'is predicated of the Forms'.

[forms], and of which they are predicated, in sensible things (for the forms of sensible things are in this matter), [and of which] the One [is predicated] among the Ideas; for the matter in them is given a form by the One.

One might ask how it is that, although Plato speaks of the efficient cause in the passage where he says, 'It is then our task to discover and to make known the maker and father of the universe' [*Tim.* 23C], and also of that for the sake of which and the end by what he again says, 'All things are with reference to the king of all, and everything is for his sake' [*Ep.*2, 312E], Aristotle makes no mention of either cause in [reporting] the doctrine of Plato.[192] [The reason is] either because Plato did not mention either of these in what he said about the causes, as Aristotle has shown in his treatise *On the Good*; or because he did not make them causes of the things [involved] in generation and destruction, and did not even formulate any complete theory about them.

[193][Having said that some philosophers had assumed that the material cause is corporeal, others that it is incorporeal, Aristotle mentioned first among those who said it is incorporeal Plato, who called it the great and the small, and the Pythagoreans, who called it the unlimited, and this was the even. But he did not mention Leucippus and Democritus, according to whom matter is both a kind of body and incorporeal, for such was the void. But he has already spoken about these men. And he added to his account the opinion of Anaximander as well, who made a principle the nature between air and fire, or that between air and water; for he speaks in both ways.[194]]

30

60,1

5

10

[192] 59,28–60,2 = Ross, *Fragmenta Selecta*, 119; Ross, *Select Fragments*, 122; Gaiser, Testimonium 22B' (op. cit., 480). At 63,23ff below, Alexander again quotes the text from Plato's *Ep.* 2, and raises the same query. On the Platonic text, see Dörrie, op. cit., 35–6 (306–7 in the reprint); and on Alexander's commentary, Jacques Brunschwig, '*EE* I 8 et le *Peri tagathou*', *Untersuchungen zur Eudemischen Ethik*, Berlin 1971, 220–1. Since Alexander here expresses the belief that Plato did have a notion of the final cause, it is surprising that Simplicius criticizes him on this very point. Alexander, he says, attributes three causes to Plato: matter, that which produces, and the model; but Simplicius himself finds a clear reference to the final cause at *Tim.* 29DE (*in Phys.* 1.2, 26,13–18; cf. 43,4–7). A partial explanation, it has been suggested to me, may be that Simplicius' source is Alexander's lost commentary on the *Physics* rather than his *Metaphysics* commentary. It is also true that Simplicius, in the text referred to, does not say that Alexander explicitly *denied* a final cause to Plato, but only that he did not include it.

[193] 60,2–10. These lines, repeated almost verbatim at 61,11–15 below, where they refer to a later text of Aristotle (*Metaph.* 988a23), are probably an intrusion in the present text. Certainly they are not relevant to the text of *Metaphysics* under consideration here.

[194] 60,8–9. On Anaximander, cf. 45,18–20 and 47,23 above; and on the doctrine of an intermediate body, see Moraux, *Aristotelismus . . .* I, 459.

988a14 Plato also attributed the cause of good and evil to the
elements, one to each of the two.

Aristotle also says this about Plato, that he 'attributed the cause
15   of good and evil', i.e. of good and evil things, 'to the elements, one
to each of the two': the cause of good to the One (since the One is
that which limits it and gives a form),[195] but the cause of evil to
the indefinite dyad; for according to him this latter is the cause
both of plurality and of inequality and indefiniteness in the things
that are. After saying that Plato had spoken of the efficient cause
(for he says that Plato assigned the efficient cause to each of the
20   two elements, the cause of good to the One, that of evil to the
indefinite dyad), Aristotle reminds us that even before Plato certain
others had both investigated and spoken about this sort of cause,
saying: 'As we say, some of the earlier philosophers too investigated
[the efficient cause], e.g. Empedocles and Anaxagoras' [988a15].
Empedocles employed not only the cause of good but also that of
25   evil, dividing the efficient cause, as Aristotle has said about Plato
too; but for Anaxagoras, as he said, Mind was the only efficient
cause of both good and evil.

[195] 60,16. Both the MSS and Asclepius read *to horizon auto* (= *to eu*), but Hayduck
says, 'exspectes *autôi*' (= *Platôni*), referring to *kat' auton*, l. 18. In that case, the
sense would be: 'since for Plato the One is that which delimits', etc. But the assertion
that the One limits the good is intelligible in view of the explanatory addition, 'and
gives it a form', because it is through this function that the One is a cause (cf.
57,25–8 above); and that Plato made the One a cause of good is Aristotle's point. This
interpretation is also adopted by Schmitz, who comments on this text of Alexander in
connection with the statement of Aristoxenus that the One *is* the good (op. cit., II,
282). A further question here: does Alexander understand by *to eu* the Good, *to
agathon*, as the above interpretation supposes? That is not certain; his explanation
of *to eu* is *ta agatha*, *particular* goods; and at l. 17 he speaks of evil 'in the things
that are', i.e. of *particular* evils.

CHAPTER 7

988a18 We have reviewed, in concise and summary fashion, [who the philosophers were who spoke about the principles and truth].

Aristotle says that he has discussed, concisely and by way of summary, who the philosophers were who spoke about the principles before him, and how they spoke. 'And about truth': it is his practice to call theoretical philosophy 'truth'. [In saying,] 'yet we have learned this much from them' [988a20], he reminds us of his purpose in undertaking this inquiry about the principles; for this was to confirm that there is no other kind of cause apart from the four that have been pointed out in the lectures [entitled] *Physics*. This fact has become obvious, for all those who spoke about causes mentioned at least one of the [four] causes; for even if they did not speak either clearly or articulately, but obscurely and inarticulately, still it is certainly clear that they apprehended these causes in some manner. But the fact that he has also given an account of the four causes, as a primary concern, in the first book of the lectures [entitled] *Physics* can be easily known by those acquainted with that work; hence he says, 'those causes that we have distinguished in our treatise on nature' [988a21]. And he will go on to show how no one had apprehended causes other than those spoken of in his treatise on nature.

60,30

61,1

5

988a23 For some of them speak of the principle as matter.

Aristotle recounts that of the philosophers who treated the principle as matter, some posited one principle, others more than one; and some made the principle a body, others made it incorporeal. After saying that some of them assumed the material principle to be corporeal and others incorporeal, he mentions first among those who posited an incorporeal principle Plato, who called it the great and the small, then the Pythagoreans, who called it the unlimited, and this was the even; for this is the number they placed in matter, since the odd number is limited and has the role (*khôra*) of form.

10

15

988a28 But Anaxagoras spoke of the infinity of the things that
are uniform.

Anaxagoras was among those who made the material principle a
body, as were those whom Aristotle next mentions. But he does not
20   mention Leucippus and Democritus, according to whom matter is
both a kind of body and incorporeal, for the void is not a body; but
he has already spoken of these men. And he adds to his account
the opinion of Anaximander, who made the principle a nature that
is between air and fire.[196]

988a32 These philosophers, then, apprehended only the
[material] cause.

Aristotle might be saying this about the philosophers whom he
25   mentioned later, when he said: 'and in addition all those [who made
the principle] air or fire or water or something denser than fire but
rarer than air' [988a29], since those before them, at any rate, did
not posit only the material cause, neither Anaxagoras nor the
Pythagoreans nor Plato. He adds that certain others mentioned
'that from which is the source of movement' [988a33], which is an
efficient cause, and says that among the latter are those who spoke
30   of friendship and strife, as he said Empedocles did, and of Mind, as
he said Anaxagoras did, or of love, as he said Parmenides and
62,3   Hesiod did.[197] Having said that Anaxagoras and Empedocles
mentioned the efficient principle too in addition to the material, he
also includes, among those who mentioned the efficient principle,
5   those who put love among the principles; and yet it might seem
that according to them, love is rather a final cause, for the object
of appetite is of this sort. Or if they had said what thing it is in the
desire for which love produced the effects that it did,[198] they would
have been referring to the final cause too; but since, [although
putting] love among the principles, they used it only as a productive
10   cause, but did not say for what purpose it [acts], they could not be
referring to this principle as an end.

62,1   **988a34** But none [of the earlier philosophers] gave any clear
account of the essence, i.e. the substance.

Aristotle shows that Plato mentioned the formal cause in some way,
for although, according to him, the Ideas are causes and principles,

---

[196] 61,11–22 = 60,2–10; see n. 193.

[197] 62,1–2. The lemma printed here by Hayduck is misplaced, since the lines that
follow are not relevant to it. I have therefore transposed it to 62,10 below, where it
introduces the passage on formal cause.

[198] 62,5–7. With this text cf. 33,4 above.

they are not causes as matter; for they do not exist in sensible things. (In saying, 'the [elements] in the Forms' [988b1],[199] he might mean the principles of the Forms, for these are not matter for sensible things but are the very elements of the Forms because they are in the Forms as their elements. For the term 'elements' is   15 not applied only to matter: strife and friendship at least are, according to Empedocles, also among the elements, but not as matter.) But neither, [according to Plato,] are the Ideas [causes and principles] as efficient causes, for it is the function of the efficient cause to impart motion, but, according to him, the Ideas are rather causes of stationariness and immobility for the things that are. But in Plato's view, the Ideas provide the form, i.e. the essence, for the things that come to be by reference to them. Therefore, just as the   20 One is cause [of the form] even for the Ideas, [so] the Ideas are causes of the form for the other things, and in such a way that these latter are given a form in virtue of their likeness to the Ideas; so that, consequently, the things that come to be and that exist by reference to the Ideas have the same form as the Ideas.[200]

988b6 That for the sake of which actions and changes and   63,1 movements occur [they say is a cause in some way, but not in this way, i.e. as it is its nature to be a cause].

Aristotle is speaking about the final cause (for this is the good and the cause as end for the things that are), and he shows that none of those before him gave an account of this cause in a manner   5 appropriate to it. For they speak of the good as being in some way a cause, not however as end, nor as that for the sake of which the other things come to be, as the good is by its nature a cause; but they employ it as an efficient cause. For in bringing in Mind and

---

[199] 62,12. At *Metaph.* 988b1, Alexander reads *ta* [*stoikheia*] *en tois eidesi* (the [elements] in the Forms); Bonitz's emendation of *ta en* to *to hen* (the One) is accepted by modern editors. Alexander is obviously puzzled by his reading; his confused explanation is that although the Platonic principles are elements, they are not material elements, since the term 'element' can be used of non-material principles as well. How the Ideas can be said to be causes of sensible things is stated more explicitly in the *alt. rec.*: 'The Platonists said that the Ideas are formal (*eidikos*) causes of sensible things, and that the principles of the Forms themselves are the indefinite dyad as matter, the One as formal cause. .... If then these are causes of the Ideas, but the Ideas are formal causes of sensible things, these principles [i.e. the indefinite dyad and the One] would therefore be principles of sensible things too.' In view of Alexander's statement here that the term 'element' is not applied only to matter, a text from Simplicius is of interest. According to him, Alexander distinguished *arkhê*, the efficient cause; *aition*, final and formal cause; and *stoikheion*, the intrinsic material principle (*in Phys.* 1.1, 10,9–12); at 13,22, he quotes Alexander directly: 'the element is matter'.

[200] 62,22. *Hôs* might suggest a criticism of the theory: 'Hence the things that come to be by reference to the Ideas are, *as it were*, of the same form as they.'

friendship respectively, Anaxagoras and Empedocles do make them
good, and causes productive of good effects, but they certainly do
10   not say that things come to be for their sake; but these very causes
are, for these [philosophers], those that produce good things.[201] He
says that those too who made the One and the Idea[202] principles
spoke in much the same way as Anaxagoras and Empedocles. (He
must mean that they spoke of being (*to on*) as well, for Plato called
the One 'being' too – he called both the One and the Idea 'being',
for these are beings in the primary sense.) For [the Platonists] do
not say that the things that come to be are generated for the sake
15   of the One and the Idea; but the latter are causes that provide being
for these things; for [the One][203] is cause of the form, but, according
to the Platonists, the things that are generated do not come to be
nor exist for the sake of the One and the Ideas. Hence they both
mention the good among the causes and also somehow leave it out,
because they do not assure it its proper role (*khôra*). Aristotle says
that they mentioned the cause as good 'only incidentally' [988b15],
20   because for it to be a cause as good, the things that come to be
[must] come to be for its sake. Therefore, those who do not ensure
that what they *call* good has this position among the causes do not
make it a cause *qua* good, but posit that which [merely] happens
to be good as an efficient cause.

One might ask how it is that Plato, who says in his *Epistles*, 'All
things are with reference to the king of all, and all things are for
25   his sake' [*Ep.* 2,312E],[204] is not, in these words, speaking of the
good as end; or, if he is, how it is that Aristotle denies that he does
so. Or [Aristotle may give the reason] when, speaking for himself,
he says at the end of book Alpha Meizon (1):

> It is evident, then, even from what we have said before, that all the
> earlier philosophers seem to be seeking the causes named in the
> *Physics*, and that we cannot name any cause apart from these. But
> they spoke obscurely about these causes, and in one sense they
30   > mentioned all, as we have also said before, but in another sense they
> did not mention them at all. For in what it says on all subjects the

[201] 63,10. Reading *agathôn* for *agatha* (Bonitz).

[202] 63,11. *Metaph.* 988b12 has *to hen ê to on* (the One or being). Either Alexander
read *to hen kai to on* (the One and being), his words at this place, and is attempting
to explain that reading; or he knew *to hen ê to on* as a variant reading, and is
attempting to explain that text by identifying *to on* and *hê idea* (being and the Idea),
as he does at 13–14 below.

[203] 63,15, *touto*. We would expect either *tauta* (= the One and the Ideas) or *hautai*
(= the Ideas), especially since *toutôn* (these) follows (l. 16); for Alexander has just
said that in Plato's view, the Ideas provide the form for the things that come to be
(62,18–21 above). But if *touto* (this) is sound, it can refer only to *to hen* (the One);
and in that case Alexander is thinking of the One as the ultimate source of form
both for the Ideas and for sensible things.

[204] 63,23–6. With these lines cf. 59,39 above, and see n. 192.

early philosophy resembles one who lisps, since it is young and only beginning [993a11–16].

988b16 [All the early philosophers seem to bear witness] that we have rightly determined [how many and of what sort the causes are].

From his account of those who have spoken about the causes it has become obvious, he says, that he has correctly determined, with 64,1 reference to the causes, how many and what they are; for these men too bear witness that the causes are of this sort because they are unable to mention any other kind of cause. 'Moreover, that when the principles are being investigated, all of them must be investigated either in this way . . .' [988a18]. And this too, he says, is evident from what has been said before: that it is necessary to 5 investigate the principles, either all of them that we have listed in making a fourfold division of cause, or some from among these four. (The words, 'either in this way', would mean the same as, 'either to investigate all of them in this way'.) Indeed, even if the present treatise does not demand the discussion of all the causes, still at least the type of cause being investigated is itself among the four; and these causes do not fall outside [the four kinds], because there 10 is no other type of cause apart from these. First, however, Aristotle proposes to state how each of the men mentioned earlier has spoken, and what difficulties result for each theory.

CHAPTER 8

988b22 Those, then, who say that the universe is one, and posit some one kind of nature as its matter, and as corporeal matter having spatial magnitude, are evidently mistaken in many respects.

64,15

He explains in what sense they thought the universe one by the words, 'and posit some one kind of nature as its matter, and as corporeal matter'; for in this way the universe is one as from one thing. After having enumerated the opinions of those before him about the principles and the causes, while examining critically both what is sound and what unsound in the things they said, he first

20 discusses those who made the principle one, and this a body; and he says they are mistaken in many respects. First because, although wishing to set forth the principles of all the things that are, these men give the principle only of bodies, when there are also certain things that are incorporeal; for it is impossible that the principle of what is incorporeal should be a body. Secondly because, although

25 bringing in generation, they left out the cause both of generation and of movement and, in short, the efficient cause; but certainly matter at least does not have movement from itself. ('About generation' means 'about generation and destruction'.) 'They attempt to state the causes and to give a physical account of all things', obviously of the things that are, most of which are in motion. 'They left out[205] the cause of movement' means 'they left out the efficient

30 cause'.) Thirdly [because] they do not posit the form as cause of anything, although all the things that are owe to their form the fact that they are just what they are; for they do not differ at all in respect to their matter, since matter is the same in all of them. It is with good reason that he calls the form 'substance',[206] for each thing has its being from its form.

The fourth error is that they readily took [whichever one] of the primary bodies suited them and made this a principle. But Aristotle

65,1 also shows that this [method] is impossible in the second book of *On Generation* [2.6], and he points out that he has spoken about this subject 'in the works on nature' [989a24], referring thus to the whole body of his physical treatises. For if either the four bodies

---

[205] 64,29. Alexander read *parelipon* for *anairousin*, 'they do away with' (*Metaph.* 988b28).

[206] 64,32. In the present text (*Metaph.* 988b28–29), Aristotle does not in fact mention *eidos* (form); he says, 'the substance, i.e. the essence (*to ti esti*)'. Either Alexander is interpreting the latter term as *eidos*, or he read *eidos* for *to ti esti*.

are principles, or some of them, or one of them, whichever it happens
to be, either they will not be out of one another, so that [thus] they
might be incorruptible, or, whenever they are generated out of one   5
another, they will remain what they at some time are while at the
same time they will also be the contraries into which they change,
and thus the contraries will actually exist at the same time – fire
and water, if these happen to be [the two bodies]; or, if they do not
remain, they will be destroyed, and thus the principle. But this
latter alternative is absurd, for a principle is that out of which
something is first generated and into which it is finally resolved,
but the principle is not generated out of anything. But although   10
this absurdity too is a consequence that results for these [philo-
sophers], it is not what Aristotle mentions here; what he criticizes
is the fact that casually, and without inquiring how the simple
bodies could be generated out of one another, they made some [one]
of the three simple bodies the sole element of the others; for with the
exception of earth, each of the other bodies was called an element by
one of these men. His criticism of them is that they ought not to
have selected the primary element, i.e. the principle, from among   15
the [three bodies] on the basis of the way in which they are generated out of one another, since to be generated out of one another is
common to all of them, and in this respect no one of them is either
prior or posterior to the others; but they did not observe this
[caution].

Aristotle himself states how the generation [of the bodies] out of
one another differs; for some of them are generated out of the others
by separation, others by combination, and from these modes of
generation it is possible to determine the prior and posterior body.
Having said this, he points out that to those who examine the   20
matter by reference to the types of generation, the primary body
will appear, in some respect, to be that out of which the generation
of the others first takes place by combination; and the one that has
the smallest parts and is most subtle would be of this kind. Hence
those who made fire the element would, by this reasoning, be
speaking rationally; and in fact each of those who call some body   25
other than fire an element agrees that the element of the bodies
must be of this sort. For this reason none of them made earth alone
an element, obviously because it has larger parts than the other
bodies. After saying this, Aristotle wonders why earth too should
not, by some reasoning, be an element of the other bodies, as most
people think it is, and especially Hesiod; for he generates earth
first of all after chaos [*Theog.* 116ff], sustaining his opinion by the   30
testimony of the majority. Perhaps Aristotle might be saying this
about earth: unless it was [only] because of the way in which generation takes place that they called those [other] bodies elements,

why in the world did they not call earth too an element, since common opinion says that it is?[207]

After this remark, he returns again to his statement that a more subtle body seems to be the element, saying that according to this opinion none of [these philosophers] would be speaking correctly if he made the element some body other than fire, [whether he made it] one of these four[208] bodies or one of those intermediate between fire and air. Having said this, he adds an argument according to which earth, on the contrary, might be called [the primary] element, saying, 'if what is prior in generation is later in nature' [989a15].[209] What he is saying is this: in nature, the more perfect seems always to be prior to the less perfect, and in generation what comes into being later is more perfect, but what exists earlier in time is less perfect,[210] as the foundation is less perfect than the house and the boy than the man. According to this argument then, he says, those who assumed that the coarser bodies are the elements will, contrary [to the previous assertion], have spoken more correctly, since these bodies seem to have been more thoroughly concocted[211] and perfected than simpler and more subtle bodies, those that are prior in generation; for the more subtle bodies are the first to be generated, for change is out of them into the coarser bodies. So that if what is prior is a principle, that which is prior in nature and being (*ousia*) would be a principle rather than what is prior in generation. For if what is prior in generation is later in nature, [then] what is later in generation would be prior in nature. But according to those for whom generation is by combination, earth is later [than the more subtle bodies]; earth, therefore, is more [truly] a principle, out of which the other bodies are in turn generated by separation.[212]

[207] 65,31–4. The point of this exegesis seems to be that had the materialists not agreed to call a body an element only if it was one into which others are combined or out of which they are separated, they might well have called earth too an element.

[208] 63,36. Since fire is one of the primary bodies, it is illogical to speak of four such bodies when fire has, *ex hypothesi*, been excluded; but *ta tessara*, 'the four', has become, for Alexander, simply a shorthand designation of the elements generally.

[209] 66,1, *to têi genesei proteron têi phusei husteron*, *Metaph*. 989a15, where both Ross and Jaeger read *to têi genesei husteron têi phusei proteron*, 'if what is later in generation is prior in nature'. See n. 212.

[210] 66,4. Supplying *atelesteron de to* at the lacuna in the text. Better sense can be had from Bonitz's conjecture, based on the Latin translation: 'In nature, the more perfect seems always to be prior to the less perfect, even if it comes into being later in generation; but what exists earlier in time is less perfect.'

[211] 66,7, *pepsis*. On the theory of 'concoction', or the overcoming of moisture by heat, see Aristotle, *Meteor*. 4.2; for the specific point made here by Alexander, 380a4.

[212] 66,14. Aristotle's point is this: the arguments in favour of making fire and earth respectively the primary element have a certain validity, but neither air nor water can claim this priority. The first argument (*Metaph*. 988b34–989a15) establishes fire, the most subtle body, as the principle because generation of the other bodies results from combination out of the primary element. The second argument (*Metaph*. 989a15–18) establishes earth, the coarsest body, as the principle because,

989a18 [Let these statements suffice,] then, with reference to   15
those who posit a single cause.

After calling attention to what has been said with reference to those
who posit a single principle, and this corporeal, Aristotle says that
a person would make these mistakes, 'even if he posits more than
one' [989a20], i.e. if he makes the corporeal principles more than   67,1
one. Or else he is not speaking simply about those who make the
principles corporeal and more than one, but also about those who
put not one but several of these four bodies among the principles,
some one of which [the philosophers] spoken of earlier made the
[primary] principle. For he mentions Empedocles, who made the   5
four bodies the matter of the things that are; 'And he too must face
the same consequences, and some that are peculiar to him' [989a21].
He is speaking, as I said, with reference to Empedocles, and says
that although he made the four bodies principles, the same absurd
consequences result for him too as for those who made one of them
a principle; but that there are other consequences as well peculiar
to him. The same consequences, because these bodies are generated   10
ouť of one another, and do not always remain constantly the same
numerically, the very thing that is a proper characteristic of the
element; for this consequence follows for those too who say that
some one of the bodies is element and matter, namely that the
principle which each of them assumes is destroyed. (Aristotle has
spoken about these matters more fully in the third book of *On the
Heaven* [3.7], and he says, calling that source to our attention, 'We
have spoken about this in our works on nature' [989a24].) For either   15
[the four bodies] will not be out of one another, if they are eternal
numerically, but will [only] appear to be coming to be; or the
contraries will exist at the same time in the case of the same thing.
Again, the fact that [Empedocles] did not put the substance, i.e. the
form, among the causes; this [objection] is in fact common [to him
and to those who posited a single material principle].[213] But [a
consequence] peculiar to Empedocles is what he says in reference
to the principles that impart motion (these would be friendship and
strife): whether, according to him, these are to be taken as two   20
principles or as one. For friendship seems clearly to produce the

---

as the final stage of generation by combination, it is 'prior in nature although later
in generation'. Alexander's lengthy commentary on the second argument not only
obscures Aristotle's point, but seems to conclude in an illogicality: in saying that
the other bodies are generated out of earth by separation, he overlooks the fact that
the other bodies already exist as stages in the combinatory process that ultimately
produces earth. Both of Aristotle's arguments assume that the process of generation
is through combination.

[213] 67,17. This remark does not correspond to anything in Aristotle's text at this
point.

effects of strife, since it divides and separates things that by themselves are wholes, to the end it might combine them and make one
68,1   body. But strife too, in his view, not only separates, but also
combines and brings together things that are similar, separating
them from their unified state, so that for him neither one of these
two opposed principles is any way more efficient cause than the
other.[214] Or else the text would be better written thus: 'neither
unreasonably (*alogôs*)', rather than 'neither commendably
(*eulogôs*)',[215] so that the sense would be that Empedocles did not
speak either altogether correctly nor altogether unreasonably.

5   **989a30** If one were to suppose that Anaxagoras said there are
two principles . . .

Next Aristotle mentions Anaxagoras. He disparages as absurd what
seem to be the direct and plain statements made by him, but points
out, through the absurdity of the things that seem to be said, that
through them Anaxagoras intended to say something else, [thus]
coming to the aid of his text and articulating its intention, as he
10   himself says. For from the fact that Anaxagoras said that all things
are mixed in all, Aristotle concludes that he is dreaming of matter,
which is potentially all things but actually none of the things it can
become. Indeed, even though Anaxagoras did not say this clearly, he
would have concurred with those who interpret his opinion thus in
the belief that he himself intended to say it, because this [way of
stating the matter] makes sense, but what he seems to be saying
15   is utterly absurd. 'For it is absurd in other respects as well' [989a33],
i.e. it is absurd to say that all things are mixed in all, [1] because
they must first exist in an unmixed state before their mixture (for
the things being mixed together must be mixed after having first
been separated, and thus the mixture is no longer first). [2] Because
it is impossible, and contrary to nature, for one chance thing to be
20   mixed with another chance thing; for how would line and white or
white and musical be mixed? [3] Because it follows, for one who
speaks in this way, that the modifications and accidents are separated from the substance and subsist (*huphestanai*) independently,
for there is also separation of things of which there is mixture; so
that if the modifications and accidents have also been mixed (for
they belong to 'all things'), they too would be separated.
        Although it is of course absurd to say [that all things are mixed
in all] (the addition of the conjunction '*kai*' (as well) [to the text]

---

[214] 67,20–68,3. This criticism is stated more fully at 35,5–23 above.
[215] 68,3–4. Aristotle's text has *out' orthôs oute eulogôs*, 'neither correctly nor
reasonably' (989a26). Alexander's proposed emendation (if he did not find this
reading in the MSS) makes a slightly better case for Empedocles.

seems superfluous),[216] nevertheless, if one will pay close attention   25
to what Anaxagoras says, articulating it carefully and interpreting
what he intends to say, he would appear to be speaking in a more
modern fashion, and more appropriately, in comparison with the   69,1
others. (The expression, 'in more modern fashion', might mean the
same as his statement at the beginning about Anaxagoras: that he
was 'older [than Empedocles] but later in his philosophical activity'
[984a11].[217] Aristotle also says how it is possible, by paying close
attention to what Anaxagoras says, to articulate [its sense]. 'For
when nothing has been separated out' [989b6], [so that] it exists   5
independently and in actuality, it is clearly impossible to predicate
truly a single one of the things that are of that substance or mixture
of which he speaks; for it is neither white nor black nor grey nor
any other colour, nor does it have any taste nor any other of the
things of this sort. For it is not possible[218] for one to predicate truly
if he says it is of such a kind or of such a size or any of the actual   10
realities (*ousia*), for [then] some [one] of these would already have
been separated out in the so-called mixture and would be actually
existent; but this is impossible if all of them are mixed [together],
since that one would not be mixed. For Anaxagoras says that all
things except Mind are mixed, and that this alone is unmixed and
pure. (Aristotle adds the phrase, 'of necessity' [989b9], to indicate
[that the separated quality] already exists and is in actuality.[219]

986b16 From this it follows, then, that we must say the prin-   15
ciples are the One [and the Other].

He summarizes Anaxagoras's opinion about the principles, the
theory to which he would subscribe if someone, following what he
says, were at the same time to express it clearly: that according to
him, 'the One' was a principle (for Mind, being simple and unmixed
according to him, would be something analogous to the One), 'and

---

[216] 68,24–5. The point of Alexander's objection to the text is not clear. Aristotle
says *atopou ontos kai allôs*, 'in other respects as well', . . . *kai dia to . . . kai dia to*,
'and because . . .' (989a33–b1). It must be the first of the correlative *kai*'s to which
Alexander is referring; although hardly superfluous, it could of course be omitted.

[217] 69,1–3. With this statement cf. his earlier interpretation of the text, 28,1ff
above, and see n. 104.

[218] 69,5. Supplying *hoion te* after *einai* (Ascl.).

[219] 69,13–14. This comment is strange, if Alexander is referring to *Metaph*. 989b8,
where Aristotle says *akhrôn ên ex anankês* (it was colourless of necessity) after
stating that no specific colour could be predicated of Anaxagoras' mixture. But
Alexander understands the phrase *ex anankês* (of necessity) as referring to the
supposed state of the separated quality. In his translation of *Metaph*. 989b14, Ross
says, 'for the particular form would necessarily have been separated out', to which
Alexander's comment would be appropriate; but *ex anankês* is not found in Aristotle's
text at this point.

20   the Other', i.e. the indefinite; for matter was this sort of thing
      before it was limited and given a form – indefinite and nothing in
      actuality, but having potentially all things that it can become, the
      sort of thing Anaxagoras assumed the mixture to be. 'So that he
70,1 speaks neither correctly nor clearly' [989b19], for he would not be
      speaking correctly in all respects even if he spoke in the way that
      Aristotle, coming to his aid, has said that he intends to speak; for
      he would be saying there are only two principles rather than four.
      Nor, again, is it possible to say he has spoken thus in all respects
      (for he appears to say that the uniform [parts] are in the mixture
5   not potentially but actually), but not even that he has stated clearly
      anything he says. 'Nevertheless, he intends to say something
      similar to what the later philosophers say' [989b19] – Aristotle is
      speaking of those around Plato, who made the One and the indefi-
      nite dyad the principles of the things that are – 'and something
      more [consistent] with things as they are perceived [to be]'. The
      word 'consistent' (*akoloutha*) is missing from the text [but fits the
      sense]; for what [he intended to say] seems more consistent with
      things as they are perceived [to be] than what he [actually] says.[220]

10   **989b21** But these philosophers are familiar only with argu-
          ments about generation and destruction and movement.

      Having reported the opinions of the ancient [philosophers] about
      the principles, Aristotle now distinguishes the natural philosophers
      from those who assume incorporeal substances, and dismisses the
71,1 former on the ground that they did not investigate the whole of
      reality (*ousia*), and that what they say is not even useful for the
      present inquiry. He goes on to examine critically the opinions of
      the Pythagoreans and Plato as more appropriate to the present
      inquiry, for these [philosophers], speaking about all the things that
5   are, posited certain other substances apart from those that are
      generated and natural, and from corporeal and sensible substances
      in general. As a result, a critical examination of their doctrine is
      more useful for the present inquiry, since our investigation does
      not deal with the sort of causes that belong to natural things or to
      those in motion, but with causes that are intelligible (*noêtos*) and
      incorporeal.

---

[220] 70,8–9. At *Metaph.* 989b20–21, Alexander read *kai tois phainomenois mallon*,
to which he proposes to add [*akoloutha*]. Jaeger gives the text thus: *kai tois* [*nun*]
phainomenois mallon ‹*akolouthei*›; while Ross reads *kai tois nun phainomenois
mallon*, translating: ' "what is now more clearly seen to be the case" – now, when
the distinction of form and matter has been clearly recognized' (*Metaphysics* I,
183 ad 20). But with the *akoloutha* that Alexander thinks must be supplied, *tois
phainomenois* takes on a different sense than that given it by Ross.

989b29 The so-called Pythagoreans use more exotic principles   10
and elements.

Aristotle criticizes the Pythagoreans, [although] they too seem to
mention the incorporeal nature, because[221] they posited principles
that are stranger and more detached from natural things and 'more
exotic', i.e. that extend more widely and transcend [na'ural things]
and are capable of being principles of other natures as well (for   15
they are incorporeal and unchanging; for numbers are of this sort,   72,1
since they are not connected with natural things). And they did
not assume ordinary principles, those that agree with the common
conceptions and the opinions of the natural philosophers; for the
principles posited by these latter are more proximate to natural
bodies and more obvious. At the same time, Aristotle gives as the
reason [for the orientation of the Pythagoreans] the fact that, since   5
they did not begin from sensible things, they posited and took the
principles not from these (for by 'received' (*parelabon* [989b31])) he
means 'took' (*elabon*)), but from mathematics – having been brought
up in the study of mathematics, they posited that the principles too
are from mathematical entities and in conformity with them. These
are mathematical objects, of which, according to the Pythagoreans,
numbers are the principles. Mathematical objects are completely
divorced from motion and are not natural, with the exception of
those of astronomy; for astronomy is indeed a mathematical science,   10
but it theorizes about natural objects and those in motion, for the
stars, with which it concerns itself, are natural and in motion.
But having posited principles of this sort, they concern themselves with nothing else than natural things, and generate these
from those [incorporeal] principles; for they generate the heaven
and its parts from the principles which they posited (these, as we
said before, are the even and the odd), and explain the phenomena   15
connected with these (by 'these' I mean the things in the heavens),
as if nothing either is or comes into being out of these principles
except sensible things and bodies – in this respect they agree with
the natural philosophers, who thought there is nothing except
natural things and those in motion. And yet principles of the kind
they posited were adequate to be called principles both of incorporeal things and of those that are above natural things, 'and they   20
are more suited to these than to theories about nature' [990a8]. And
Aristotle [also] criticizes them for this, that they did not adequately
explain the causes even of natural things. For how does movement,

---

[221] 71,13. It becomes clearer, from 72,12ff below, that Aristotle's criticism is not
of the aspect of the Pythagorean doctrine that is here discussed, the exotic character
of their principles, but rather of their failure to employ the immaterial principles
they posited. *Mentoi*, 72,12, is an echo of *men*, 71,13; the latter has an adversative
sense.

obviously the proper characteristic of natural things, come to be in
them, if they exist and come into being from such principles as
these, the limited and the unlimited? Of these principles, the
25   limited is the odd, which Aristotle calls limit, and the unlimited is
what the Pythagoreans call the even. For numbers are motionless,
and are not responsible for any motion whatever. But they do not
even explain that it is possible, without movement and change, for
the things which they generate from those causes to come to be,
nor [do they explain] even the actions of the stars, which are
brought about by their motion and movement; for the actions of the
30   stars are their risings and settings and things of this sort, and how
is it possible for these to occur without movement? By his reference
to the stars, whose activity is through movement, Aristotle shows
with all clarity the inadequacy of the theory.

But even if they should be conceded the possibility that spatial
magnitudes and bodies can be composed out of numbers and things
that have no extension whatever, something that is most assuredly
35   impossible – not even if this be posited do they explain the source,
in natural bodies, of the internal inclinations (*rhopê*) natural to
them, lightness and heaviness;[222] for certainly these bodies are not
73,1   potentially light or heavy, as they are for those according to whom
a kind of matter, which is either a kind of body or potentially a
body, underlies [these qualities]. For what they say about bodies is
not more applicable to natural than to mathematical bodies, since
equality and inequality and shape are common both to the latter
5   and to the former. But if they do not explain the properties (*ta idia*)
of natural bodies in virtue of which they are natural (these are
heaviness-lightness, heat-cold, moisture-dryness), they would not
even by speaking about natural bodies, about which they intended
and proposed to speak.

[222] 73,26, *rhopai*. On the various senses of this term in Aristotle, see Bonitz, Index,
668b. In the present text, Alexander uses the term in the first sense specified by
Bonitz: inclination downwards, or weight, that which causes a downward inclination;
cf. Aristotle *Metaph.* 1052b29, where Ross translates *rhopê* as 'gravity'. The more
dynamic sense of *rhopê* = *dunamis* is found in Alexander *in Metaph.* 5, 357,27–9;
earth and fire, and also animate beings such as man and the other animals, are all
what they are in virtue of their form; in living things this form is the soul, in earth
and fire it is *rhopê*; and id. 421,18–20: how natural things are prevented from moving
in accordance with their *hormê* (natural impulse or drive) and their *rhopê*; also *de
Mixtione* 237,9, where Todd translates 'impulse'. On *rhopê*, see Fritz Zimmermann,
'Philoponus' impetus theory in the Arabic tradition', in Richard Sorabji (ed.), *Philoponus and the Rejection of Aristotelian Science*, London and Ithaca N.Y. 1987, 121–2
and 128.

990a18 And again,[223] how ought we to understand that the
modifications of number and number itself are causes of what   10
[exists and happens] in the heavens?

Aristotle points out this further absurd consequence that results
for [the Pythagoreans]: that while saying that the causes of the
things that exist and happen in the heavens, from the beginning
and now, are the modifications of numbers and numbers themselves
(for they think that there is nothing else except the things in the
heavens),[224] they do not speak of nor admit any other numbers
outside of these, from which, in their view, the universe is consti-   15
tuted. Now the cause ought to be something other than the effect
(*to aitiaton*); but although saying that numbers are the universe
and each of the things in it, and assuming that numbers are the
principles of these things, they speak of no other number apart
from this – as Plato did in speaking of one number, the ideal
number, which he also made a cause, and of another number that
is in sensible things. But speaking as they do, [the Pythagoreans]   20
would be saying that number itself is its own cause, if it is in fact
the cause of the things existing in the universe, but is itself these
things.

990a22 When they place opinion and opportunity in this
particular place . . .
                                                                       74,1
By these words Aristotle shows how the Pythagoreans made the
universe and the things in it numbers. While forever talking of
numbers and making numbers the causes of these things, they did
not speak of other numbers apart from these, but said that numbers   5
themselves are their own causes; and [thus] the same thing becomes
for them both cause and effect. For they said that opinion is established in a particular part of the universe, and opportunity in
another, and in yet another in turn, whether below or above these,
either injustice or decision (*krisis*) or mixture or some other of the
things in the heavens.[225] The proof they offered that these things   10

---

[223] 73,9. The lemma has *eti hai*, Ross and Jaeger *eti de*.
[224] 73,13. On this text, see Philip, op. cit., 70, n. 2.
[225] 74,7–76,5. With this description of the Pythagorean doctrine, cf. 38,8–41,5
above. As n. 131 points out, there are certain discrepancies between the arrangement
of the heavenly bodies as described there and in the present text. The principal
difference is that here the number 1 is at the centre of the universe, whereas in the
earlier description the hearth, or central fire, held this place. See Burkert and Raven
as cited in n. 131, and Philip, op. cit., 169, n. 10. The *alt. rec.* offers some additional
information of interest: 'When questioned, they said that for each of the things
mentioned there is a number, and that just as an orderly arrangement is discerned
in the case of numbers, so [such an arrangement is found] in the case of the universe,
since it is a number and has its being out of numbers. . . . In these numbers,

are established according to an arrangement such as this is that each of them belongs to a number,[226] and there is a particular number proper to each place in the universe. For at the centre is 1 (for the centre is the first place in the universe); after the centre is 2, which they called both 'opinion' and 'daring'; and in this way the number of things being constituted becomes greater as they keep moving away from the centre, because the numbers too from which they are constituted, or rather with which they are identical,[227] are of this kind. For they said that numbers and their modifications follow the places in the heavens, and are proper to them; and that for this reason spatial magnitudes too come into existence at a later stage out of these numbers.[228] – The words, 'There happens to be already in this place a plurality of spatial magnitudes composed [of numbers]' [990a25], could refer to the places in our vicinity, i.e. on earth, in the sense that in this place a plurality of spatial magnitudes is constituted because the number already in this place is also greater, so that,[229] being greater, it produces the differences with respect to the plurality of spatial magnitudes; for [the Pythagoreans] say that the numbers and their modifications follow in accordance with their relationship (*oikeiotês*) with the particular places. Or a simpler and more literal [interpretation] is to say[230] that the causes themselves of the plurality [of spatial magnitudes] are established in a particular place and that there are already more numbers in this place, in the sense that the multiplicity of things follows on the multiplicity of these numbers, because things *are* numbers for those who construct even the universe itself according to a num-

---

therefore, and in the powers resulting from them [i.e. the numbers raised to their second, third, and higher powers], are discerned both the unequal 1, which is proper to injustice, and the equal 1, which is proper to decision or justice. Moreover, mixture too consists in equality, the symbol of which is the right angle.' (74).

[226] 74,11, *hekaston tou arithmou estin*, lit. 'is of the number', probably because each of the things mentioned was said to be identified with a particular number. The *alt. rec.* gives what seems to be a better version of the doctrine: 'each of them *is* a number.'

[227] 74,15. Reading *tauta* for *tauta*, by analogy with 75,21.

[228] 74,12–75,2. See Ross's criticism of Alexander's interpretation of *Metaph.* 990a25–27; 'spatial magnitudes', he says, 'is inapplicable to opinion and the like' (*Metaphysics* I, 185 ad 26). But does Alexander in fact equate *megethê*, 'spatial magnitudes', with opinion? He seems rather to say that the latter come *after* the things identified with the numbers 1, 2, etc. Perhaps too, as the *alt. rec.* implies, *megethê* are to be understood of extended mathematical entities: triangle, square, etc.

[229] 75,6. Reading *hôste* for *hôn ta* (Hayduck), and omitting the bracketed [*te*].

[230] 75,8–10, *tou en tini ... topôi toutôi*. The text is corrupt at this point; the minimal sense that can be obtained from *tou ... aitia* results from adopting Bonitz's *to* for *tou* (l. 8).

ber.[231] But is it this number in the heavens that we should consider the cause of the things that come to be in the heavens, so that it is its own cause, or is some other number the cause of this one? It is surely more reasonable to say there is another number, as Plato   15 too did. (In the second book of his treatise on the doctrine of the Pythagoreans, Aristotle mentions the arrangement of the numbers in the heavens which the Pythagoreans devised.)[232]

990a23 A little above or below [were located] injustice and decision.

Those who said that things are numbers allotted to things that place in the heavens that, they believed, the numbers with which   20 these things are identical also occupy. They said, for instance, that opinion occupies that place in the universe which, they believed, 2 occupies, since for them 2 was opinion.[233] To opportunity they gave in turn that place in the universe which 7 occupies, since they also thought that the number 7 is opportunity. And a little above or below opportunity they located injustice or decision, whichever it   25 happened to be, because the place of the numbers themselves was also the same for these things. Certain transcriptions of the text have the reading *anikia* instead of *adikia* (injustice). [Some] say that the Pythagoreans called the number 5 *anikia* because the first of the rectangular triangles having rational sides is that, one of whose sides enclosing a right angle is three [units long], the other   30 four, and the hypoteneuse of which is five [units long]. Since therefore the square of the hypoteneuse is equal (*ison dunatai*) to that of both the sides together,[234] it is for this reason called the one

[231] 75,2–12. Alexander struggles to find an intelligible explanation of *Metaph.* 990a25–7; on that text, see Ross as cited in n. 228. He first states that the *megethê*, magnitudes or extensions of some sort, come into existence out of a combination of the numbers 1, 2, etc., but presumably while the constitution of the celestial cosmos is still in process. He then offers two additional interpretations: that Aristotle is referring to spatial magnitudes on earth, or that the causes of plurality pre-exist in a place; the question, whether this place is celestial or terrestrial, is left undetermined. These 'causes' seem again to be simply numbers, and the multiplicity of the *megethê* to be consequent on them. This last interpretation he calls 'simpler and more obvious', but it is, if anything, more complicated and confusing than the others.

[232] 75,15–17 = Ross, *Fragmenta Selecta*, 137; Ross, *Select Fragments*, 141.

[233] 75,23. '. . . [Alexander's] equation of dyad and *doxa* is not Pythagorean', Philip, op. cit., 70, n. 3. But if *duas* here means the number 2, as the sequence shows, that criticism may not be justified.

[234] 75,31–2. '*Dunasthai*: valere in potentia, in quadrato, . . . to be equivalent in square': Charles Mugler, *Dictionnaire historique de la terminologie géométrique des Grecs*, 150. The play on *dunatai-dunamenê–dunasteuomenai* can be brought out only imperfectly in English. The meaning is that the square of 5 (25) equals the sum of the square of 3 and 4 (9 + 16). Thus the hypoteneuse is, as Alexander says at first, *equal* to the two sides taken together, and it is not 'defeated' by them; but how can it be said to 'dominate' (l. 33) except in a contest with the sides taken separately?

'having power' (*dunamenê*), while the sides are called those 'that are overpowered' (*dunasteuomenai*); and the hypoteneuse is 5. And they called 5 *a-nikia* because it is not defeated (*nikômenê*), but is unconquered and dominant. But whether the reading should be

76,1 *anikia* or *adikia*, it is easy to understand the sense of what is being said.

'Let us leave the Pythagoreans for the present,' says Aristotle, 'since it is sufficient only to have touched on them' [990a33], [thus] excusing himself from a more lengthy examination of them at this stage, because they included among the things that are nothing more than did the natural philosophers. He will, however, still discuss their entire doctrine about the principles towards the end

5 of this treatise.[235]

[235] 76,4–5. Perhaps a reference to *Metaphysics* 14, 1090a20–35, although in that passage Aristotle merely recapitulates his criticism of the Pythagorean theory given in Book 1.

CHAPTER 9

990a34 Those who made the Ideas causes, firstly, in seeking
to grasp the causes of the things around us, [brought in others
equal in number to these].

Those who made the Ideas causes he criticizes [for the following
reasons].[236]

[**Obj. 1**] In seeking the causes of the things constituted by nature
(for surely this is the force of the words, 'of the things around us'),   76,10
they added other substances, equal in number to these things, as
if things would be more intelligible if there were more of the same
things; for in no other respect did they make the Ideas differ from
the things that are by reference to them than by their eternity,[237]
so that, since these things are unknowable, the Ideas too would be
unknowable in the same way as these things, of which, they say,
they are the models. By positing, then, other things equal in number
and similar to those the knowledge and understanding of which   15
they were seeking, they thought that by means of these they would
be able to comprehend those things too which they were seeking,
as Aristotle will show a little later. Or his criticism is that, wishing
to know the causes of the things that are, they sought, by means
of these things, the causes of the things themselves.[238] For they
thought they were explaining the causes of these things by adopting
a procedure similar to that of those who wish to count a certain
plurality, but then, on the ground that these things could not be
counted if there were so many of them,[239] add to them another   20
plurality equal in number to the first, and then count in this way.
But the real force of the objection would be, not that the plurality
of things the Platonists posited is equal in number to the things
they were seeking, but that these things are similar [to the ones

---

[236] 76,8ff. To bring some order into Alexander's lengthy commentary on ch. 9, I
have broken up the text by introducing Ross's enumeration of Aristotle's various
arguments against the Platonists. On the insertion of 'the Platonists' throughout
these pages, see n. 163.

[237] 76,12, *tôi aidiôi*. The term may have been suggested to Alexander by Aristotle's
kai epi tois aidiois (*Metaph.* 990b8), although *aidios* in Aristotle's text refers to the
heavenly bodies, as Alexander later interprets that passage (77,26).

[238] 76,17–18, *ê ho . . . ta aitia*. The text here is corrupt, and yields no acceptable
sense. The unsatisfactory translation follows the Latin version (S) given in
Hayduck's apparatus.

[239] 76,20, *tosauta*. This is unexpected, for Alexander must have in mind Aristotle's
elattonôn ontôn, 'because they were so few' (*Metaph.* 990b3). But Alexander's way of
stating the case makes the absurdity of the supposed method more obvious.

being sought], and for this reason are similarly unknowable. Aristotle will say that, according to the Platonists, the Forms do not
25   differ at all, except by their eternity, from the things that exist by
reference to them; but by the comparison with number he has
pointed out that the Forms are unknowable in the same way [as
the things referred to them]. And he will soon show that the things
they added to those they were investigating are not causes. Or his
77,1   criticism is that the Platonists, having added things almost equal
in number to those they were investigating, were thus investigating
all things, and were explaining the causes both of the first things
and of those added on; for his example of number also agrees with
this interpretation. In saying that the Forms 'are almost not fewer
than these things' [990b4], he is speaking not of particular things
and individuals but of classes (*eidê*) over these individuals.[240] For
5   the Platonists were not seeking the causes of Socrates or Plato but
of man and horse, for according to them the Forms are almost equal
in number to these classes. But he adds 'almost' perhaps because
they did not posit Ideas of all common things; for they did not posit
them either of [the universals] over artefacts (*ta tekhnêta*) or of
those over evil things, even though, as he will soon say, the consequence was that they said there are Ideas of these things too because
of what they said about the Ideas.
10   To show that the Ideas are no fewer than the things whose causes
the Platonists were seeking when they proceeded [to postulate] the
Ideas, he adds: 'for to each thing there is something homonymous'
[999b6], saying 'homonymous' rather than 'synonymous' because
Plato too spoke of the Ideas in this way [*Tim.* 52A, *Parm.* 133D].
Aristotle is pointing out that it was because the Platonists posited
some Form synonymous with each of the things they were investigating that they say the Forms are equal in number to sensible
15   things. Or the term 'homonymous' could mean that, as the Platonists speak of [the Ideas], the latter would contribute nothing to our
knowledge of the things in this world (*ta entautha*). After saying,
'for to each thing there is something homonymous', he shows how
this is so 'in the case of each thing'. His statement that 'and apart
from the substances [there is something homonymous], and of the
other things too that are a one-over-many,[241] both in the case of the

---

[240] 77,5. Ross argues that *toutois* (*Metaph.* 990b2) means individual things, not
classes of things, as Alexander here interprets it; he points to *tôndi tôn ontôn* (b1)
as evidence (*Metaphysics* I, 191 ad b2). In the sequence of the commentary (77,10ff),
Alexander is of course constrained to understand individual things because of
hekaston in Aristotle's text (*Metaph.* 990b6).

[241] 77,18–19. The text of *Metaphysics* that Alexander quotes here (990b6–8)
presents problems. Jaeger reads: *kath' hekaston gar homônumon ti ésti ‹kai para tas
ousias› tôn te allôn hôn éstin hen epi pollôn ‹kai para tas ousias›*, 'for to each thing
there is something homonymous, both of the other things of which there is a one-

things here below and in that of eternal things' [990b7], would be equivalent to saying that apart from the substances here below (*têide*) there are Forms homonymous with them, and similarly [Forms] apart from the other things that exist in addition to substance, which are the other genera,[242] over which there is something one and common to the many particulars. For in cases in which there are common things,[243] those that are above the particulars, the Ideas would, according to the Platonists, be causes of the being and of the coming to be of the common things. The words, 'both in the case of the things here below and in that of eternal things', would mean both for the things [subject to] generation and destruction ('things here below' indicates these), and for eternal things; for according to the Platonists, both the universe and the things in it possess their being eternally.[244] Hence it is reasonable to say that there is an equal number [of Forms] 'of the other things too of which there is a one-over-many', in the sense that [there are Forms] of the other things too of which there is a one over many instances;

20

25

over-many, and apart from the substances . . .' Ross reads: *kath' hekaston gar homônumon ti esti kai para tas ousias, tôn te allôn éstin hen epi pollôn*, translating: 'for to each thing there answers an entity having the same name as it and existing apart from the substances, and in the case of non-substantial things there is a one-over-many' (*Metaphysics* I, 191 ad 6). Alexander's reading differs from both the above: *kath' hekaston gar homônumon ti esti* (this part quoted separately at 77,16–17), *kai para tas ousias tôn te allôn ha estin hen epi pollôn*, although at 27 below, Alexander has Jaeger's reading: *tôn te allôn hôn estin hen epi pollôn*. The reading of the present text would be more consistent with what follows if a second *estin* were inserted after *ousias*: 'And . . . [there is] a one-over-many of the other things that are', those scl. that are in addition to substance, as he later explains.

[242] 77,20–2. Earlier in the commentary, Alexander has interpreted Aristotle's *ousiai* of sensible substances (76,10), and the Platonic *eidê tôn ontôn* in the usual sense of man, horse, etc. (77,5). But here he understands Aristotle's statement that there is a one-over-many in the case of things other than substance to mean that there are also Forms for the Aristotelian categories other than substance: quantity, quality, and the other accidents. This interpretation, however, is not carried out in what follows.

[243] 77,22.23.29, *ta koina*; 77,32, *to koinon*. The translation of these terms is difficult. Martin Tweedale translates the singular as 'the common item' ('Alexander of Aphrodisias' views on universals', *Phronesis* 29, 1984, 279–303), and 'common entity' is also possible; but I prefer the more concrete 'common thing' or 'things'. (See Greek–English Index for a listing of subsequent occurrences of these terms.) It would be simpler to render *to koinon* as 'the universal', for such of course it is, but it seems better to reserve this translation for *to katholou*. As to whether Alexander distinguishes between *to koinon* and *to kathoulou*, see R.W. Sharples, 'Alexander of Aphrodisias: scholasticism and innovation', *Aufstieg und Niedergang der römischen Welt* 36.2, Berlin, 1987, 1202, n. 72, with the sources there cited.

[244] 77,26–7. By *tois aidiois* (*Metaph.* 990b8) Aristotle means the heavenly bodies, as his expanded expression at 991a shows: *tois aidiois tôn aisthêtôn*; thus Ross believes, and thus Alexander interprets both here and in his commentary on the later text (96,2ff below). Harold Cherniss, however, thinks that *tois aidiois* refers to the Ideas; see his lengthy discussion of the point, and of what he takes to be Alexander's error: *Aristotle's Criticism of Plato and the Academy* I, Baltimore 1944, 199, n. 117.

for he adds this with the intention of making clear the meaning of
30   'other things', since, according to the Platonists, the Ideas are causes
of the common things that are over the [many] particulars.[245] Or
else he says, 'the one-over-many', with reference to the Idea; for
even though there is not an Idea of particular things, still there is
an Idea of the common thing in these particulars; for there is an
Idea of man, although not of Socrates or Plato, and this 'man' must
be common both to Socrates and to Plato and to all those who have
the same form as they, because it is in all of them.
35   [**Obj. 2**][246] 'None of the ways in which we prove that the Forms
78,1   exist is convincing' [990b8]. The words 'we prove' show that in
stating the doctrine of Plato, Aristotle is speaking as if in reference
to his own opinion; for it is not as one refuting another's arguments
and theories, but as one testing and critically examining his own
opinion, that he refutes [Plato] in order to discover the truth. He
5   attempts to show that none of the arguments offered to establish
the Ideas proves that there are Ideas. For some of them neither
conclude correctly (*sullogizesthai*) nor prove the point at issue, in
addition to the fact that they posit Ideas even of things for which
the Platonists did not wish there to be Ideas; and others, although
they seem to reach some valid conclusion about the Ideas, do not
escape the charge of establishing Ideas even of things for which the
Platonists did not wish there to be Ideas. For the case is not that
10   some of these arguments are stated in a completely invalid way
(*asullogistôs*), while others establish Ideas even of things for which
the Platonists do not wish to say there are Ideas, but that some of
the same arguments fail in both these respects and others fail, at
any rate, in one or other of them.
    Or else Aristotle is charging that some of the arguments stated
by the Platonists are totally false and prove nothing, such as would
be the one that says: if there is anything true, the Forms must
exist, for none of the things in this world is true. And: if there is
15   memory, there are Forms, for memory is of that which is permanent.
And the one that says: number is of being (*ontos*); but the things

---

[245] 77,24–30. See n. 241 on the reading of Aristotle's text adopted here by Alexander. In the commentary above, he interpreted 'the other things of which there is
a one-over-many' as the genera of accident (genera in categories other than substance); here he understands them as the particular instances that are under the
universal. In this interpretation, the 'common things' or universals are themselves
under a Form or Idea, which is their cause. It is difficult, at first reading, to see how
Alexander's second interpretation (77,31–4) differs from his first, although it might
possibly be taken to mean that the Idea *is to koinon*, the thing common to particular
instances and in them; but this would be to make the Ideas immanent in sensible
things, and Alexander will later say that the Platonists rejected this view.
[246] 77,34ff. Aristotle's second criticism of the Ideas (*Metaph.* 990b8–17) actually
contains several distinct arguments. These I have marked a, b, etc. from 79,3
onwards in Alexander's extended commentary on this text.

here below are not beings (*onta*); but if that is so, [number is] of the Forms; therefore, the Forms exist. And similarly the one saying that definitions are of things that are, but that none of the things here below *is*.[247] But arguments such as these are false and do not at all prove what should be proved. For this reason Aristotle does not, at this time, mention any argument of this sort, but censures some of the arguments that seem to prove something; and first the 20 one that attempts to establish the Ideas from the sciences. If the very arguments stated by the Platonists to establish the Ideas are such that either they do not prove the point at issue, or bring in Ideas of certain other things and not of those they wish, there is no need for other arguments from another source, but to have shown the weakness of what they say suffices in itself to destroy the theory 25 [of the Ideas].

990b11 For according to the arguments from the sciences, 79,1 there will be Forms of all the things of which there are sciences.

[**Obj. 2a**][248] The Platonists also used the sciences to establish the Ideas, and in a number of ways, as Aristotle says in the first book of *On Ideas*; and the arguments to which he seems to be referring 5 here are such as the following. [i] If every science does its work by referring to some one and the same thing, and not to any particular

---

[247] 78,13–18 is printed by Harlfinger (see n. 248) as being doubtfully a quotation from the *de Ideis*. Janine Bertier comments on these minor arguments in proof of the Ideas, 'Les preuves de la réalité des nombres et la théorie des idées d'après Métaphysique N2, 1090a2–3, 1090b5', *Mathematics and Metaphysics in Aristotle*, Bern 1987, 294–7; and S. Mansion (cited in n. 248) examines them at length, 174–81 (104–11 in the reprint).

[248] 79,3–83,30 = (with certain omissions) Ross, *Fragmenta Selecta*, 122–5; Ross, *Select Fragments*, 125–8. Alexander 83,34–89,7 = (with certain omissions) Ross, *Fragmenta Selecta*, 125–8; Ross, *Select Fragments*, 129–32. In ROTA, these two fragments are printed continuously, II, 2435–40, but Alexander 88,20–89,7, included by Ross, is omitted. Gaiser prints 85,15–86,23 as his Testimonium 48B (op. cit., 527–8), and this same text is given, with French translation, by Richard (op. cit., 260–5). Translations of portions of the *de Ideis* will be found in Terry Penner, *The Ascent from Nominalism*, Dordrecht 1987, 245–50, and in the studies listed in the following notes. A new edition of the text of the *de Ideis* by Dieter Harlfinger is included in Walter Leszl's *Il 'De Ideis' di Aristotele e la teoria platonica delle Idee*, Firenze 1975, 22–39. Numerous additions to the fragment as printed by Rose were proposed by Wilpert, first in *Die Reste . . .*, 378–85, then in *Zwei . . . Frühschriften . . .*, 15–120; for a list of these, see Suzanne Mansion, 'La critique de la théorie des Idées dans le *Peri Ideôn* d'Aristote', *Revue Philosophique de Louvain* 47, 1949, 169–202; reprinted in her *Études Aristoteliciennes*, Louvain 1984, 99–132. Scholarly interest in the *de Ideis* was stimulated by the seminal studies of Léon Robin, *La théorie platonicienne des idées et des nombres d'après Aristote*, Paris 1908; repr. Hildesheim 1963, and of Harold Cherniss (op. cit.); the latter work contains copious references to the older literature. For the secondary literature to 1975, see Leszl's comprehensive study of the *de Ideis* noted above; more recent sources are reported in the studies referred to in the following notes.

thing, there must be, in the case of each science, something else apart from sensible things which is eternal, and a model of the things that come to be in each science. But the Idea is a thing of this sort. [ii] Again, the things of which there are sciences *are*; but the sciences deal with certain things apart from particular things,
10 for these latter are unlimited and indefinite, whereas the objects of the sciences are determinate (*hôrismenos*). Therefore, there are certain things apart from particular things, and these are the Ideas. [iii] Again, if medicine is the science not of this particular health but simply of health, there will be a health-itself; and if geometry is not the science of this equal and this commensurable but simply of equal and simply of commensurable, there will be an equal-itself
15 and a commensurable-itself; and these are the Ideas.

Such arguments, however, do not prove the point at issue, which was that there are Ideas, but prove [only] that there are certain things apart from sensible particulars. But it is not at all the case that, if there are certain things apart from particular things, these things are Ideas; for apart from particular things there are the common things, which we say are also the objects of the sciences. Again, [this also applies to the argument] that there are Ideas too
20 of the things subject to the arts, for in fact every art refers to some one thing the things that come to be from it, and the things with which the arts deal *are*, and the arts deal with certain things apart from particular things. And the last argument, in addition to the fact that it does not prove that there are Ideas, will also be seen to establish Ideas of things for which the Platonists do not wish there to be Ideas. For if, because medicine is not a science of this health
80,1 but simply of health, there is such a thing as health-itself, there will also be [something of this sort] in the case of each of the arts. For [an art] does not deal with the particular thing nor the 'this', but simply with that which is its object, as carpentry simply with bench, not with this bench, and simply with bed, not this bed; in
5 similar fashion both sculpture, and painting, and building, and each of the other arts is related to the things subject to it. Therefore, there will also be an Idea for each of the objects of the arts, the very thing the Platonists do not wish.[249]

990b13 And according to the 'one-over-many [argument]' that there is one attribute common to many things there will be Forms even of negations.

[**Obj. 2b**] They also use an argument such as the following to establish the Ideas. If each of the many men is a man, and each of

[249] 79,3–80,6. On the argument 'from the sciences', see Daniel Frank, 'A disproof in the *Peri Ideôn*', *Southern Journal of Philosophy* 22, 1984, 49–59.

the many animals an animal, and so in all the other cases, and if　10
in none of these cases is the same thing predicated of itself, but
there is something predicated of all of them that is not the same
as any of them, there must be something belonging to [all of]
them,[250] apart from the particular things, that is separated (*kekh-*
ôrismenos) and eternal; for it is always predicated in the same way
of all the [particular] things that keep changing numerically. But
that which is one over many, separated from them and eternal, is
an Idea; therefore, there are Ideas.　15

This argument, Aristotle says, establishes Ideas even of negations
(*apophasis*) and of things that are not; for one and the same negation
is in fact predicated of many things, and even of things that are
not, and is not the same as any of the things of which it is predicated
truly. For 'not-man' is predicated of horse and dog and of everything
apart from man, and for this reason is a one-over-many (*hen epi*　20
pollôn) and is not any of the things of which it is predicated. Again,
it always remains predicable in a like way of things that are alike;
for 'non-musical' is predicated truly of many things (of all those
that are not musical), and similarly 'not-man' of all things that are　81,1
not man, so that there are Ideas even of negations. But this is
absurd; for how could there be an Idea of not-being? For if one
accepts this – [that there are Ideas of negations] – there will be a
single Idea of things generically dissimilar and totally different –
of line, for instance, and man; for both of these are 'not-horse'.
Again, there will be a single Idea even of an unlimited number of　5
things. Moreover, there will also [be a single Idea] of what is
primary and what is secondary; for both man and animal are 'not-
wood', but one of them is primary, the other secondary, and the
Platonists do not wish there to be either genera or Ideas of such
things. It is clear that not even this argument proves that there
are Ideas, but that it too tends to prove that what is predicated in
common is other than the particular things of which it is
predicated.[251]　10

Again, the very people who wish to show that what is predicated
in common of many things is one thing, and that this is an Idea,
construct [a proof] of this from negations. For one who denies some-

---

[250] 80,12, *eiê an ti toutôn.* I follow Ross in translating, 'there must be something
belonging to them', although ROTA has adopted a new version: 'there will be something', and *sic* Gail Fine, 'The One over Many', *Philosophical Review* 89, 1980, 199.
But *toutôn* must be accounted for; and that the *ti kekhôrismenon* (something separated) 'belongs to' the particulars is a valid statement, since, as Alexander has just
pointed out, it is properly predicated of them. Cf. 88,17–18 below: 'the fact that one
thing is predicated in reference to many, a thing that, [being] the same, belongs
(*huparkhei*) to all of them', etc.

[251] 80,8–81,10. On these lines, see Cherniss, op. cit., 260–72; Fine, op. cit.; Schmitz,
op. cit., II, 402–6.

thing of several things will do so by reference to one thing; for if he says, 'Man is not white', and 'Horse is not white', he is not denying, in each case, an attribute proper to man and horse, but,
15   referring to one thing, he denies one and the same whiteness of each of them. [But if this is so, then] neither would one who affirms the same attribute of several things be affirming, in each case, a different attribute, but there must be some one thing which he affirms – [he predicates] 'man', for instance, by reference to one and the same thing; for as with negation, so with affirmation (*kataphasis*). Therefore, there exists something else that is apart from what is in sensible things, something that accounts for the affirmation that is true of several things and common [to them]; and this is the
20   Idea. Now this argument, Aristotle says, creates Ideas not only of things that are affirmed but also of those that are denied; for in both cases there is a similar [reference to] one thing.[252]

990b14 According to [the argument] that it is possible to think of something even when it has perished, [there will be Forms] of perishable things; for there is an image of these.

25   [**Obj. 2c**] The argument that attempts to establish that there are Ideas from thinking (*noein*) is as follows. If, when we think of man or footed or animal, we are thinking of something that both is one of the things that are and is not any of the particular things (for in fact the same thought (*ennoia*) remains even after these things have perished), it is clear that there is something apart from sensible particulars, of which we think both when these latter exist and when they do not; for certainly we are not then thinking of some-
82,1   thing non-existent. And this is a Form or Idea. Now Aristotle says that this argument establishes Ideas even of things that are perishable or that have perished, and in general of particular and perishable things, such as Socrates or Plato; for in fact we think of these men, and retain [their image in] imagination and preserve them even when they no longer exist; for there is also an image (*phan-*
5   *tasma*) of things that no longer exist. Moreover, we also think of things that do not exist at all, such as the Horse-Centaur and the Chimera; so that not even such an argument proves that there are Ideas.[253]

---

[252] 80,10–22. On this part of the argument, see especially Schmitz, op. cit. II, 404.
[253] 81,25–82,7. Cherniss discusses this argument, op. cit., 272–5; he thinks it '. . . simply a special form of the proof that the common predicate which is the object of knowledge is other than the particular sensible . . .' (273).

990b15 Again, some of the more accurate arguments lead to Ideas of relations, of which we say there is no independent class; and others involve (*legousin*) the third man.[254]   10

[**Obj. 2d**] The argument that attempts to establish Ideas from[255] relatives is the following.[256] When the same term is predicated of several things not homonymously, but in such a way as to indicate a single nature, it is predicated truly of them either because they   83,1 are in the proper sense that which is signified by the predicate, as when we call Socrates or Plato 'man'; or because they are likenesses of things that are truly [what is signified by the predicate,] as when we predicate 'man' of men in pictures (for in the case of these latter we indicate the likenesses of men by signifying the same particular nature in all of them); or because one of them is model and the   5 others likenesses, as if we were to call both Socrates and his likenesses 'men'. But we predicate equality itself of the things here on earth, although it is predicated of them [only] homonymously; for neither does the same formula apply to them all, nor are we signifying things that are truly equal, for the quantity (*to poson*) of sensible things is not precisely determined, but shifts and continually changes, nor does any of the things here on earth admit exactly   10 of the formula of equality. But neither [are they related] as model and likeness, for none of them is more model or likeness than any

----

[254] 82,10, *legousin*. Ross explains this word (crediting Jackson) thus: 'Aristotle has previously pointed out certain *consequences* of Platonic arguments; he now points out certain *implications actually stated* (*legousin* can mean nothing else) in Plato's more accurate arguments ...' (*Metaphysics* I, 194 ad 15); and he translates, '. . . others *introduce* the "third man" ' (italics added). Cherniss, however, defends Alexander's interpretation of *legousin* in the sense of 'involve', 'imply', 'say *in effect*' (op. cit., 276, n. 184). The meaning of Aristotle's 'the more accurate arguments' is also debated. Ross does not accept Alexander's interpretation (83,17–22 below) that these arguments, unlike the previous ones, establish the existence of Ideas as models (*paradeigmata*); but see Schmitz, op. cit., I,2, 445, for a criticism of Ross's view. See further Gail Fine, 'Aristotle and the more accurate arguments', *Language and Logos*, Cambridge 1982, 158, with a discussion of Cherniss's opinion.

[255] 82,11. Reading *ek tôn pros ti* for *kai tôn pros ti* (Harlfinger).

[256] 82,11–83,33. On the 'argument from relatives', see S. Mansion, op. cit., 181–6 (111–16 in the reprint). This argument has elicited much discussion since G.E.L. Owen published, in 1957, 'A proof in the *Peri Ideôn*', *Journal of Hellenic Studies*; reprinted in R.E. Allen (ed.), *Studies in Plato's Metaphysics*, London and N.Y., 1965, 293–312, and again in G.E.L. Owen, *Logic, Science and Dialectic*, London and Ithaca N.Y. 1986, 165–79. Listed here, in chronological order, are studies that have appeared more recently. Julia Annas, 'Forms and first principles', *Phronesis* 19, 1974, 257–83; Leszl, op. cit. (1975), 185–224; Robert Barford, 'A proof from the *Peri Ideôn* revisited', *Phronesis* 21, 1976, 198–218; C.J. Rowe, 'The proof from relatives in the *Peri Ideôn*: further reconsideration', *Phronesis* 24, 1979, 270–81; Michel Narcy, 'L'homonymie entre Aristote et ses commentateurs néo-platoniciens', *Études Philosophiques*, 1981, 49 and note aditionnelle, 50–2; Fine, op. cit. 1982; Schmitz, op. cit., I,2 (1985), 446–50, and II *passim* (specific references given in the following notes).

other. But even if one were to admit that the likeness is not [merely] homonymous with its model, the conclusion is always that these particular equal things are equal [only] as likenesses of what is
15 equal in the true and proper sense. But if this is so, there is an equal-itself, one that is equal in the proper sense, by reference to which the things here, as likenesses of it, come to be, and are said to be, equal; but this is an Idea, a model[257] for the things that come to be by reference to it.

Only this last argument, then, one that also establishes Ideas of relatives, seems to aim more carefully and more accurately and more directly at a proof for the Ideas. For this argument, unlike
20 the ones that preceded it, seems to show not simply that the common thing is something apart from particular things, but that there is some model of the things here on earth, [a model] which [itself] *is* in the proper sense;[258] for this is what is thought to be characteristic of the Ideas most of all. Aristotle says, then, that this argument establishes Ideas of relatives as well. At all events, the proof just given proceeded by reference to the equal, and this is a relative; but the Platonists denied that there are Ideas of relatives because
25 Ideas, being for them substances of some kind, subsist independently, whereas relatives have their being in their relation to one another.[259] Again, if the equal is equal to an equal, there would be more than one Idea of the equal; for the equal-itself is equal to the equal-itself, for if it were not equal to anything it would not be equal at all. Again, according to this same argument there will have to be Ideas of unequals too, for the situation is similar: [either] there will be Ideas of [both] opposites or there will not be Ideas; but
30 even the Platonists admit that the unequal involves more than one thing. – Once again, Aristotle makes common cause with [Plato's] theory, speaking with reference to it as if it were his own by saying, 'things of which we say there is no independent class'. By 'class' (*genos*) he means substantial being (*hupostasis*) or nature, if indeed relation is like an offshoot [of being], as he said elsewhere (*EN* 1096a21).

But the argument that brings in the third man is the following.[260]
35 The Platonists say that the things predicated in common of subst-

---

[257] 83,16. Deleting *kai eikôn* (Harlfinger).

[258] 83,20–2. According to Alexander, then, the 'argument from relatives' is more accurate because it establishes the existence of Ideas specifically as models; on that point, see the citation to Ross in n. 254.

[259] 83,24–6. On the interpretation of these lines, see Schmitz, op. cit., I,2, 407.

[260] 83,34–85,12. On Alexander's version of the arguments 'that involve the third man', see Curt Arpe, 'Das Argument *Tritos Anthrôpos*', *Hermes* 76, 1941, 171–207; S. Mansion, op. cit., 186–92 (116–22 in the reprint); Fine, op. cit., 161–9; Schmitz, op. cit., II, 194–200 and 211. Of the four arguments, only the last (84,21–85,12) is directly attributed to the *de Ideis* by Alexander.

ances both are in the proper sense such things [as they are said to
be], and that they are Ideas. And again,[261] [they say] that things   84,1
similar to one another are similar by participation in the same
thing, which is this thing in the proper sense; and that this thing
is the Idea. But if this is so, and what is predicated in common of
certain things, if it were not to be the same as any of those things
of which it is predicated, is something else apart from it[262] (for that
is why man-himself is a genus: because, while being predicated of   5
particular men, it was not the same as any of them), there will be
some third man apart both from particular men such as Socrates
or Plato, and from the Idea, which itself is also numerically one.

There was an argument stated by the sophists that brings in the
third man; it is as follows. If we say, 'Man walks', we are not saying
either that man as Idea walks (for the Idea cannot move), or that   10
any particular man walks. (For how [could we say this about one]
whom we do not know? For we know that a man is walking, but
we do not know which of the particular men it is of whom we say
this.) [Hence] we are saying that some other man apart from these
[two], a third man, walks; therefore, there will be a third man of
whom we predicate walking. Now the occasion for this argument,
which is sophistic, is provided by those who separate the common   15
thing from particulars, as do those who posit the Ideas. In his book
against Diodorus [Cronus], Phanias says that the sophist Polyxenus
brought in the third man by saying, 'If it is both by sharing
(*metokhê*) and participating in the Idea, i.e. in man-himself, that
man exists, there must be some man who will have his being by
reference to the Idea. But neither man-himself, which is an Idea,
[exists] by sharing in an Idea, nor does any individual man. It
remains that it is some other man, a third man, who has his being   20
by reference to the Idea.'[263]

The third man can also be proved in this way. If what is predicated truly of more than one thing is also [some] other thing apart
from the things of which it is predicated, being separated from them
(for this is what those who posit the Ideas think they are proving;
for the reason why, according to them, there is something, man-
himself, is because 'man' is predicated truly of particular men, who   25
are more than one, and is other than particular men) – but if this
is so, there will be some third man. For if [the 'man'] predicated is

---

[261] 84,1. Reading *eti te* for *eti* (Harlfinger).

[262] 84,4. Reading *ekeino* for *ekeina* (Harlfinger).

[263] 84,16–21. These lines are excluded by Ross, *Fragmenta Selecta*, but are retained
by Harlfinger, and are given in the ROTA translation of the *de Ideis*. On this
version of the 'third man' argument, see Andreas Graeser, 'Der "Dritte Mensch" des
Polyxenos', *Museum Helveticum* 31, 1974, 140–3, with references to the Polyxenus-
literature; and Schmitz, op. cit., II, 206–8, with a discussion of various
interpretations.

other than those of whom it is predicted and subsists by itself, and
'man' is predicated both of particular men and of the Idea, there
85,1   will be some third man apart both from particular men and from
the Idea. And in this way there will be still a fourth man, the one
predicated of the third man and of the Idea and of particular men,
and similarly a fifth, and so on *ad infinitum*. This argument is the
same as the first, [and follows] because the Platonists posited that
5   things similar to one another are similar by participation in some
identical thing; for particular men and the Ideas are similar. Now
Aristotle refuted both these arguments, although they appear to be
more accurate: the first on the ground that it establishes Ideas of
relatives as well, the second on the ground that it brings in the
third man, then increases [the number of] men *ad infinitum*; and
each of the other things of which the Platonists say there are Ideas
10   will be similarly increased. Others have in fact made use of the
first explanation of the third man [argument], and Eudemus clearly
does so in his work *On Diction*; but Aristotle himself [uses] the last
explanation in the first[264] book of *On Ideas*, and a little later on in
the present treatise.

990b17 And in general, the arguments for the Ideas destroy
the things the existence of which those who say there are Forms
desire to safeguard more than the existence of the Ideas.[265]

15   [**Obj. 3**] What the Platonists desire more, and desire above all else,
is that the principles should exist; for the principles are, for them,
also principles of the Ideas themselves. These principles are the
One and the indefinite dyad, as Aristotle both said a little earlier
[52,1ff] and as he reported in his treatise *On the Good*; moreover,
these are, according to the Platonists, principles of number as well.
Now these arguments, he says, that establish the Ideas destroy
20   these principles; but if the principles are destroyed, the things after
the principles will also be destroyed, on the supposition that they
come from principles, so that the Ideas too will be destroyed.[266] For
if there is something[267] separated, i.e. an Idea, over all the things
that have a common predicate, and if 'dyad' is predicated even of
the indefinite dyad, there would be something prior to the indefinite
dyad and an Idea [of it]; and thus the indefinite dyad would no
longer be a principle. But neither would the dyad, in turn, be both

---

[264] 85,11. Reading *prôtôi* for *tetartôi* (Harlfinger).

[265] 85,13–14. The lemma has *boulontai* rather than the *boulometha* printed by
both Ross and Jaeger, and *hôi legontes eidê*, bracketed by both these editors.

[266] 85,15–88,2. The arguments 'that destroy the principles' are discussed in detail
by Annas, 'Forms . . .'; see also Cherniss, op. cit., 300ff; Schmitz, op. cit., II, 114–18.

[267] 85,22. Reading *khôriston ti* for *te* (S).

prior and a principle, for number is predicated in turn of it too,   25
since it is an Idea, for the Platonists assume that the Ideas are
numbers, so that for them number, being a kind of Idea, would be
the first thing. But in that case, number will be prior to the indefi-   86,1
nite dyad, which for them is a principle, not the dyad to number;
but if this is so, the dyad would no longer be a principle, if it is in
fact what it is by participation (*metaskhesis*) is something else.

Again, [the dyad] is assumed to be a principle of number, but
according to the argument just stated number becomes prior to the   5
dyad. But if number is relative (for every number is the number of
something), and if number is first among the things that are (if it
is in fact prior even to the dyad, which the Platonists assumed to
be a principle), [then] according to them what is relative would be
prior to what exists independently. But this is absurd; for whatever
is relative is secondary. For the relative signifies the relation of an
antecedent underlying nature which is prior to the relation that
belongs to it [only] incidentally;[268] for (as Aristotle says in the   10
Ethics) relation is like an offshoot [of being] [1096a21]. But even if
someone were to say that number is a quantity and not a relation,
the consequence for the Platonists would be that quantity is prior
to substance; and the great and the small are themselves among
the relatives.[269] Again, the consequence is that they must say that
what is relative is both a principle of, and prior to, that which
exists independently, inasmuch as the Idea is, according to them, a
principle of substances, but the Idea's being an Idea consists in its   15
being a model, and a model is relative; for the model is a model of
something. Again, if the Ideas have their being by being models,
the things that come to be by reference to them, and of which they
are the Ideas, would be likenesses of them; and in this way one
might say that, according to the Platonists, all the things constituted by nature become relative, for they are all [either] likenesses
[or] models.[270] Again, if the Ideas have their being by being models,
and a model exists for the sake of that which comes to be by
reference to it, and that which exists on account of another is less
estimable than the latter, the Ideas will be less estimable than the
things that come to be by reference to them.

[268] 86,8–10. The first use of *skhesis* (relation) obscures the point of this statement.
If A is said to be larger than B, the implication is that A, before any comparison
with B, already has a certain size or extension (its 'underlying nature'); and when
it is called 'larger', the meaning is only that it has acquired a quite adventitious
modification (the second *skhesis* of the text) that does not in any way affect its own
nature.

[269] 86,10, *paraphuadi ... êthikois*, and 86,12–13, *auto de ... pros ti*, are omitted
by Harlfinger from the text of the *de Ideis*.

[270] 86,16–20. For a translation of, and commentary on, these lines, see Schmitz,
op. cit., II, 105–6.

87,1   **990b21** And all the other points in which certain people, by following the theory of the Ideas, have contravened the principles.

The following are some of the arguments that, in addition to those already mentioned, because of positing the Ideas destroy their principles. [i] If that which is predicated in common of certain things
5   is their principle and Idea, and if 'principle' is predicated in common of the principles and 'element' of the elements, there would be something prior to, and a principle of, the principles and the elements; and thus there would be neither a principle nor an element. [ii] Again, an Idea is not prior to an Idea, for the Ideas are all equally principles. But the One-itself and the dyad-itself and
10   man-himself and horse-itself and each of the other Ideas is alike an Idea; therefore, none of these will be prior to any other, so that none will be a principle; therefore, the One and the indefinite dyad will not be principles. [iii] Again, it is absurd that an Idea should receive its form from an Idea, for all Ideas are Forms; but if the One and the indefinite dyad are principles, there will be an Idea that receives its form from an Idea: the dyad-itself, that is, from the One-itself. For it is thus that Platonists say these [two] are
15   principles, in the sense that the One is form, the [indefinite] dyad matter; therefore, they are not principles. But if they say that the indefinite dyad is not an Idea, [then] in the first place there will be something prior to it, although it is a principle: the dyad-itself, that is, by participation in which the [indefinite] dyad is itself a dyad, since the indefinite dyad is not the dyad-itself; for it is [only] by participation that 'dyad' will be predicated of it, as it is of the [particular] dyads. [iv] Again, if the Ideas are simple, they would
20   not be [derived] from different principles; but the One and the indefinite dyad are different. [v] Again, the number of dyads will be astonishing if one dyad is the dyad-itself, another the indefinite dyad, another the mathematical dyad we use in counting, which is not the same as either of these, and again, besides these, the dyad in sensible numbered things. These [consequences] are absurd, so that it is clearly possible, by following up the very assumptions
88,1   about the Ideas made by the Platonists, to destroy the principles, which are for them of greater importance than the Ideas.[271]

---

[271] 88,2. Here concludes the lengthy excerpt from Aristotle's *de Ideis* that began at 79,3. Ross, following Wilpert, prints 88,20–89,7 as a continuation of the fragment (*Fragmenta Selecta*, 132); Harlfinger, however, does not include these lines in his edition, although printing them among the *dubia*, and they are omitted from the translation in ROTA.

990b22 Again, according to the supposition by which we say that the Ideas exist, [there will be Forms not only of substances but of many other things as well].

[**Obj. 4**] Aristotle says that as a consequence of the arguments that 5 establish the Ideas, the Platonists must say that there are Ideas not only of substances but also of many other things, as has been proved by what has already been said. For the argument based on the fact that something common to several things can be thought of, and that it [continues] to be thought of even when the particular things no longer exist, brings in Ideas of perishable things and proves that there are Ideas not only of substances.[272] Moreover, the arguments from the sciences similarly prove that there are Ideas 10 not only of substances but also of many other things; for it is not only in the case of substances that thinking continues after the substances of which [something common] is predicated have perished, but also in the case of qualities and quantities and of each of the things that are in this way, nor are there sciences only of substances. Moreover, if there are Ideas of the virtues, there would not be Ideas only of substances, for the virtues are not substances. He says, 'and a thousand other consequences follow' [990b27], 15 because there are certain other arguments aimed at proving the Ideas that result in saying that there are Forms not only of substances. For the argument from the fact that one thing is predicated in reference to many, a thing that, [being] the same, belongs to all of them although they differ from one another, and that is other than each of them, does not introduce Ideas only of substances; for that one thing is predicated with reference to many [is the case] not only with substance but with the accidents too. And the argu- 20 ment that says that the reason things come to be in an orderly way is that they come to be by reference to a fixed model, and that this 89,1 is the Idea, does not apply only to substances. Moreover, there is the argument that [begins] with the statement that whenever we make a true assertion [about something], that thing exists. But when we say there are five or three harmonies (*sumphônia*)[273] and three concordances, we are making a true assertion; therefore, they

---

[272] 88,9. Bonitz suspects a lacuna in the text before *monôn*. Hayduck indicates the lacuna, and suggests supplying *ideas eisagei kai ou tôn ousiôn*; I adopt this reading in the translation.

[273] 89,4. *Sumphônia* is opposed to *diaphônia*, 'dissonance' (Chailley, op. cit., 214 s.v.). Aristotle defines it as 'such-and-such a blending of high and low' (*Metaph.* 1043a10), and this definition is repeated by later authors: 'the blending of two sounds of which one is higher and the other lower' (Cleonides), and, 'the coincidence and blending of two notes different as to acuteness and depth' (Aelianus); (Solon Michaelides, *The Music of Ancient Greece: an Encyclopaedia*, London 1978, 308). *Sumphônia* thus signifies the agreeable sound produced by two contrasting notes struck in unison, so that 'harmony' (Ross) seems an apt translation, although Chailley and Michaelides

5   are just this many. But surely the number of things in this world
is unlimited; therefore, there exist certain other and eternal things
by reference to which we make true assertions.[274] Now this argument too does not [apply] only to substances; and there are many
other arguments of this sort.

But in conformity with what is necessary, and with what is
consistent with the opinions about the Forms, according to which
the Platonists say that they can be participated in, there will be,
in their view, Ideas only of substances.[275] For if, according to them,
the Ideas are causes of the being of the things that are by reference
10   to them, and if it is by participating in them that the things that
are by reference to them have their being, clearly it would not be
per accidens that they are participated in and are causes for the
things that are by reference to, and through, them, but *per se*,
inasmuch as they are Ideas. Things might be said to participate *per
accidens* in certain [others] if they participate in them in some
respect which is not that in virtue of which the things participated
in have their being. But the Ideas, if they are participated in *per
15   accidens*, would not confer being on the things that are by reference
to them; for what participates in some accidental attribute of man
is not a man, but [only] what participates in man *qua* man. But
the Ideas are substances (for certainly the Platonists would not say
that the principles are not substances, for thus what is not substance would be prior to substance); therefore, the things too for

---

render as 'consonance' and 'concord' respectively. (Both 'harmony' and 'concord' are
found in ROTA.) By definition, then, *sumphônia* seems to be something quite
different from *harmonia* (see n. 123), and Alexander here seems to distinguish the
two terms; but it is not clear how the three *sumphôniai* to which he here refers
differ from the three *harmoniai* (those of the octave, the fourth, and the fifth) that
he describes at 39,19–22. A concordant pair of notes is produced by strings whose
lengths stand in certain simple ratios (1:2, 1:4, 1:3, 2:3, 4:3, on ancient reckoning).
Accordingly, Aristotle describes *sumphônia* as a ratio (*logos*) of numbers (*Metaph.*
1092b14; cf. *Probl.* 921b8, 'a blending of contraries which have a *logos* to one
another'), and so too Alexander in his later discussion of the term (108,19–109,2),
where the description of *sumphôniai* seems indistinguishable from that given of
harmoniai at 39,19ff.

[274] 89,2–6. Because of the vague statement that serves as minor premise ('But
surely the number of things in this world is unlimited'), the argument is obscure.
Its point seems to be this: if we can assert *with truth* that there is a specific number
of combinations of musical notes, the reason cannot be the proportion or ratio (*logos*)
that we discover by tuning the strings of the lyre in various combinations, because
such proportions, being only very imprecise imitations of the true mathematical
proportions they seek to reproduce, are not specific in number but unlimited. Therefore, the truth of our assertion can be validated only by reference to the exact
mathematical ratios 2:1, 3:2, etc., and these are Ideas.

[275] 89,7–9. Alexander is here paraphrasing *Metaph.* 990b29–30, 'For [the Forms]
are not participated in *per accidens*, but things must participate in each Form in
such a way that they are not predicated of a subject.' From 89,9 to 90,2, he develops
the implications of this text.

which the Ideas are causes of being by participation [of these things]
in them must necessarily be substances as well. For the Platonists,
then, there will be Ideas only of substances. For if there are Ideas   20
too of things that are not substances, such as accidents, why, in the
first place, are there not Ideas of all the accidents rather than of
some but not of others? Again, either the Ideas of accidents will in
their turn be substances, or they will not. If they are not substances,
there will be Ideas that, although principles, are not substances;
but the Platonists say that the principles are substances. Again, it
is absurd that all the Ideas should not be, to the highest degree, of
the same nature. And if someone were to say that the Ideas are   90,1
objects of thought (*noêma*) or substances,[276] how is it that some of
the things participating *per se* in them[277] come to be and are substances, but others are not substances?

990b30 But things must participate in each Form in such a
way that they are not predicated of a subject.

That is, 'But things that are by reference to the Forms must partici-   5
pate in each of them in such a way that they do not in any way
have their being[278] in a subject', i.e. in such a way that they are
not predicated *per accidens* and from some accident that belongs to
the Forms – for here Aristotle uses [the expression] 'of a subject'
instead of 'of an accident'. Therefore, he says, since the things that
come to be and are by reference to the Ideas, and exist because of
them, participate in them *per se*, they would not [participate] in
some accident belonging to the Forms. But thus the things that are   10
by reference to the Ideas must be substances because they participate *per se*, and not *per accidens*, in the substances [of the Ideas].
He adds an example of participation *per accidens*. If the dyad that
is dyad by participation in the [ideal] dyad participates in eternity,
it does so *per accidens*, because the [ideal] dyad, by participation in
which it is dyad, is eternal.[279] But it does not participate *per acci-*
dens in the [ideal] dyad, for [then] it would be dyad in the same   15

---

[276] 90,1. 'Object of thought *or* substances' is strange; one would expect either
mallon ê, or *ouk* for *ê*, since at 92,18–26 below, where Alexander mentions and
criticizes the theory that the Ideas are *noêmata*, one of his arguments is: 'If the Ideas
are *noêmata*, they are *not* substances.' But in the present text, 'that the Ideas are
thoughts, not substances', can scarcely be reconciled with the sequence of the argument. These lines are perhaps suspect because there is no mention of *noêmata* in
LF, which reproduces the text of A that precedes and follows.
[277] 90,1. Reading *autôn* for *ousiôn* (LF, 89).
[278] 90,6. Reading *to einai* for *kai auto* (Bonitz after L).
[279] 90,14, *epei aidiou hê duas metekhousa duas estin*. For this reading, which
yields no acceptable sense, I adopt Hayduck's conjecture, *aidiou ousês tês duados
metekhousa*, a reading almost identical with that given by L. *Duas*, 'dyad', is Alexander's adaptation from Aristotle's *diplasion*, 'double' (*Metaph.* 990b34).

way as it is eternal; but the [ideal] dyad is not dyad inasmuch as
it is eternal, but eternity is incidental to it. Hence, if something
that participates in the [ideal] dyad should be said to participate in
eternity too, it would participate *per accidens* in the dyad.[280] Since
then it participates *per se* in the [ideal] dyad, but *per accidens* in
eternity, it is dyad, and to that extent similar to that dyad, but it
20   is not eternal; for things that participate in certain [others] *per
accidens* are not similar to those in which they participate in this
way. If then the things in this world are similar to the Ideas,
they do not participate in them *per accidens* but *per se*; but what
participates *per se* in substance is substance. Therefore, there will
be Ideas only of substances, in conformity with what is consistent
91,1 with [the opinion of] the Platonists and a necessary [consequence]
for them, if the Ideas are in fact substances, and the things participating *per se* in substances are substances. For the same terms
signify substance here and in reference to eternal things, as man
is substance in this world and in the ideal world, and heat a quality
both here and there. And if this argument is sound, the consequence
will be that the Platonists must say that of the things around us,
5   there are Ideas only of substances, if the Ideas are substances.

In certain manuscripts we find the reading: 'But things must
participate in each Form in such a way that it *is* predicated of a
subject.' And by this reading Aristotle would be saying that things
participating in the Idea must participate in it *per se*, and that in
this way the Idea will be predicated of them as subjects. As a result,
if the formula of dyad applies to something that is said to participate
10   in the [ideal] dyad, that thing participates in the dyad; but if the
formula that applies to the thing participating is not that of dyad,
but of eternity, it participates in eternity. But in saying, 'so that
the Forms will be substance' [990b34], he means, 'so that if the
Forms exist, they will be substance'; or, 'so that the Forms will be
only substance';[281] for this point is assumed.

'The same terms[282] signify substance in this world and in the
ideal world' [990b34]. For if what is quality among us is substance
among the Forms, it would certainly not be necessary to say that
15   of the things in this world, there are Ideas only of substances; for
if the Ideas are substances, it is surely not possible to say that some
of the things that come to be by reference to them are substances,
but others something else. 'For the same terms signify substance

---

[280] 90,17–18. This point is stated more clearly in the *alt. rec.*: 'The dyad-itself has
its being not *qua* eternal ... but *qua* dyad. If then its being belonged to it *qua*
eternal, but the dyad [belonged to it] *per accidens*, and the sensible dyad were
to exist by participation in this [eternal] dyad, the sensible dyad would be *per se*
eternal, but *per accidens* dyad' (90).

[281] 91,12. Reading *monê ousia* for *monêi ousiai* (Bonitz).

[282] 91,13.17.27. Reading *tauta* for *tauta* (cf. *Metaph.* 990b34).

in this world and in the ideal world, or what can it mean to say that there is something apart from these things, the one-over-many?' [991a1]. If the things in this world do not participate *per se* in the Ideas, but [only] *per accidens*, what, Aristotle asks, does it signify for the Platonists to say that there is something apart from these 20 things, i.e. the sensibles, something that, being one, is predicated of many and is the one model of the many things in this world? For there will not be the one-over-many if this one is predicated *per accidens* of the things that come to be by reference to it (for in that case, all things could participate in all things); and what participatessin something *per accidens* neither participates in it in the proper sense, nor has its being from that thing inasmuch as it is 25 that thing, nor is made like it. Or else the question, 'What can it mean to say that there is something apart from these things, the one-over-many?' could be asked as a consequence of the statement that 'The same terms signify substance in this world and in the ideal world'. For if this latter is not [true], what is the meaning of their assertion that there is something apart from sensible things, the one thing that is predicated of many? For this assertion is made on the ground that the same nature is manifested both by the one thing that is over many and by the many of which the one thing is 30 predicated.

Now that this point has been made, one might add to it the following. If it is in respect to substance that the things here partici- 92,1 pate in the Ideas, and if these things differ, either the same differences are also in the Ideas by reference to which these different things exist, or something analogous to these differences. For since the things in this world have their being from the Ideas, they will also have from these latter the fact that they differ, because they have their differences in virtue of the substance which they receive from the Ideas. For it is because of this that one Idea confers this 5 form and another Ideas confers that form, since otherwise nothing would prevent one Idea from being the source of all forms.[283] As a result, each Idea either will be the same in substance and form as the things that come to be by reference to it, or will in any case at least possess some power whereby one Idea produces and confers this particular form and another that particular form, in virtue of which the things that have their being by reference to these Ideas also have their differences. But the [same] kind of difference that 10 is in the things here that differ from one another will be in the Ideas too, or at least something analogous. But among the things in this world, one is rational animal, another irrational (*alogos*) animal, and it is an Idea that confers each of these proper differ-

---

[283] 92,6. Reading *einai* after *pantón* (Brandis).

ences; therefore, the rational and the irrational, or something analogous to these, in virtue of which one Idea confers the rational and
15   another the irrational, are in the Ideas too. And the things, [rational
and irrational animal,] that have their being by reference to, and
from, the Ideas have the same relationship (*logos*) to each other as
do the things, [the rational and the irrational,] by reference to
which these [animals] came into being, whether these [differentiae]
are contraries, or one of them a possession, the other a privation
(*sterêsis*).284 Both the rational and the irrational, therefore, are in
the Ideas too. But if this is the case, how are the Ideas still simple?
Again, if the Ideas are objects of thought, as some say, and their
reality (*hupostasis*) consists in their being thought of, how will the
one who thinks of them think of them at the same time? For it is
20   impossible to think of contraries or opposites at the same time,
seeing that these are not simply a plurality. But if the Ideas are
thought of by turn, they are perishable, not eternal; for when they
are not being thought of they will not exist, if indeed their being
consists in their being thought of. Things that are impossible by
their very nature285 are impossible in all instances, just as, [once]
it was impossible for the diagonal to be commensurable with the
25   side, this is similarly the case everywhere and for everyone –
indeed, even for the gods. Again, if the Ideas are objects of thought,
they are not substances, and the principles will not be substances.
Again, how will substance come to be by reference to something
not substance? For as it is absurd that what comes to be by reference
to substance should not be substance, so it is also absurd that
what comes to be by reference to what is not substance should be
substance.

991a12 And if the Ideas and the things participating in them
have the same form, [there will be something common to these].

The argument is from a disjunction, and from a disjunction divided
93,1   into contradictory [propositions]. For either the form and formula
of the Ideas and of the things participating in them is the same, or
it is not the same.286 If it is in fact the same, just as there is

---

284 92,14–17. This is badly stated. Alexander has argued that the differentiae
found in sensible things must be based on something analogous in the Ideas, and
here he means that in light of that premise, the rational and irrational that differen-
tiate animals will also exist in the Ideas. But in making this latter point, he speaks
of the rational and the irrational as if it were these differentiae in which rational
and irrational animal participate, rather than in the Ideas in which, according to
the argument, these differentiae are found.

285 92,23. Reading *autêi têi phusei* for *têi autêi phusei* (Bonitz).

286 93,2. Two consequences of the second half of the disjunction are given, the first
at 93,14ff below, the second at 94,2ff below.

something common in (*epi*) the things that participate, since they
have the same form, so there will be something common in, and
predicated of, these things and the Ideas from which they are; for
that Idea has the same form as these things. But in that case, what   5
is predicated in common of them will be an Idea, and thus there
would be an Idea of an Idea; and this process would continue *ad
infinitum*. What Aristotle says here is the second argument we gave
in explaining the third man [84,21ff]. Having shown previously
that the things participating in the Ideas will not participate in
them *per accidens*, given that these things have both their being
in general, and the fact that they are particular things of this
kind, through participation in the Ideas, he introduces the present   10
statement as being equivalent to [the following]: if therefore the
Ideas and the things participating in them have the same form, as
has been proved, there will be something common both in each Idea
and in the things that are by reference to each Idea; but in this
way the things here below, having as they do the same form as
things in the ideal world, will also be substances because the Ideas
by reference to which they are are substances; and thus there would
be Ideas only of substances. But if [the form of the Ideas and of the
things participating in them] is not [the same], he will state the
absurd consequence that follows in this case as well. 'For why   15
should 2 be one and the same in the perishable 2's or in those that
are many but eternal, and not the same in the 2-itself as in the
particular 2?' [991a3]. This question serves to establish that there
will be something common both to the Ideas and to the things that
are by reference to them. For if, because the 2's in sensible and
perishable things have the same form as the imperishable 2's by
means of which we count sensible things (these would be the math-   20
ematical 2's, for the Platonists said that mathematical objects are
between sensible things and the Ideas [52,10ff], being eternal but
multiple [and] similar to one another), we predicate 2 of these as
one and the same predicate, disregarding the fact that one 2 is
eternal and the other not, but, since they have the same form
inasmuch as they are 2's, predicating 2 in common of all of them
similarly because each 2 has its being in virtue of its participation   25
in 2-itself[287] – if [we so predicate, then] it will be no less the case
that 2 is predicated in common both of the Idea itself, the 2-itself,   94,1
and of the particular 2's that have their being from it: because,
[that is, the ideal 2 and the particular 2's] have the same form.

But if, [again,] the things that are by reference to the Ideas should
not have been made like them either in substance or in form, they
would be [only] homonymous with the Ideas. But in that case, why

---

[287] 93,24. Reading *tôi kata* for *to kata* (Bonitz).

5   would a particular Idea be the cause of the being of things [only]
       homonymous with it any more than of some other things, if these
       things called by the same name (*homonumôs*) as the Idea are not
       in fact made like it in substance and form? The case will be the
       same as if one were to call both Callias and a wooden image 'man',
       although the two are not at all alike with respect [to their being]
       men. And, in general, how could things be said to participate in the
       Ideas if they have no community (*koinônia*) whatever with them in
10   respect to their substance? And this [objection] would be equivalent
       to the one stated shortly before: 'What can it mean to say that there
       is something apart from these things, the one-over-many?' [991a1].
       For if we were to say that as likenesses [are called] by the same
       name as the things from which they are derived, so things here
       below too [are named after] the Ideas, in what respect will the
       Platonists claim that these things have been made like the Ideas
       if not in their substance? Are they likenesses by their shape or
15   colour? but there is nothing of this sort in the Ideas. But have they
       been made like the Ideas in eternity or incorporeality or immuta-
       bility? but that is impossible. If we examine the matter in this way,
       we shall discover [the similarity can be] in respect to nothing except
       substance. And indeed, even if it were the fact that things partici-
       pating [in the Ideas] do so in virtue of some one of the other [proper-
       ties] that belong to them, in virtue of which of these [properties]
       that the Ideas have in common with one another would things
       participate in them: their eternity, for instance, or incorporeality,
20   or immutability? But if things did participate in virtue of some one
       of the common properties, why in the world is one of the things
95,1   that participate man, another horse, another the number 2? [This
       is] not inasmuch as these [Forms are Forms of man and horse, etc.],
       or [inasmuch as] those [particular things are men and horses, etc.]
       by participating in the Forms[288] – but on account of which of the

---

[288] 95,1–2, *mê katho tauta estin ê kai ekeina metekhonta autôn.* The heavily-inter-
polated translation is an attempt to make some sense of this cryptic statement. The
general idea, at any rate, is clear. Since, *ex hypothesi*, sensible particulars do not
participate in the substance of the Forms, these particulars, which do in fact exist
as man and horse and other things, are not differentiated because there are different
Forms corresponding to the substantial differences among sensibles. Hence the
differentiation of sensibles must be explained by their participation in one of the
properties belonging to the Forms; but since these are common to all the Forms, they
cannot account for the differences in things participating in them. This argument is
stated more clearly in the *alt. rec.*: 'If then it were in virtue of one of these common
properties that things here below have been made like the Ideas, why is man-himself
responsible for the fact that man exists as man, but is not responsible in the same
way for the fact that horse too exists as horse? And so for all other things. And in
this way, one Idea would suffice as the thing responsible for the fact that all things
exist as what each of them is, but the other Ideas would be useless and superfluous'
(94).

common properties of the Forms, [then, are particular things differentiated]?

991a8 But above all one might raise this difficulty: what do the Forms contribute to sensible things, either to those that are eternal [or to those that come to be and perish]?

[**Obj. 5**] By this question, Aristotle might be pointing out that he   5
was right in saying, at the beginning of his refutation of the Ideas: 'In seeking to explain the causes of things in this world, the Platonists first of all bring in other things, equal in number [to natural things' [990b1]. For if, as he now shows, the things they posited contribute nothing to the things they were investigating, they did nothing except add other things equal in number to the things under investigation, as if they would have a better understanding   10
of the things that are if they had more, even twice as many, of these. The difficulty that he now raises is this: what is it of which   96,1
the Ideas are causes for the things of which there are said to be Ideas? He says, '[What do they contribute] to sensible things, either to those that are eternal or to those that come to be and perish?' because for the Platonists there are Ideas of the divine bodies too, such as the sun, the moon, and the stars; for they posited Ideas of   5
these bodies too and of the entire heaven. (For it was for this reason that he said shortly before: 'There is a one-over-many both in the case of the things here below and in that of eternal things' [990b7].) He therefore speaks of the heavenly bodies as eternal but sensible, but of those in this world as coming to be and perishing. He is puzzled, then, about what the Ideas contribute to the things that exist by nature, either to those that are divine or to those in generation and destruction. And first [with reference to] movement, which is the thing most characteristic of natural bodies; for the   10
divine bodies move forever and continuously in a circular motion, but those in generation change by reason of all the changes that are in accordance with their natures. He shows that in this respect the Ideas certainly contribute nothing to bodies, neither to generation nor to any sort of movement whatever, for the Ideas would be causes of stationariness rather than of motion for the things that   15
are, since in fact they are motionless according to the Platonists; so that the Ideas would not be even an efficient cause.

Secondly, he says that the Ideas do not contribute anything to the understanding and knowledge of the things in this world, those that are apart from the Ideas. For the knowledge of each thing comes about through knowledge of its form, since each thing has its essence in virtue of its form; but neither are the Ideas forms of

20   the things in this world, nor is it possible[289] that, because the form of
the things in this world, in virtue of which they are these particular
things, e.g. men or horses or dogs, is the Idea, there should be
knowledge of these things through knowledge of the Forms. For if
[the Forms] in the ideal world were the form, i.e. substance, of
things in this world (for the substance of each thing in the proper
sense is the form in virtue of which it has its being, and a thing is
knowable through this form), they would be in these things, since

25   the substance, i.e. the form, of each thing is in the thing whose
substance it is; but the Ideas are not in the things in this world, if
they do in fact exist by themselves in separation. But neither do
[the Forms] contribute anything to the being of the things in this
world. Aristotle has shown that the Forms cannot be responsible
either for movement or for change in general in the things said [to
be] by reference to them, nor yet for [our] understanding or knowledge of these things, because they are not in them. Next, using the
following argument in addition to what has already been said, he

30   shows, by what he [now] says, that the Forms do not contribute
anything to the being of these things either. For things that
contribute to the being are in the things they assist to this end,
[as] either their matter or their form; the Forms, however, are not
in things in this world, but separated from them.

   He has said that the Forms cannot contribute to the being of
things constituted by nature because they are not in them. (Here

35   he must be speaking of a 'contribution to being' in the sense in
which the elements are said to contribute to each of the things that
have elements, for as elements complete these things by being in
them, so too do both matter and form; for he has [already] shown
that the Forms [do not contribute] as efficient causes because they
cannot be responsible for any movement or change in these things.)

   He goes on to say how things mixed in certain [other] things are

97,1   responsible for their being the sort of things they are, although he
has pointed out that it is reasonable to assume that [the Forms]
are separated from the things in this world. For if the Forms were
responsible for the being of these things by being mixed with them,
they would be so in the way in which white would be said to be
responsible for the white body's being white because white is mixed
with it as a kind of nature capable of existing independently; for it

5   is in this way that white, by being intermixed, would be responsible
for the fact that the things with which it is mixed are white. As a
result, the Ideas too, if they were mixed with the things that are
by nature, could be responsible for their being the kinds of things
they are, so that man would be man through the admixture of the

---

[289] 96,20. Adding *dunaton* after *einai* (Bonitz).

Idea, man-himself. But after stating how the Ideas could be said to be responsible for the fact that the things constituted by nature are the kinds of things they are (for it would be by being intermixed), Aristotle immediately shows that it is impossible to assert that the   10
Forms have been mixed with the things said to have their being by reference to them, saying that the argument making this assertion is too easily upset [991a16], and is unsound. And he does at least add what [philosophers] held the opinion that says that each of the things that are is what it is because there is something mixed with it on account of which it is what it is. For Anaxagoras said that each of the things that are has been mixed out of all the   15
uniform bodies, but that the substance of the thing seems to be out of that body of which most has been mixed in, so that each thing was what it was because the other particular bodies had been mixed in it [in greater proportion]. And Eudoxus, one of the friends of Plato, thought that each thing is by the admixture of the Ideas in the things that are by reference to them; and there were certain others [who held this opinion], as Aristotle remarks. But he says that the argument saying that each of the things that are owes the   20
fact that it is a 'this something' to participation in something [else] is too easily refuted. And he showed, in what he said in reference to Anaxagoras [989a30ff], that in general the nature of the things that are is not constituted in this way. For not everything is by nature [such] that it can be mixed with every other thing, since a mixture is of things that can be separated and subsist independently, but accidents are not things of this sort; but if what has been intermixed can be separated, the modifications of substance   25
would be separable. Both generation and destruction too are done away with according to those who speak in this way; and there are all the other objections that Aristotle stated against this opinion in the first book of the lectures [entitled] *Physics* [1.4].

But [to prove] that the other things do not exist by an admixture of the Ideas, as Eudoxus and some others thought, it is easy, he says, to assemble many impossible consequences of this opinion; and they would be as follows.[290] If the Ideas are mixed with the   30
other things, [i] in the first place, they would be bodies, for a mixture   98,1
is of bodies. [ii] Again, the Ideas will be contrary to one another, for a mixture is in respect to contrariety. [iii] Again, the Idea will be mixed in such a way that either the whole of it will be in each

---

[290] 97,27–98,24 (continuation of the *de Ideis*) = Ross, *Fragmenta Selecta*, 128; Ross, *Select Fragments*, 132; ROTA, 2440. On this passage, see Kurt von Fritz, 'Die Ideenlehre des Eudoxos von Knidos und ihr Verhältnis zur platonischen Ideenlehre', *Philologus* 62, 1926/27, 8–10; criticized by Schmitz, op. cit., II, 157–61; Cherniss, op. cit., App. VII (525); Gail Fine, 'Immanence', *Oxford Studies in Ancient Philosophy* IV, Oxford 1986, 87–96.

of the things in which it is mixed, or [only] a part. But if the whole Idea, what is numerically one will be in more than one thing, for the Idea is a numerical unity. But if [it is mixed] by parts, what

5 participates in a part[291] of man-himself will be man, not what participates in man-himself as a whole. [iv] Again, the Ideas would be divisible and capable of being broken into parts, although they are impassible. [v] Then the Forms will be uniform, if all the things containing a part of a particular Form are in fact similar to one another; but how is it possible for the Forms to be uniform? For a part of a man cannot be a man, in the way in which a particle of

10 gold is gold. [vi] Again, as Aristotle himself says a little later, there will be not one but many Ideas mixed in each thing; for if there is one Idea of animal and another of man, but man is both an animal and a man, he would participate in both Ideas. And the Idea, man-himself, inasmuch as it is also animal, would itself participate in animal; and thus the Ideas would no longer be simple, but composed

15 from many components, and some Ideas would be primary, others secondary. But if [the Idea, man-himself,] is not animal, how is it not absurd to say that man is not an animal? [vii] Again, if [the Forms] are mixed with the things that are by reference to them, how would they still be models, as the Platonists say they are? For it is not in this way, by being mixed, that models cause the resemblance to themselves in their likenesses. [viii] Again, the Ideas would be destroyed along with the destruction of the things

20 in which they are. But they would not even exist independently in separation, but would be in the things participating in them. [ix] In addition to these objections, they will no longer be even immutable. And there are all the other absurd consequences of this opinion that Aristotle pointed out in examining it in the second book of his treatise *On Ideas*. This is why he says here, 'It is easy to assemble many impossible consequences of this opinion'; for they have been assembled there.

99,1   **991a19** But it is impossible[292] for the other things to be from the Ideas in any of the usual senses of 'from'.

[**Obj. 6**] Aristotle has shown that the Ideas are not causes of movement or change for the things in this world, and that they do not contribute anything to [our] knowledge and understanding of these

5 things, nor to their substance and the fact that they exist, as things mixed in particular things contribute to their being by being in them – in fine, that they are not causes at all. He [now] adds, 'But

---

[291] 98,4. Reading *merous* for *meros* (Harlfinger).
[292] 99,1. The lemma has *ésti* for the *esti* printed by Ross and Jaeger.

it is impossible for the other things to be from the Ideas in any of
the usual senses of "from" ', perhaps[293] pointing out that it cannot
be shown that the things referred to the Ideas[294] come from them
in any of the ways in which to come 'from something' is used. Now
the usual ways in which 'from something' is used are, in the proper
sense, from matter and form; for we say that enmattered things are   10
from the matter, and likewise from the form too, but also from both.   100,1
But the things referred to the Ideas are not from the Idea in any
of these ways, as has been shown, for the Ideas would be in these
things. 'From something' also means as a thing is from the one who
makes it; and as what is perfect is from what is imperfect, as we
say that a man comes to be from a boy; and as a whole is from the   5
parts; and as the contraries are from the contraries. That which
comes after is also said to be from something, as the Isthmian
games from the Olympian. But certainly the things in this world
are not from the Ideas in any of these senses of 'from something'.
For the Ideas are neither the matter nor the form of these things,
as has been proved, nor are they parts of them. Nor are these things
from the Ideas as from contraries, for when something comes to be   10
from a contrary, it does so while the same substrate remains and
changes from the contrary; but if [things came to be from the Ideas]
in this way, the Ideas and the things referred to them would have
the same substrate, so that the Ideas would be contrary to the
things that come to be by reference to them, but not similar to
them. Again, the Ideas would be destroyed in the generation of
these things, as the latter [came to be] from the Ideas and the Ideas
from them; for it is in this way that generation from contraries
takes place. But neither do the things referred to the Ideas come to   15
be as [if] the Ideas remained [in them] while acquiring some kind
of additional perfection, as a man was said to come from the boy;
for the Ideas are not in these things, nor are they perfected by
them. For the Ideas[295] would be less perfect than these things and
would be in them and perishable, since the destruction of things
that have reached perfection is the destruction of the Ideas as
well.[296] But neither are the Ideas efficient causes of things in this   20

---

[293] 99,7. The text has *êtoi*, 'either', but Alexander does not state the alternative
interpretation until 100,25 below.

[294] 99,9, *ta pros auta*. The antecedent is *tôn ideôn*, so that we must either read
autas, or consider this another instance of the loose reference of a neuter plural to
a feminine antecedent (see n. 175). A further possibility is that Alexander, having
mentioned *ideai*, identifies these with *eidê*.

[295] 100,17–18. Here, as in 99,9 above, we find neuter plurals (*ekeina, atelestera,
phtharta*) in reference to a feminine antecedent (*hupomenousôn, proslambanousôn*),
clearly the Ideas.

[296] 100,18–19. The point of this obscure argument may be that, on the hypothesis
that the Ideas derive their perfection from things subject to destruction, the Ideas
would perish when these things have reached their maturity and perished. But this

world, as a father is of his child, for the Ideas cannot move; and a
particular man generates a particular man, but man-himself does
not [generate]. But neither [do things in this world come to be after
the Ideas,] as the Isthmian games from the Olympian.

    Thus Aristotle says, 'But it is impossible for the other things to
be from the Ideas in any of the usual senses of "from"', either
because 'from something' [is used] in a number of senses, and this

25   point has been shown; or else he might be saying, 'in any of the
usual senses in which "from" is used' by those who posit the Ideas,
as some have understood him [to mean]. For in asking in what way
there is participation in the Forms, the Platonists say it is either
in this way, that the Idea is in each thing separately, as man-
himself in each particular man; or that part of the Idea is in each

30   thing; or that the Form is model for the things participating in it.
The first two of these modes of participating are impossible, as we
showed shortly before, and as Aristotle himself said in mentioning
Eudoxus: 'It is easy to assemble many impossible consequences of
this opinion', to which he added, 'But it is impossible for the other
things to be from the Ideas in any of the usual senses of "from"',

35   meaning by this that it is not possible for the other things to be
from the Forms even in the one way, besides these [two], that still
remains.[297] For once this point has been proved, it will also have
been proved that [participation is impossible] in any of the usual
ways used [by the Platonists]. This is the way that says that the
things here below [that are] referred to the Ideas also come to be
by reference to a model, and he mentions it at once, saying, 'But
to call the Ideas models ... [is to use empty words and poetical

40   metaphors]' [991a20]. Either he added this remark for the reason
[just stated], or because, even though it was his [original] intention

101,1 to point out that it is impossible for the other things to have come
to be from the Forms in any of the usual ways in which 'from
something' is used, he now goes on at once to show that what the
Platonists say – their statement that the Ideas are models, and that
it is in this way that the things here below participate in them[298]

5   – is to use empty words and poetical metaphors (this because it is
typical of poets to use metaphors). [The notion of] a model is
borrowed from painters, who are said to paint by reference to a
model. Aristotle shows that those who say the Ideas are models are

---

and the preceding argument should not be pressed too closely – Alexander is piling
up a farrago of objections, doubtless taken from stock arguments collected by the
Peripatetics, without being overly concerned about their philosophical validity.

  [297] 100,35–6. Reading *ek tou para toutous eti kataleipomenou tropou* (Bonitz).

  [298] 101,3–4. It is all but impossible to get a satisfactory sense from the text as
printed by Hayduck. I therefore adopt the reading he himself suggests in the apparatus, based on the Latin version (S): *hoti to paradeigmata legein autas einai kai
houtô metekhein.*

speaking empty words by his question, 'For what is it that does its work while looking at the Ideas?' For if the Ideas are models, there ought to be something that produces its effect by referring to them, as we see painters painting by reference to their models.   10

991a20 But to say that the Forms are models in which the other things participate is to use empty words.

Having asked how the Ideas are causes of the things in this world and what it is that they cause, Aristotle has shown that it is not possible for them to be causes either of the movement of these things, or of [our] understanding and knowledge of them, or of their   15
being, but that it is also impossible for the things in this world to come to be from the Ideas in any of the ways in which 'from something' is used. In addition to these points that have been proved, he discredits, with good reason, the term 'participation' used by the Platonists, on the ground that it is meaningless. For they say that the Ideas are models, and that the things here below participate in them; now to speak in this way, he says, is to use empty words and to speak in metaphors, as do the poets; for those who use   20
'participation' in the case of the Ideas do not indicate any of those things in which the participant participates.[299] He gives a brief proof that what they say is empty talk by his question, 'For what is it that does its work while looking at the Ideas?' [991a22]. For in every instance in which a thing comes to be by reference to some model, it comes to be through the agency of something that makes it like the model and produces it; but in the case of the Ideas, what is it that produces the things in this world while looking at the   25
Ideas? For we see that a particular man is generated by a particular man, and a horse by a horse, and so in all other cases; but none of these [agents] does what it does while looking at the Idea, but both the generation and the role of each agent is something natural: one agent implants the seed,[300] the other receives it, nurturing and developing it in a kind of sequence. Nor do those learned in the   30
sciences produce the objects proper to the sciences while looking towards some Idea.

---

[299] 101,20–1. This obscure statement must be understood in the context of a theory of participation in which the Ideas are said to be models. To say that they are such, and that it is thus that things 'participate' in them, is to give no information about the Ideas as beings in which other things share; for a likeness does not share in its model in any real sense, i.e. as actually having some part in, or of, it.

[300] 101,28, *arkhê*, lit. 'beginning'. The translation is adapted to the kind of generative process Alexander has in mind.

102,1   **991a23** It is possible for a thing both to be and to become like
          another without being copied from it.

The present statement is made against the theory that the Ideas
are models. For even if it were to be conceded that there are Forms,
and that the things in this world are similar to those things called
5   Ideas, the Forms would certainly not also be models of these things,
unless indeed there were to be something that produces by reference
to them. For it is possible for some things to resemble certain others
even though there is nothing that makes them like, or produces
them, by reference to the latter. And Aristotle shows this clearly
in the case of Socrates; for if Theaetetus resembled Socrates, he had
not therefore been copied from Socrates as well, for whether
Socrates is living or not, it is possible for someone to resemble him,
10   as Theaetetus did, even without being copied from him – for even
now a man could both be and become such as Socrates was. But if
one thing can become like another that no longer even exists, it is
clear that some things become like certain others without there
being anything at all that makes them like, and produces them, by
reference to a model. For as one who resembles the man who no
longer exists did not become such by reference to him, so, even if
15   there were some eternal Form, and it were granted that there is
some nature of this sort, the resemblance to it will not be as by
103,1   reference to a model, so long at least as there is nothing that
produces this likeness by reference to that Form.[301] This objection
might also be made against certain arguments that say the Ideas
are objects of thought. For even if they are, it does not thereby
follow that the things here below also come to be by reference to
them, since there is nothing that produces these things by reference
to the Forms.
5   One might also prove that none of the things constituted by
nature comes to be or has come to be by reference to a model by
the following argument.[302] If the world is eternal, and if none of

---

[301] 102,1–15. The lemma introducing this passage has *endekhetai de*, where Ross
and Jaeger read *endekhetai te*, thus introducing, as Ross notes (*Metaphysics* I, 199
ad 23), a new objection. And the objection, as stated by Aristotle, is simply that one
thing can be like another without being made like it. Alexander, however, seems to
consider this objection connected with the preceding one, that there must be a maker
who produces likenesses from models, so that his exposition is somewhat confused.
[302] 103,4–104,18. On this interesting text, one of the rare instances in which
Alexander departs from the text of *Metaphysics* to express a personal reflection, see
Charles Genequand, 'Quelques aspects de l'idée de la nature d'Aristote à al-Ghazali',
Revue de Théologie et de Philosophie 116, 1984, 113–17. Alexander's attack is
certainly directed in part against the Stoics; Genequand points to a similar passage
in the *de Mixtione* (225,18–27; Todd, 139–41), and in the *de Fato* we find a statement
of the position Alexander here refutes (191,30–192,17; Sharples 70–1). But beyond
this, 'Il s'agit . . . de réfuter une philosophie de la nature incompatible avec certaines
doctrines fondamentales de l'aristotelisme, en particulier l'éternité du monde et

the things that now come to be in accordance with nature comes to be by reference to an Idea as model, then neither would anything have come to be in this way in the past. But the world is indeed eternal, as they say;[303] and none of the things that now come to be in accordance with nature comes to be by reference to an Idea as model, as I shall prove. Therefore, neither did any of the things   10
that came to be naturally in the past come to be as [if] by reference to a model; for all things always come to be in the same way in the world, since it is eternal. But if this is so, the Ideas would not be models.

But that none of the things that now come to be naturally comes to be by reference to an Idea [as] model is clear from the following. All the things that come to be are particular instances of particular things that exist,[304] and are generated by a particular instance of particular things, so that things [generated] naturally also [come   15
to be in this way]: this man, for instance, is naturally generated by this man, and this horse by this horse, and this vine by this vine. But surely each of the things too that produce something naturally does so[305] in virtue of the nature in it, i.e. in virtue of the cause and principle and power in it to move in some way. For those things both exist naturally and have a nature that have a principle of   20
movement within themselves inasmuch as they are also these particular things, but not *per accidens*; and the horse in fact produces the horse in virtue of this sort of principle in it. But certainly neither a man nor a horse nor any other of the things that generate and produce naturally produces the thing it generates while looking to a model; for it is not by giving any thought whatever to how the

---

l'immanence de la génération' (116). To be compared with this text is a lengthy quotation given by Simplicius (*in Phys.* 2.3, 310,25–311,27), in which Alexander, commenting on the words 'form and model' in a text of Aristotle (*Phys.* 194b25), rejects the notion that nature works towards an end as does the human artisan. Nature does not produce by first taking thought, so that its thought might be said to be a model of the things that come to be naturally. In agents that operate 'by choice and art and reason' (310,33), the end must be cognized as the goal and model of the things to be produced, but it is otherwise with nature, 'for nature is an irrational power' (311,1). This does not mean, however, that nature produces by chance and not for the sake of something, i.e. for an end; 'for the term "for the sake of" is not the name of rational generation involving choice, but whatever comes into being in an orderly manner and for the sake of another comes to be for the sake of something; and this [comes about] in a similar manner whether [it happens] by choice and reason or without reason, as we say is the case with nature' (311,22–5). With this conclusion cf. Aristotle, *Phys.* 199a17–18.

[303] 103,8, *hôs phasi*. 'La démonstration prend appui sur un point qui . . . est posé comme un axiome: l'éternité du monde' (Genequand, op. cit., 113).

[304] 103,14, *tôn kath' hekasta tina estin ha esti*, where *ha esti* might seem superfluous; but Alexander perhaps wishes to emphasize that the proximate cause of natural generation is an existing instance of the being to be produced.

[305] 103,18. Reading *poiei* after *phusin* (Bonitz).

25   thing that is to be should come to be that they set about producing
what they produce, as we see in the case of the arts. For it is for
this reason that the arts are only in those capable of exercising this
kind of foresight over the things that will be as a result of art, for
they are in men; but many things are generated in accordance with
nature both by irrational and even by inanimate things. Therefore,
none of the things that now produce something in accordance with
30   nature does so by reference to a model; but if not now, not in the past
either, for the generation of things that come into being naturally is
always similar.

There is both truth and falsity in saying that the things that come
to be naturally do so according to certain numbers, determinate and
arranged in a fixed order (*tetagmenos*)[306] (for they do not come to
be as a result of chance or spontaneity, for it is for this reason that
a man generates a man), and on this account to think that nature
produces its effects by reference to a kind of model or plan (*logos*)
35   while looking to this latter. For all natural things come to be
according to a certain order and certain determinate numbers, and
not by chance or spontaneity, but surely this does not mean that
they also come to be by reference to a model. For it is not by
reflecting (*ennoein*) that nature produces what it does (for it is an
irrational power), but it is responsible for the fact that [generation]
takes place in an orderly progression of movements, so that a first
movement is followed in orderly sequence by a second, although not
40   as the result of any reasoning process, and this second movement is
104,1   followed in turn by a third, until the movements have progressed
to the end for the sake of which they occurred. It is this order that
art imitates, for it puts things together in a rational way and [thus]
produces its object. Hence art is a rational power, but nature is
irrational. But it is not correct to say that nature, being a kind of
divine art, produces nothing irrationally, nor to think that, because

---

[306] 103,31, *arithmous*. There is a similar reference to numbers in the text from
Simplicius referred to in n. 302: 'This succession [of movements in the process of
natural generation] takes place according to certain numbers and a [certain] order,
until it has been terminated in the form that is coming into being, unless there
should be something that hinders [the process]' (311,18–19); and again in the *de
Fato*: 'For those things which have nature as the cause of their coming to be progress,
according to a definite and numbered order (*kata tinas arithmous kai taxin hôrismenon*), to some end, and cease from coming to be when they arrive at it; unless
something obstructs them and prevents them from following the natural path to the
end before them' (168,3–7; translation of Sharples, 44). The precise meaning of
'numbers' in this context is not clear, although, in combination with Alexander's
insistence that the process of natural generation has a fixed order (*tetagmenos, taxis*),
and that the numbers are definite or determined (*hôrismenos*), the term might
suggest what Genequand, in commenting on the text from Simplicius, calls '. . . une
vue purement mécaniste de la nature' (op. cit., 116). It may also point to the regular
sequence of the stages in the generative process that Alexander later describes
(103,38–104,1).

it is divine, it possesses from the gods this gift of producing what 5
it does [by looking] to some fixed and determinate model. For it is
not in this way that nature is called a divine art, as if the gods
were employing this art, but because, being a power from the gods,
it is capable of preserving the right order of movement according
to a certain harmonious sequence, not in virtue of any reasoning
process or thought (*noêsis*), but because it is from the gods. But the 10
gift it possesses from the gods could not be that of producing by
reference to a model, for how could it produce anything by reference
to a model of which it has no knowledge whatever? One might,
however, more reasonably say that nature has from the gods this
similarity to the [rational] agent, in whom the thing coming to be
exists and from whom it takes its origin, that nature produces
according to the regular order (*eutaxia*) of movements that is
without reason.[307] Again, it is possible to discover [this] regular 15
order even in evil things and in those that come to be in a way
contrary to nature, such as abcesses, wounds, boils, and periodic
illnesses. But the generations of certain living things too are in fact
orderly, but not by reference to an Idea, those e.g. of worms, gnats,
and grubs.[308]

---

[307] 104,8–9. The movements referred to, as Genequand explains (op. cit., 115), are
those of the heavenly bodies, whose revolutions produce in turn the generation of
animals. The influence of the movements of these bodies on sublunary coming-to-be
is a central theme in Alexander's theory of providence; on this point, see Sharples,
op. cit., 25–6, and *Mantissa* 172,17–19: 'Of the things that are brought about and
put together by the divine power that comes to be in that body that is subject to
coming to be, as a result of its proximity to the divine . . .' (translation of Sharples,
97). Alexander (?) also devotes one of his *Quaestiones* to the topic, 'What is the
power, from the movement of the divine body, that comes to be in the body adjacent
to it that is mortal and in [process of] coming to be' (*Qq.* 2.3, 47,30–50,27).

[308] 104,17–18. 'These are the lowest form of animal life, spontaneously generated
from matter' (Todd, *Alexander . . .*, 227). In saying that a regularity can be discerned
even in things generated by chance or contrary to nature, Alexander may be over-
stating his case, but his intent in the present text is to reject completely the notion
that nature operates 'by reference to a model'. At the conclusion of the Simplicius
text, however, he concedes a sense in which the form may be called a *paradeigma*
(the word used by Aristotle), 'because nature inclines towards the form – not by
choice, but rather as puppets do'. The characteristic of a thing made by reference to
a model, he continues, is that it be produced for a definite end (*pros hôrismenon*)
and that it resemble its model, so that 'if something comes to be for a definite end
and is like its model, it would come to be by reference to a model; and it is in this
way that the things that come to be naturally come to be; therefore, [they come to
be] by reference to a model' (311,29–37). One senses here the same ambiguity that
characterizes Alexander's attempt to explain the acceptable sense in which nature
can be called a divine power and a gift of the gods.

991a27 And there will be more than one model of the same thing, hence more than one Form as well.

20   This text, up to, 'again, one would think it impossible' [991b1], is not contained in certain manuscripts, and for this reason [some commentators] did not even mention it. By it Aristotle shows this further absurd consequence of the theory about the Ideas; for if

105,1   they are models of things here below, there will be more than one model of the same thing, and more than one Idea of that thing. For if man is animal and two-footed and man, and these are different, there would be a model and Idea of each of them, and man will

5   participate in man-himself and animal-itself and two-footed-itself. But if [all these] exist together in man-himself, being different from one another, the Idea will not be something simple, but will be composed out of Ideas. But if each of these is an Idea, there will be an Idea prior to an Idea (for animal-itself is prior to man-himself, since animal is genus of man-himself), or the Idea, [man-himself,] will be separated from animal. But this is impossible, and man-

10   himself does participate[309] in animal-itself, at least if man-himself too is animal, so that the model of man would be not only man-himself but animal-itself;[310] therefore, [there will be] a single likeness of man-himself and animal-[itself], for [man] participates in animal.[311] But [man-himself] will participate not only in animal-itself but in two-footed-itself as well, so that the one Idea will also participate in more than one Idea. For if it does not, one of the things of which man is composed exists without participation in an

15   Idea; for man is two-footed neither inasmuch as he is animal (since there are certain animals that are not of this sort), nor inasmuch as he is man (since there are other two-footed animals as well). And again, if animal does not have its being from being man, neither would it have two-footedness from the Idea of man; but thus it would be conceded that the things here below do not have their being entirely by reference to an Idea.[312] Again, there will be some-

20   thing prior and something posterior in the Ideas. But if man-himself

[309] 105,9. Reading *metekhei* for *metekhon* (Hayduck).

[310] 105,9–10. The text is corrupt at this point. I adopt Hayduck's conjecture, based on LF, *hôste eiê an anthrôpou ou monon ho autoanthrôpos alla kai to autozôion paradeigma.*

[311] 105,11–12. This point is stated more clearly in the *alt. rec.*: 'Hence man will be a single likeness of man-himself and animal-itself' (104). The argument shifts from the multiplication of Ideas to its consequences: that the sensible participant, although a unity, participates in more than one Idea.

[312] 105,16–18. This argument turns on the previous statement that 'animal' and 'two-footed' are not identified with 'man', and assumes that the Idea in question is 'man-himself'. Since 'animal' and 'two-footed' can be found apart from man, they exist among sensibles without an Idea to support them, so that man as a whole does not exist by participation in an Idea.

does not participate in animal-itself but is nevertheless animal (for to say that man-himself is not animal, although he is man, would be the height of absurdity),[313] it is also unnecessary that animal in this world should exist by participation in animal-itself, [and] thus that [man in this world should exist by participation in] man-himself.[314] 'Again, the Forms are models not only of sensible things but of the Ideas themselves' [991a29];[315] we have already said how. For animal-itself is model of man-himself, for the genus will be model of its species because each of them is also what the genus is; and thus the Forms [as species], while being models of sensible things, will themselves be likenesses of the Forms.   25

991b1 Again, one would think it impossible that the substance and that of which it is the substance should exist apart.

[**Obj. 7**] What Aristotle is saying is that it is impossible for the   30
substance of something to be separated from that of which it is substance, for the substance of each thing is in it. If then the Ideas are substances [of things], they are not separated from them; but   106,1
if they are separated, they are not substances of these things. But those who say that the definitions of things in this world are formulated according to the Ideas certainly make the Ideas substances of sensible things, for definitions express the substance of each thing and are formulated by reference to the forms proper [to things]; for each thing has its being, which its definition expresses, in accord-   5
ance with its proper substance. And thus the Ideas would be the forms of things here below.

991b3 We say[315a] in the *Phaedo* that the Forms are causes both of being and of becoming.

'We say' is said in the same way as in previous instances, for Aristotle joins in the opinion as being his own too, and shows that   10

---

[313] 105,22–3, *to gar legein . . . atopôtaton*. In the translation, this clause has been inserted as a parenthesis after *zôion estin* (20), since the explanatory *gar* (for) makes sense only as a comment on the supposition that man-himself is not animal.

[314] 105,21–2. The text says only, *houtôs de oude tou autoanthrôpou*, 'or in man himself either'. But the point of the argument is, not that animal does not participate in man-himself (some animals, in fact, are not men), but that, if the Idea, man-himself, can be animal without participating in the Idea, animal-itself, then men in this world can be men without participating in the Idea, man-himself.

[315] 105,24. Alexander read *kai autôn ideôn*; Ross and Jaeger omit *ideôn*, although in his apparatus the latter says, 'i.e. idearum', and Ross translates, 'but of the Forms themselves also'.

[315a] 106, 7, *legomen* (we say). With two exceptions, the MSS have *legetai* (it is said). Werner Jaeger accepted this reading in his 1957 edition of the *Metaphysics*, while reporting Alexander's (and Asclepius') *legomen* in his *apparatus criticus*, with the query *an recte*? But at the very end of his life, in an unfinished article published

what is said in the *Phaedo* [100D] is false. For [there] it was said
that the Forms are causes both of the being and of the becoming of
the things in this world; but this is not true, at least if (as has been
stated above) it is impossible for the substance and that of which
it is substance to exist apart. Having said, '[causes] both of being
and becoming', he now says [that they cannot be causes] even of
15   becoming. For how is it [that they cannot be causes] even of
becoming?[316] For even were the Forms to exist, still they would not
be causes of things either being or becoming by reference to them,
for there will be nothing at all by reference to them if there is not
something that imparts motion and produces things – for certainly
107,1   the Ideas are not causes of things as producing them. He shows
that the cause of things that come to be is what produces them, and
not a model, from the fact that many things both come to be and
are of which the Platonists say there are no Ideas, such as artefacts;
for neither a house nor a ring is by reference to Ideas. But if these
things are not prevented from either becoming or being, even if
there are no Forms, because they have that which produces them,
5   neither will the things of which the Platonists say there are Ideas
be prevented from either being or becoming even if there are no
Ideas; for the things too of which they say there are Ideas will be
through causes similar to those through which the things of which
they say there are no Ideas come into being. For as these latter
come to be because of art, not by reference to any Idea, so natural
things too will be because of nature without a model, the one gener-
10   ating being analogous to the artisan, and the female taking the
role of matter. For models are useless if there is nothing that

posthumously ('We say in the *Phaedo*', *Harry Austryn Wolfson Jubilee Volume*,
Jerusalem 1965, English section, vol 1, 407–21), he argued that *legomen* represents
the indirect textual tradition of the Greek commentators, a tradition that antedates
by eight centuries the oldest and best manuscripts of the text of *Metaphysics*. The
first person plural should therefore be read at *Metaph.* 991b3 as being on a par with
the twelve other instances in *Metaph.* 1.9 where Aristotle uses this form of expression
(990b9, 11, 16, 18, 23; 991b7; 992a11, 25 (*bis*) 27, 28, 31); *legomen* goes back to 'the
purer text [of *Metaphysics*] that was read by Alexander of Aphrodisias in the third
century AD or by Simplicius in the sixth century AD and that is quoted in their
commentaries' (408).
      Jaeger also discusses the relevance of Alexander's comment on *legomen* (106,
9–10) to the question, whether Aristotle had at one time subscribed to Plato's theory
of Forms. The present text does not answer that question, but 'What we can say
with certainty is that Alexander ... saw here a genuine problem, and took for
granted that Aristotle was speaking of his (former) adherence to Plato's assumption
[of the Forms] as a fact and not merely as a matter of polite form ...' (410). In
commenting on Jaeger's article, Philip Merlan agrees that *legomen* is genuine, but
thinks that Jaeger's interpretation quoted above goes beyond what can be concluded
from a literal reading of Alexander 77,35–78,4 ('Nochmals: War Aristoteles je
Anhänger der Ideenlehre? Jaegers letztes Wort', *Archiv für Geschichte der Philosophie* 52, 1970, 35–9, also a posthumous publication).
      [316] 106,14–15, *pôs gar ... gignesthai*. Bonitz thinks this sentence corrupt.

produces by referring to them, but that which produces something is not prevented from doing so even without a model, as the Platonists themselves admit is the case with artefacts.

991b9 Again, if the Forms were to be numbers, how will they be causes?

[**Obj. 8**] Aristotle also attempts to refute the argument in support   15
of the theory according to which the Platonists said that the Ideas are numbers; for if they said that the Ideas are numbers, but the Ideas cannot be numbers, it is obvious that according to the Platonists there would not be Ideas.[317] Again, he asks this question: if the Ideas *are* numbers, how will they be causes for the things in this world? Is it because these things too are numbers, as the Ideas also are, although obviously different numbers than those [that are Ideas], but differing too from one another, as the Ideas also differ   20
from one another? Is one number man, another horse, another Plato and another Socrates, and do the things that are differ from one another according to the differences of their numbers? But in that case, how will those numbers belonging to the Ideas be causes for the numbers in this world in which the things that are exist? For even if these latter numbers were to be equivalent to[318] those [ideal] numbers, so that, for instance, the number 5 would be both man-   25
himself and the perceptible man, but one 5 would be eternal and the other not, how will that [ideal] 5 be a cause of being for this [perceptible] 5? For certainly numbers are not causes of being for one another [because they are] numerical equivalents; for how is it, in general, that a number is a cause of being for a number?

991b13 But if [the Forms are causes as numbers] because the   108,1
things in this world are ratios of numbers ... [there is obviously some one particular thing of which they are ratios].

Aristotle has set out to prove that if the Ideas are numbers, they cannot be causes for the things in this world. With this purpose in mind, he first took up the point that the things in this world, which the Platonists say come to be by reference to the Forms, are also said by them to be numbers equivalent to those [ideal] numbers

---

[317] 107,16–17. This *reductio ad absurdum* is Alexander's contribution; Aristotle's objection is that stated in the lemma, and Alexander develops it in what follows, although his *eti* (again) seems to suggest that Aristotle is posing a new question.

[318] 107,24, *isoi*, lit. 'if the numbers are equal', which might suggest a recurrence of the argument that there are as many entities in the ideal world (in this case, numbers) as there are in the sensible world. But as Alexander's example shows, his meaning is that each ideal and perceptible number has the same numerical value as its counterpart, a point repeated at 108,2–7 below.

5   that are eternal, although these [perceptible] numbers are not
     eternal; and he showed that numbers equivalent to [certain others]
     cannot be causes of being for the numbers equivalent to [them],[319]
     not even if the former are eternal and the latter not. Now he takes
     up the point that the Platonists do not say that the things in this
     world are [actually] numbers, but that they consist in some ratio
     (*logos*) of numbers, and that this is what they wish to assert; and
10   he shows that not even in this way can the Ideas and those eternal
     numbers be causes for the things in this world that exist in a ratio
     of numbers. Wishing to show what it means to say that the things
     in this world are ratios of numbers, he adds the example of
     harmony; for harmony is not a number but some ratio of numbers,
     i.e. certain things having a numerical ratio to one another. For to
     be in the proportion of 2:1 is to be in a ratio of numbers, that pre-
15   cisely which the harmony of the octave has because its being consists
     in this ratio; and again, the being of another harmony consists in
     turn in the proportion 4:3, and again, that of another harmony in
     turn in the proportion 3:2, and these are ratios of numbers.

     Now even if one were to say that all the things that exist are
     ratios of numbers, the Ideas and the [ideal] numbers will not be
     causes for these things even in this way; for in that case, the
     numbers will no longer be over those things.[320] For if the things in
20   this world are particular ratios of numbers, there are obviously
     certain things in them possessing this ratio in which each of them
     has its being, just as harmony, being a ratio of numbers, has some
109,1 one substrate and some underlying nature of which the harmony
     is the definition and formula; and this substrate is the musical
   ′ notes. If then the things said to have their being by reference to
     the Forms are in a ratio of numbers, there is some substrate in
     them which, by receiving the ratio of numbers, becomes at one time
5   man, at another time something else, becoming different things at
     different times in accordance with the different ratios, as [there are
     different] harmonies because of the difference of ratios in their
     sounds. But this thing [that receives the different ratios] will be
     found to be nothing other than the substrate and the matter, in the

---

[319] 108,6, *isoi arithmoi tois isois*, lit. 'equal numbers cannot be causes of being for
equal numbers'; but to translate thus is to mislead because of the sense of the
English 'equal number', so that the clumsy paraphrase adopted in the translation
is necessary.

[320] 108,18–19. That is, if sensible things are ratios of numbers, the ideal numbers
will not be 'over' them in the way in which an Idea is said to be a 'one-over-many';
therefore, the Ideas are not numbers. This conclusion is that in which the line of
argument that began at 107,15 should terminate, and is in fact stated formally at
109,10–12. But the argument is made more complicated by the additional assertion
that if the Ideas are numbers, they cannot be *causes* of sensible things, as the
Platonists are assumed to hold that they are. Cf. the final conclusion to this section:
'Consequently, either the Ideas are not numbers or they are not causes' (109,21–2).

particular number and ratio of which each of the things that are
will exist, e.g. in the ratio of fire or air or water or earth or of
whatever the particular thing might be;[321] for it is in the ratio of
these things to one another that the things [composed] out of them
have their being and receive a form. But if this is the case, the   10
Ideas too, since they are models of these things, will themselves
have to be numerical ratios and not simply numbers; for if Callias,
for example, or the man who has been made like the Idea, is a ratio
in certain numbers of fire and earth and water and air or of other
particular substrates, the Idea too, the number said to be man-
himself, by reference to which the [perceptible] man was, will be a   15
numerical ratio and not number-itself – [a ratio] either of the
numbers themselves, if this should be the substrate in them, or of
something else, whatever might be [the substrate] in them.[322] (This
is what Aristotle signifies by the words, 'whether [man-himself] is
a number in a sense or not' [991b19].) For number is certainly not
what causes [something] to be in a numerical ratio, since there are
different ratios in the same number; for in 6 there are the ratios
2:1 and 3:2. But if this is the case, the Idea is not simply number, for   20
number and numerical ratio are not even the same thing; neither,
therefore, is there number-itself, the Idea. Consequently, either the
Ideas are not numbers or they are not causes for the things that
have their being in a ratio of numbers.

This argument first of all does away with [the possibility] that
the Ideas are numbers, then proves that they are composite
(*sunthetos*) too, not simple. For if there are ratios of numbers
[composed] of many sounds, there will also be some substrate in the   25
Ideas which will make the being of each of them [consist] in a ratio
of numbers;[323] and the consequence of this will be that there is not

[321] 109,8. According to the explanation up to this point, each of the elements and
other sensibles is a distinct numerical ratio; but the following statement (9–10)
seems to say that each sensible consists in the proportion in which the individual
ratios are found in it. This latter view is consistent with Aristotle's example (Ross
refers to the description of the animal body as a mixture, in certain ratios, of the four
elements, *Tim.* 73BC (*Metaphysics* I, 199 ad 13)), and with Alexander's expansion of
that example (12ff below).

[322] 109,16. Hayduck indicates a lacuna in the text after *en autois*, and suggests
the addition of *ê allou tinos, ho ti pot' an êi en autois* (Ascl.); the translation follows
this reading.

[323] 109,24–6. Alexander here returns to Aristotle's earlier statement, 'If it is
because the things in this world are ratios of numbers' (*Metaph.* 991b13); but his
argument is compressed. Sounds, as has been said above, are the substrate of these
ratios in sensible harmonies; if then the Ideas as numbers are models of sensible
things, there must also be a substrate in the Ideas to support the numerical ratios
which are in them, or, more properly, which they are. This last point, however,
although it may explain his previous statement that the argument of the Platonists
makes the Ideas composite beings, is not really relevant to what follows. We would
expect Alexander to say, 'The consequence is that *the Idea* is not a number at all';
but from this point to l. 30, he is arguing that even *numbers* cease to be on the
assumption that the Ideas are ratios of numbers.

any number, for if there is no number-itself, neither would there
be number, nor would the things that are [exist] by reference to
number [as] a model. But if there is no number, there would
certainly not be a ratio of numbers either, so that the Platonists
cannot say that the things that are exist even in a ratio of numbers.
30   The statement, 'nor will it be a kind of number for this reason'
110,1   [991b20],[324] might mean that [because] the Idea [is a numerical
ratio], it will not for that reason be a number, since what is in such
a ratio is not thereby a number.

991b21 Again, one number comes from many numbers, but
how can one Form come from many Forms?

5   [**Obj. 9**] Aristotle also shows that the Ideas cannot be numbers from
the fact that one number results when many numbers are combined
(for when 3 and 4 are combined they produce 7), but that it is
impossible for one form to come from many forms; for if the forms
of man and dog, for instance, are combined they do not produce one
10   form. For the fact that animal is included in man does not mean
that man is a composite (*suntheton*) of animal and another form,
since neither is animal a form subsisting independently, nor can
man exist apart from animal; but animal is part of each of the
animals that actually exist. But each of the numbers in a combination becomes part of the whole while remaining itself. Conse-
15   quently, the Ideas would not be numbers. But if one were to say
that each of the Ideas too is from many Ideas, as man, e.g., from
animal and two-footed, a first [consequence] for the Platonists is
that the Ideas will no longer be simple, but composite; then that
some of the Ideas will be primary, others secondary, since the form
of animal comes first, then that of man or horse. Again, in the case
of numbers a single number results from a combination of all the
20   different numbers, but this is impossible in the case of the Ideas;
for all the different forms do not produce one composite thing, such
as horse or dog. Again, things that are combined exist in their own
right before they are combined; but it is impossible either to find
(*labein*) or to think of man and animal ever [existing] in separation.

[324] 109,30. Jaeger inserts ‹*idea*› after *tis*: 'Nor will any Idea be a number for this
reason'. The addition agrees with Alexander's subsequent commentary.

991b22 But if the number does not come from the numbers   111,1
themselves, but from the things that are in the numbers,[325] e.g.
in 10,000, how is it with the units? For if they are specifically
similar, many absurdities will result, and also if they are not
specifically similar, nor the same with one another.[326]

Someone might say, says Aristotle, that one form does not come
from a combination of the forms themselves, because not even in   5
the case of numbers does it happen that one number results from
the combination of numbers, but from that of the units; for every
number results from a combination of units, not of 3's and 4's, if
the numbers are very large, for 10,000 is in fact composed of units,
not of thousands or of hundreds. But if this too is the case, [(he
would say),] then the Ideas at least are not like numbers inasmuch
as one number comes from many numbers, but inasmuch as it is   10
composed of units. [If the Platonists argue thus,] we may rightly
[demand] to learn from them whether the units from the combination of which the Ideas are composed are specifically similar
(*homoeidês*) to one another, or whether they are dissimilar. For if
they are specifically similar, Aristotle says, many absurdities will
result, which he does not bring forward here because they are
well known; but he speaks about them in Book 13 of this treatise
[1081a18–29, b35–37]. For the result is that every combination of   15
those units will produce an Idea; for if all the units are specifically
similar, why in the world do some of them produce Ideas and others
not? And in this way, every number will be an Idea – not a number
just so large and from just the number of units from which they
wish the Idea too to be composed, or from just so many of them, if the
units from which the numbers are [composed] are in fact specifically
similar.[326a] Again, all the Ideas will be specifically similar to one

---

[325] 111,1. The modern text of *Metaphysics* reads *en tôi arithmôi* for Alexander's
enarithmôn.

[326] 111,3. The modern text of *Metaphysics* reads *mête [hai] autai* for Alexander's
mêde hai autai. Alexander's subsequent paraphrase of this text (112,6–7 below)
indicates that he read *mêde hai autai kata to eidos*, taking these words as explanatory
of Aristotle's *mê homoeideis* (*Metaph.* 991b24).

[326a] 111,17–18, *pas arithmos . . . ek tosônde*. Both language and sense are obscure;
it is difficult to see how *ek tosônde [monadôn]* differs from the preceding *ek tosoutôn
monadôn*. I understand Alexander to mean that since the Ideas must be supposed
to differ from one another, there should be, on the hypothesis that Ideas are numbers,
a specific and different number corresponding to each Idea – a number composed 'of
just as many units' as there are distinct constituents in the Idea which that number
represents. But if the units are qualitatively identical, they cannot account for the
essential difference among the Ideas, so that any and every number, no matter how
many units it contains, will be an Idea, but an Idea that cannot be distinguished
from any other Idea except by reference to the larger or smaller number of units
which its corresponding number contains, a point stated more explicitly in the next
objection.

20 another, differing from one another in no respect except in the multiplicity of their units; and thus the things participating in them will also be specifically similar to one another. But the rational and

112,1 the irrational do not seem to differ by reason of a multiplicity of certain things, but rather by reason of a quality (*poiotês*). For if they were to say that the irrational consists in fewer units, it is obvious that the irrational will become rational if only the number of units were added to it by which the rational exceeded it. Such then are the absurdities that follow on the assumption that the units are specifically similar.

5 Aristotle himself adds the absurd consequences that follow if the Platonists were to say that the units are not specifically similar. For if neither those units [in a number] are specifically similar [to one another], nor all the units [in other numbers] similar to all others nor the same with respect to their form (this is what he means by 'nor the same'), but if there will be some differentia in them, so that some of them produce Ideas and other do not, or some of them produce these Ideas, others those, what differentia will there be in the units, all of them without qualities (*apathês*) as

10 they are and incapable of receiving any differentiation whatever in respect to anything in them? For the only differentia in units, as Aristotle says in the first book of *On the Soul*, is position [409a20]; but if the units have position they will no longer be simply units, but points. For none of these consequences is reasonable, nor consistent with the way in which we think about the units. – But with reference to the text: after saying, 'How is it with the

15 units?' [991b23], he adds why he said, 'How is it?'; for they must be either specifically similar to one another, or specifically dissimilar.

991b27 Again, it is necessary to establish another kind[327] of numbers, with which arithmetic deals.

[**Obj. 10**] If the units [in a number] are not specifically similar to all the others, it is obvious that there will be some from which the Ideas [are constituted], and others which the arithmeticians use, so that there will be one particular kind of numbers with which arithmetic deals and another particular kind from which the Ideas [are constituted]. But by this same line of reasoning, all the math-

113,1 ematical objects too will involve [yet] another kind, i.e. these objects will have another sort (*eidos*) of numbers; for mathematical objects

---

[327] 112,17, *heteron genos*, which Ross translates 'a second kind'. But Aristotle at least suggests three kinds, and Alexander definitely understands him to mean three: ideal numbers, sensible numbers (the object of arithmetic), and a kind 'different' from these two, the object of mathematics, intermediate between the first two kinds.

are the things said to be intermediate between those that have their being by reference to the Ideas, which[328] are sensible forms and in sensible things,[329] and the Ideas by reference to which[330] these things have their being. Therefore, these [numbers] that, underlying mathematical objects, are in addition to sensible and ideal [numbers], will be some other kinds [of numbers] and of another sort (*eidos*), if there is a difference in species between the numbers from which [are constituted] the objects with which the mathematicians deal and [the numbers] from which the Ideas [are constituted][331] (for, in the view of the Platonists, the principles of mathematical objects too are numbers, if [numbers] are in fact without qualification [the principles] of all the things that are).[332] 'But how,' says Aristotle, speaking of the mathematical objects, 'do they exist, or from what principles are they?'[333] if not from the same principles from which [are constituted] both the Ideas and the ideal number, and which the Platonists assumed to be the principles of all things. And how will mathematical objects still be, for them, intermediate between sensible things and the Ideas, when they are of another nature and from other principles? For things that are intermediate between certain [others] are intermediate in virtue of some community and relationship.[334] But since these mathematical objects are of a different kind and nature, how could they be intermediate between the Ideas and the things said to have their being by reference to them if the Ideas do not differ from the intermediates and sensible

5

10

15

[328] 113,3. Reading *ha* for *ho*, the latter either a scribal error or a misprint.

[329] 113,3. Alexander might seem to be saying that *ta mathêmatika* (the mathematical objects) are between the Ideas and sensible forms in general. This, however, is not Aristotle's point, and later (19–20) Alexander restricts the meaning of sensible forms to those of numbers used in counting.

[330] 113,4, *hai tôn ideôn pros ha tauta to einai ekhei*, with which cf. 13–14 below, *tôn te ideôn kai tôn pros auta legomenôn*. The translation assumes that this is another instance of loose reference of neuter plurals to a feminine antecedent (see n. 175).

[331] 113,5–6, *hetera tina genê estai kai heteron eidos*. The plural *genê* (kinds) is strange: according to the argument to this point, the numbers from which mathematical objects are constituted are a single *genos*; see l. 1 above. How then can there be *genê* (plural) of these, and what is the relation of these *genê* to the *eidos*, mentioned here and also in l. 1? Both *genos* and *eidos* are obviously being used in a wide sense in this passage, although the following *eidêtikê* suggests that *eidos* at least may have a more technical sense. The most satisfactory explanation would be to regard *genos* as the genus 'number', of which the ideal, mathematical, and arithmetical numbers are species, but the text does not warrant this interpretation.

[332] 113,8–9. Omitting *hetera genê estai*, which cannot be construed here and is probably interpolated from l. 5 above. Bonitz thinks the text faulty at this point.

[333] 113,9–10. The translation follows the reconstruction of the text proposed by Bonitz, based on *Metaph.* 991b29: *ha pôs* (for *haplôs*), *phêsi, legôn peri tôn mathêmatikôn, ê . . .*

[334] 113,13. Adopting Hayduck's reconstruction of the text, based on the Latin version (S), to supply the lacuna after *arkhôn: ta gar metaxu onta tinôn kata koinônian tina kai oikeiotêta metaxu ti esti.*

things do not differ from them either?[335] For these too [i.e. sensibles] will require other principles. For things taken as from abstraction are intermediate, but abstraction is not possible in the case of things that are from the same principles.[336] Again, it is absurd to call mathematical objects intermediate for this reason too, inasmuch as the Platonists did not say there are any intermediates between the sensible substances of man or horse and the Ideas, but they did say this in the case of number and mathematical objects; what is the reason for this? – In saying, 'the things themselves' [991b31], Aristotle means the Ideas, since the Platonists make it clear [that they are speaking of the Ideas] by adding the word 'itself'.

991b31 Again, each of the units in the dyad must come from a [prior dyad].

[**Obj. 11**] Since the dyad is a principle (Aristotle must be speaking of the indefinite dyad),[337] and all the things that are are either

---

[335] 113,14–15. The sense of these lines is uncertain. Alexander has argued, in the previous sentence, that the special class of numbers supposedly intermediate between ideal and sensible numbers is of a different nature than either of the other classes, and so cannot be intermediate between them. In the present sentence, the text of which is dubious, he first repeats this point of the *dissimilarity* of mathematical numbers, then concludes with the apparent assumption that they do *not* differ. It seems possible that the text contains segments of what were originally *two* arguments against the possibility of mathematical intermediates. (1) If they are from principles different from those of ideal and sensible numbers, they have nothing in common with these, hence cannot be intermediate between them. (2) If there is no distinction between the mathematical intermediates and either ideal or sensible numbers, they are not intermediate, but identical with one or the other class.

[336] 113,15–17. The sense is again obscure. *Gar* suggests that these lines offer an explanation of the previous statement: that sensibles (if *toutois*, l. 15, is correctly referred to the preceding *toutôn*, as in the translation) need other principles, presumably than those of the mathematicals. Alexander seems to be arguing, then, that mathematicals are intermediate because they are derived by abstraction, presumably from sensibles, but that they could not be so abstracted if they and the sensibles from which they are abstracted have the same principles. But if that is the thrust of the argument, is he not saying that mathematicals, which are intermediate because abstracted, cannot *be* intermediate because they have different principles than sensibles? To remove that objection, Hayduck suggests that the reading at l. 17 should be: *ei mê ek tôn autôn arkhôn*, 'if they are *not* from the same principles', and this conjecture, based on LF, may well be right. Because the argument is stated more simply and clearly in LF, it seems useful to append the text of the *alt. rec.*: 'But how are the objects of mathematics intermediate if they are of a different nature, and have nothing in common with either sensible things or the intelligible Forms? For intermediates are said to be such in virtue of some community and relationship with the extremes. But neither could mathematical objects be derived from abstraction if they are, as they have been said to be, from other principles and not from those that are common; for the things derived by abstraction are from common principles' (112).

[337] 113,24, *têi duadi* (*Metaph.* 991b31). See Ross's discussion of this text, *Metaphysics* I, 201 ad 31. He believes that *hê duas* is the number 2, not the indefinite dyad, as Alexander understands it.

principles or from principles, and there are also units in the dyad   114,1
that the Platonists posit [as] a principle, the units in it will be from
principles because they are not principles (for the dyad is this
principle). From what principles, then? For each unit will have to
come from the dyad; but it is absurd to say that the parts of the
dyad are composed from the dyad and that the unit is from the
dyad,[338] for certainly each of these units in the dyad will not be   5
reduced to the unit[339] which, because it confers form in some way,
is said to be a principle; for these units would be much prior to the
dyad.[340] 'And yet this is impossible' [992a1], if the units in the dyad
will be prior in definition to the dyad, [as they will be] at least if
the dyad has its being from them, and if the principle of that which
comes from something [else] is that from which it comes. But it is
impossible for those who say that the dyad is a principle to assert
this, [namely that the units are prior to the dyad]; for [then] there
will be some principle of the principle and something prior to the   10
principle.[341]

992a1 Again, why is a number a unity when taken together?

[**Obj. 12**] Since each Idea is a unity (*hen ti*) and each Idea a number,
why is number a unity (*heis*)? And when a particular number comes
forth from the units, by what agency does that which comes from
them become a unity? And which of them [i.e. the units] is it that
confers a form and produces a unity?[342] And how does some one
thing come into being? For if [the number] is not a unity, neither   15
is the Idea a number; for the Idea is a unity. But if [the number]
is a unity, why is it such? And by what agency does it have its

---

[338] 114,4, *ou gar dê* . . . 114,9, *ex hou*. Hayduck's text, with the emendations I have
adopted (see the following notes), gives at best a confused reading. The point of the
argument, stated quite clearly at the end, is that the indefinite dyad must have
units in it (because it is a 2), and according to the doctrine of the Platonists, these
units must come from the One and the indefinite dyad, the principles of all numbers.
Thus the units *in* the indefinite dyad will be prior to that dyad; and since these
units must come from an indefinite dyad as *their* principle, there must finally be
another indefinite dyad prior to that formed from the units – an absurdity.

[339] 114,5. Reading *tôn en têi duadi monadôn eis tên monada anakhthêsetai*, Bonitz
after S.

[340] 114,6. Adopting the conjecture, *polu gar hautai ekeinês an* for *pollai gar hautai
ekeinên an* (Brandis).

[341] 114,10. Alexander is perhaps playing on the double sense of *arkhê*, so that the
final words would mean: 'And there will be something before the beginning.'

[342] 114,14, *kai ti* . . . *autôn*. If *autôn* is retained, it must refer to the units, so that
the sense is that some one of the units from which a specific number is produced
must be capable of conferring the form which makes that number a unity, e.g. 5 or
6. But ll. 16–17 suggest that the correct reading here might be *autous* = *arithmous*
(numbers): i.e. there must be some agency other than the units that confers a form
on the specific numbers.

being? For if there is something that confers unity on the numbers and produces the Ideas, it is no longer the Ideas that will be in numbers, but rather that which puts an end to their multiplicity and makes each of them a unity; for the number 10 is something other than ten things.

20   **992a2** Again, in addition to what has been said, if the units are different, [they ought to have stated the case as do those who say there are four, or two, elements].

[**Obj. 13**] If the text were written, 'if the units are *not* different',[343] what Aristotle would be saying is the following. For those who assume that the One is a principle there would be the further absurd consequence of saying that the common predicate is an 115,1 element of the things to which it belongs in common; but this is impossible. For if the units are of the same nature, the assumption will be that the term 'unit' is predicated of them; but surely what is common is posterior, and has its being from these units and in them. That they face this consequence he shows by the fact that, 5 on the one hand, the units are specifically similar (for he says, 'if they are specifically similar',[344] as if it were agreed that they are such), but that, on the other hand, if they are specifically similar, the unit, taken without qualification as the unit predicated in common of all the units, is taken as species. But the Platonists ought not to have assumed in this way that the One without qualification is a principle, but [should have done] as do those according to whom 10 the element is a body. For the latter do not call the common [element] 'body', but, specifying some [one] body among those that are under the common body, for instance this particular body fire or air, they call this body, which already exists with some difference, the element; for body without qualification is common to all bodies, which are not different with respect to their being bodies. For neither does there exist some common body that could be an element, nor 15 anything else[345] more common that is not [the] universal (*koinon*) itself as such, because the very question, whether something, 'the universal' (*to koinon*), exists at all, is a matter of controversy.[346]

---

[343] 114,22. Although the lemma at the head of this passage has *ei hai monades diaphoroi*, the text of *Metaph*. 992a2, Alexander first comments on a contradictory reading, *ei hai monades adiaphoroi*, without however stating that he found this reading in the MSS. Later, he expresses his dissatisfaction with this reading (116,25 below). On the text, see also n. 344.

[344] 115,5, *eiper homoeideis*. These words, which Alexander specifically refers to Aristotle, are not found in our text of *Metaphysics*.

[345] 115,14. Reading *allo ti* before *mallon* (Bonitz).

[346] 115,14–16. The *alt. rec.* quotes Aristotle's text, 'whether there is [something] common [to them], body, or not' (992a6), then explains that the supposed common

The Platonists too ought therefore to have specified a particular
One in a similar way, as do those who say that a particular body
is an element, and to have assumed this particular One as a principle; but as it is, they say that the One in an unqualified sense is
a principle, not as if the units were many and separated from one
another, and the One predicated in common of them, but as if the
unit were a whole of some kind, and one, and uniform, and had the   20
units as parts similar to itself, as [do] fire and water;[347] for each of
these is indeed some one thing and uniform. 'But if this is the case,'
says Aristotle, 'the numbers will not be substances' [992a7]. If, that   116,1
is, the Platonists were to speak of the One in this way, as uniform,
the numbers will no longer be substances and Ideas for them, but
material substrates (for uniform things are of this sort); moreover,
the whole will not be an Idea of its parts.[348] Again, the substance
of each thing in the proper sense is its form, but the numbers will   5
have the status (*logos*) of matter, not of form.[349]

Or the text could [mean] the following. If the Platonists were to
say that the One is such as one particular nature, as fire or water,
and that, being such, it is a principle, the numbers will no longer
be substances or Ideas and principles for them. For number does
not [come to be] from the combination of a one of this kind[350] (for

---

body cannot be anything other than the Aristotelian universal, body as genus, so
that to suppose the reality of such a common body is to raise the disputed question,
'whether the genera exist independently, having their own existence apart from the
bodies that are seen in the species [of bodies]' (115).

[347] 115,18–21. Reading *oukh hôs* for *hôste* (18) and *all' hôs* for *all' oukh* (Ascl.).
With these emendations, the text yields a tolerable sense, but the point is stated
more succinctly in the *alt. rec.*: 'But as it is, speaking thus of the One without
distinction, they talk of it as having uniform parts, just as the parts of fire or water
are called fire and water synonymously' (115).

[348] 116,1–4. This explanation of why the numbers will not be substances is
surprising. According to the Platonists, the *two* principles of number are the One
and the indefinite dyad, and the latter, as Alexander recognizes, is analogous to a
material substrate on which the One confers a form; hence it is not the numbers
themselves that are substrates. Aristotle's own criticism is that, if the One is the
same wherever it is found, the 1's produced from it are not substances but ordinary
mathematical numbers; thus Ross, *Metaphysics* I, 201 ad 6, who cites *Metaph.*
1018a5: 'If all the units are combinable and undifferentiated, mathematical numbers
result, and only this one kind, and the Ideas cannot be numbers.' This argument is
in fact found in the *alt. rec.*: 'If, then, the units are uniform, or [if] they speak of the
One without any distinction, the number of the Forms is indistinguishable from the
number from which natural things [are constituted]; and if this is so, the number
of the Ideas is no longer a principle, because it is composed out of the same kind of
units as those of the number here below' (115). And Alexander seems to adopt this
explanation in his next interpretation of the text (116,5ff).

[349] 116,4–5, *eti ... hexousin*. The text is corrupt at this point; the translation
follows Asclepius: *eti te ousia hekastou kuriôs to eidos, hoi de arithmoi hulês ouk
eidous logon hexousin.*

[350] 116,8–9. Reading *tou toioutou henos suntheseôs* for *tou toioutou suntheseôs*
(Ascl.).

it is one single thing and the same thing that comes to be from a combination of a one of this kind, as in the case of the combination [of parts] of fire), but from the combination of a [one] of this kind, [i.e.] a one that is obviously uniform, the Ideas and principles [come to be], but a number does not.[351] The numbers will therefore no longer be substances and Ideas for the Platonists, but clearly that thing, if it exists, the One-itself.[352] And if, according to them, this latter is something and is a principle, one must be said in many ways,[353] for otherwise it would be impossible for them to call the One a principle. [But] Aristotle could have introduced the statement, 'Evidently, if there is a One-itself' [992a8], on the ground that it is reasonable for the Platonists to say this. For [then] they would be speaking of the One not as a genus and common, nor as uniform, but as that One which, because it has some other nature, is a principle apart from all other things. To this he adds that the One will [then] be, for them, one of the things that are said in many ways, and will be homonymous. But he has [already] said that if the things in this world are homonymous with things in the ideal world, these latter would no longer be models of the things in this world, nor eternal beings.[354] But if there is a One-itself, and if this One-itself is, for the Platonists, a principle, being of another nature apart from the other 1's, the evident consequence is that the units are said in many ways and are not specifically similar. Obviously,

---

[351] 116,5–11. The argument is: the Platonists assert that the numbers, which are Ideas and principles, are substances, and that they proceed from the One, which is (as Alexander, after Aristotle, understands it) undifferentiated. But a combination of one's of this sort will produce only a single, uniform thing, as the combination of parts of fire produces only one fire; such a combination will not, however, produce numbers, presumably because numbers such as 3, 5, etc., are different entities, not a single thing such as fire. Although it may be true, as the Platonists are assumed to say, that the *Ideas* proceed from the (undifferentiated) One as their principle, the *numbers* do not; hence the numbers are not substances, nor Ideas and principles. Note that the conclusion of Aristotle's own argument is simply that 'the numbers will not be substances' [992a7], i.e. they will be only non-substantial entities such as ordinary mathematical numbers. Throughout the present text, however, Alexander extends this conclusion to include the Ideas, i.e. the principles, so that it is not clear whether his principal point is that the numbers are not substances, or that they are not Ideas.

[352] 116,11–13. This statement seems, on the face of it, unintelligible, for the above argument does not show that the numbers *are* the One-itself. A possible solution is found by comparing this statement with 7–8 above: 'The numbers will no longer be substances or Ideas *and principles.*' If 'principles' were read in the present text, the sense would be that it is not the numbers which are principles (if they are not Ideas they cannot, for the Platonists, be principles), but that *the principle* will be the One-itself.

[353] 116,14–15, 'one must be said in many ways'. This comes close to saying that the *term* 'one' has many senses. In fact, however, Aristotle and Alexander do not use this linguistic mode (the *term* 'one'), but the material mode (one), saying that one is predicated in many ways.

[354] 116,20. Reading *onta* for *on* (Brandis).

however, this conclusion is absurd; for what differentiae will there be among the units, and what will be the formulae differentiating them? And [a further absurdity is] that that unit, [One-itself], will not be an Idea and a model of these [other units].   25

In my opinion, however, the text does not read thus: 'Again, in addition to what has been said, if the units are *not* different', but, 'if they *are* different'; for it was this point about which Aristotle was arguing, and this was what the Platonists thought: that the units are different, and that some of them are those in the Ideas and others the mathematical units. If the text is read in this way, what he is saying would be as follows. If, according to the Platonists,   30 the units are different and not all specifically similar, they ought to have specified this particular unit and said that it is an element and principle, but not unit without qualification, the universal (*to koinon*). For those who speak about the corporeal elements do not call body without qualification an element, but, since the bodies differ according to their form, they specify, saying which of the bodies they think to be an element – that it is air or fire or something of this sort; but they do not [say] that the common body   117,1 without qualification [is an element]. (For whether or not there is some common body apart from those of which 'body' is predicated, they do not call this common body an element; for it would be possible for them to call an element something else of which 'body' is predicated rather than one of these bodies which they [actually] so designate.) Thus the Platonists too ought to have specified what   5 kind of One and what kind of unit they call an element, since the units differ. But as it is, in speaking of 'the One' without qualification, they talk as if all the units were uniform and undifferentiated; for this is what Aristotle signifies by saying, 'as if the One were uniform, like fire or water' [992a6]; for by using the term 'uniform' he is pointing out the lack of differentiation of the units and their specific similarity. But if this were to be the case with the   10 units, the numbers, i.e. the Ideas, would no longer be substances; for it is about those [ideal] numbers that he is speaking. For if all the units are specifically similar, [then] just as the number in our world is not substance, so neither would that [ideal] number [be substance], composed as it is of units that are specifically similar to this [sensible] number. Obviously, however, the Platonists do not say this, but there is, according to them, a One that is not the same as, nor specifically similar to, the other [1's], and this One is a   15 principle; but if this is so, the units are not specifically similar, for otherwise it would be impossible to say that the One [is] a principle. Consequently, they ought to have specified what kind of thing they call a principle. But if they say that the units are not specifically similar, they face the difficulty stated above [991b26]: what differentia is there among units that are without qualities?

20   **992a10** When we wish to reduce substances to their principles, we posit that lines come from the short and the long.

[**Obj. 14**] Here too, Aristotle says, 'we posit', consistently with what he said previously, for he is refuting the theory about the Forms as if it were his own. He sets forth the doctrine of the Platonists, which he has also given in his treatise *On Philosophy*.[355] They wished to
25   reduce the things that are – for he always calls the things that are 'substances' – they wished then to reduce these things to the principles they assumed (their principles were the great and the small, which they called the indefinite dyad). Wishing therefore to reduce all things to this principle, they said that the principles of length (*mêkos*) are the short and the long, on the ground that length originates from a long and a short, which are great and small, or that every line (*grammê*) is [included] in one or another of these; and [they said that the principles] of the plane (*epipedon*) are the
118,1 narrow and the wide, which are themselves also great and small. Having said this and set forth their doctrine, he adds to this the absurd consequence this doctrine entails, saying: 'And how will either the plane contain a line, or the solid a line and a plane?'
5   [992a18]. What he means is this. The limit (*peras*) of a body, which is a solid, is thought to be its surface (*epiphaneia*), which he calls 'plane', and the limit of the surface or plane the line, which he calls 'length'; so that length is in the plane too, and both plane and length in the solid (*to stereon*) – at any rate, the surface (which he calls 'plane') is said to be that which contains length and breadth (*platos*), and the solid that which has depth (*bathos*) too in addition to these.
10   It is in this way, then, that these things are naturally constituted. But since the Platonists say that the short and long and the narrow and wide and the deep and shallow are different genera, and posit that they are under different genera and are not subordinate to one another, how will it still be possible for either length to be in the plane or length and plane in the solid? For just as not even number is in any of these things because, according to the Platonists, the
15   principles of number were different (for the principles of number are the many and the few, which are different than the things spoken of above), so neither, in the case of these things, will any of them that are higher be in those that are below, i.e. none of those

[355] 117,23–118,1 = Ross, *Fragmenta Selecta*, 78; Ross, *Select Fragments*, 83; ROTA II, 2391. Gaiser prints this text as his Testimonium 26B (op. cit., 488), and Richard reproduces it, with French translation (op. cit., 276–7).

that are prior will be in those coming later. For the first of the three, and the one above, is the line, second the plane, and third the solid, since the former are more simple than the solid and are 20 thought of before it; but number is prior to all of these. Therefore, just as number, although prior, is not in these things because the many and the few, [the genus] under which number is, is a different genus than each of [the genera] under which these things are, so not even in the case of these things themselves will one of them, according to the Platonists, be in the other. For neither will length be in the plane, because length is from short and long but the plane 25 from narrow and wide, which are different genera, nor will these [two] be in the solid. Nor is it possible to say that these genera 119,1 differ indeed from one another and are other, but that they are nevertheless subordinate to one another, so that the deep is under the broad and similarly the broad under the long, and that for this reason [length and plane] can be in the solid, as both 'winged' and 5 'animal' are in bird. For [animal and winged and bird] have a community of different genera[355a] in relation to one another, inasmuch as they are subordinated to one another; for the genus of something is predicated essentially of that thing too, and what is subordinate to something as being under a genus is just what the genus is – man just what animals is, white just what colour is. Consequently, if the broad is genus of the deep, and the solid is something deep and the plane [something] broad, the solid will be 10 just what plane is; and bird, in fact, is just what animal is. But it is absurd to call body a plane, and similarly [to call] the plane length.

992a19 Again, from what [principle] will the points be present [in the lines]?

What Aristotle is saying is this. Points[356] are thought to be present in the length, i.e. in the line, just as the line is present in the plane 15

[355a] 119, 5. If *genôn* has the sense of 'genus', one consistent with its use in this passage, we must assume that Alexander is speaking imprecisely in order to illustrate his principal point: that long and broad and deep, which *are* different genera according to the Platonists, cannot be subordinated to one another as 'winged' is subordinate to 'animal', and 'bird' to 'winged'. Possibly, however, *genôn* should be understood as 'classes' or 'kinds', so that Alexander would mean that genus and specific difference and species are different sorts of logical entities.

[356] 119,14, *ta sêmeia kai hai stigmai*, two terms for 'points', as at 55,24 above, where Alexander says that *sêmeia* is the mathematicians' term, but that Plato and the Pythagoreans used the term *monades*, 'units'. 'Sêmeion: Nom désignant le point géométrique. L'ancienne expression était *stigmê*; elle fut remplacée, à la suite de l'épuration des fondements de la géométrie par Platon et son école, par *sêmeion* = signe': Mugler, op. cit., 376. On this text see Stenzl, op. cit., 74–5, and Ross, *Metaphysics* I, 207: '*stigmê* claims reality for that which has position but no magnitude, while *sêmeion* means simply a conventional mark'.

and the plane in the solid, but to be of another nature [than line, plane, and solid], as these latter differ from one another. What then are the principles of these points? and under what genus can they be placed? and how can they be reduced to the great and the small? and how will they be in length? After raising this difficulty, he next reports Plato's opinion about points. For he says that Plato simply did not accept [the theory] that there is any nature of a point, but said that this was a kind of geometrical doctrine and thesis which is not in the nature of the things that are. He therefore denied that the point is anything, and would not even use this name, but would often call [the point] 'principle of the line', which, he used to say, was the indivisible line. Aristotle reports that Plato too, and not only Xenocrates, posited indivisible lines, and clearly they located this line under the same genus as that of the [divisible] line, the short and long. Expressing his complete bafflement at this theory, he says, 'And yet these too' (obviously lines) 'must have a limit' [992a23], whether they are indivisible or not; for in fact [the reason that] the line was seen to be some other nature than the plane is not because it exists independently. For neither did the plane fail, because of being a limit of the solid, to be something different in its own right from the solid; just so, then, there is some limit of the line too, and this is the point.[357] Similarly, therefore, and according to the same argument, the point will exist as the line also does, so that the point will have been proved to exist by the same argument by which both the line and the plane are proved to exist. As Aristotle reported in what precedes this passage, Plato posited the great and the small as the material principle of the things that are; for his formal principle was the One.

992a24 In general, although wisdom seeks the cause of perceptible things, we have given up this attempt.

[**Obj. 15**] Aristotle brings this charge too against those who concerned themselves in any way with the Ideas: that the purpose

---

[357] 120,10–13. Stated more clearly, the argument is this: even indivisible lines must have limits, which are points. It cannot be argued that these points are not *distinct* from the lines they limit, and hence do not exist, on the ground that they do not exist *independently* of the lines; for lines are distinct from planes, though not independent of them, and planes too are distinct from solids, though not independent of them. The argument is reported more fully in the *alt. rec.*: 'And just as the line was of another nature than the plane and yet existed, and the plane [was of another nature than] the solid and yet it too existed (for if something is different than something [else] that exists, it is not thereby not-being), so too the point, which is different than the line and its limit, will not be not-being; but by the same argument [used in reference] to the line and the plane, which are limits, the latter of body, the former of plane, the point too, which is limit of the line, will exist no less [than line and place]' (120).

of [philosophical] investigation is that those who undertake to speculate about the things that are should discern what could be the efficient cause of these sensible and perceptible things, and how each of them comes to be. The Platonists, [however,] neglected to investigate what this cause might be (for they say nothing about the cause from which movement begins, the one that is the efficient cause; for the Idea cannot produce anything), but, in the belief that they were giving the substance and the formal cause as the explanation of things (for the causes, taken together, are four in number), they assumed certain other substances and Forms apart from those of perceptible things (for these are the Ideas). But they never say how those Forms are forms of these [sensible] things; for the [word] 'participation' they introduced [is] a sound without meaning, since they do not make it clear how these [sensible] things participate in the Ideas, as Aristotle has already said [991a20]. Hence it was with good reason that, at the beginning [of his criticism] too, he accused them of having added other things, equal in number to those being investigated, which contribute nothing at all to their [explanation] of the things under investigation.

[**Obj. 16**] Having shown that the Ideas are neither efficient nor formal causes (for the form is in that of which it is the form, but neither are the Ideas in sensible things, nor does the term 'participation' signify anything), he says in addition that according to the Platonists, the Ideas are not even causes for the things that are as that for the sake of which and the end, the cause that is cause in the most proper sense in all things that come to be in accordance with intellect and knowledge and nature. For all the things that come to be in accordance with nature and art and knowledge, and those moreover that [come about] in accordance with choice (*proairesis*), come to be for the sake of something, and this is the cause in them in the most proper sense. But it is not in this way, according to the Platonists, that the Ideas are causes for the things that are, for they do not say the Ideas are causes of the fact that the things coming to be by reference to the Ideas exist in the right way,[358] but [only] of their existence in general; for they say the Ideas are models, not ends. For how could they even be ends of these [sensible] things? For the end does not exist before that of which it is the end, but is only thought of before [this latter],

121,1

5

10

15

20

---

[358] 121,19. In his brief reference to the final cause (*Metaph.* 992a29–32), Aristotle says only that the Forms have no connection with it. Alexander's expansion of the objection seems an instance of random polemic. If the distinction between *to einai* and *to eu einai* is to be taken seriously, it means either that the Forms, unlike nature, are not causes that provide for an orderly process of generation (cf. 103,4–104,18, and notes ad loc.), or that they are not responsible for the fact that natural things achieve the perfection to which they are ordinated (see the discussion of these terms in n. 5).

and comes to be along with that of which it is the end; but the Ideas both exist before [the things referred to them], and neither come to be [with] nor are in the things that come to be.

25   [**Obj. 17**] Having shown that the Ideas are neither efficient causes, nor forms nor ends of the things that come to be, Aristotle states the reason why the Platonists went astray in regard to the Ideas. For because of their enthusiasm for mathematics, and because they supposed that philosophy too [consists] in speculation about these matters, and for this reason spent all their time on

122,1   mathematical studies alone, they came to assume that the principles of the things that are are those which they thought to be the principles of mathematical objects, even though saying that mathematics should not be made an end, but should be pursued for the sake of other subjects. They said, at any rate, that mathematical speculation is a propaideutic, and Plato used to call the mathematical sciences co-workers with philosophy [*Rep.* 533D]. But that,

5   despite these statements, they philosophize about and concern themselves with nothing other[359] than mathematics, they make clear both by saying that numbers are principles of all the things that are, and by assuming that the Ideas are numbers, and by generating natural things from those that are mathematical. For the very substance which they assume to be principle, as matter,

10   of the things that come to be by nature (this is the indefinite dyad, i.e. the great and the small) is in fact mathematical rather than natural; for the dyad is a principle of number rather than of the things constituted by nature, being too mathematical a nature and not the kind that underlies, and it would seem to be something predicated of matter and different from it rather than being itself a kind of substrate and matter. After saying, 'and [one might suppose] that it is rather a predicate' [992b2], Aristotle makes clear

15   how it is predicated by adding, 'and that it is a differentia of the substance, i.e. of the matter, rather than matter'. For just as, according to those who [include] the rare and the dense among the principles of natural things, these are not matter but differentiae of matter, i.e. of the substrate, whether this be air or water or what is intermediate between these, so too the great and the small and excess and defect would seem rather to be certain differentiae of a

20   substrate in virtue of which, for the Platonists, change [takes place], but not themselves substrates. He says, 'These are a kind of excess and defect' [992b6], with reference to the rare and the dense, pointing out their similarity to the great and the small and to excess

123,1   and defect in general, which are not matter but its differentiae; for the rare is analogous to excess and the dense to defect.

---

[359] 122,5. Reading *allo khôris* for *allo peri* (Ascl.).

He has [previously] stated his difficulty with the One, the principle which was, for the Platonists, the formal principle, and his
further difficulty with the indefinite dyad, which they posited as
matter. [Here he notes] that they do not even say anything about
the movement of things that come to be by nature, [i.e.] from what
source it is in them, and yet nothing is so necessary, for one who   5
talks about natural things and makes the Ideas models, as a
reasoned account (*logos*) of movement. For if these things, excess
and defect, are movement, the Forms will be in motion, at least if
they have excess and defect in themselves as principles, since [these
two] are movement; but the Platonists are unwilling [to accept] this
conclusion, for, according to them, the Forms are motionless. But
if [excess and defect] are not movements, what is the source of   10
movement in the natural things that are what they are in virtue
of participation in the Forms?[360] For what has its being by reference
to a model must also possess its innate movement either from its
model, the model too being of this sort, or from some other cause.
But if movement is destroyed, the whole theoretical inquiry about
nature is also destroyed.

992b9 And what seems easy – to show that all things are one   15
– is not accomplished; for all things do not become one by
exposition, but a One-itself results, if we grant all their assumptions. And not even this follows, unless we grant that the
universal is a genus; and in some cases this is not possible.

[**Obj. 18**] Since those who posited the Ideas supposed that the One
is the supreme reality (*ousia*),[361] as of course the Pythagoreans also   20
did, they were convinced that it is the formal principle and cause
of the things that are. [This was] because they observed that the
nature of the one is the cause, for each thing, of its being and of its

---

[360] 123,7–9. On Alexander's interpretation of *Metaph.* 992b4, see Cherniss, op. cit.,
224, n. 132. Alexander is mistaken, he believes, in understanding 'the great and the
small' as an element in the Ideas rather than as the material principle of sensible
existence.

[361] 123,19. The meaning of *ousia* in this Platonic context is uncertain, but since it
is identified with the One, and the method of *ekthesis* to be described goes beyond
substance to being and the One, I give it the sense of 'reality'. Janine Bertier, who
offers a translation of, and commentary on, this text ('Une hénadologie liée au
Stoïcisme tardif dans le commentaire d'Alexandre d'Aphrodisie à la *Métaphysique*
d'Aristote (990b9)', *Les Stoïciens et leur logique*, Paris 1978, 41–57), translates *ousia*
as '*essence*'; but although that sense might be appropriate at 124,10, it is hardly
suitable to the present text except on the assumption that Alexander is using the
word as a Platonist might. That *ousia* has its usual sense of 'substance' at 124,21 is
shown by the subsequent reduction of *ousia* and *poiotês* (quality), (to which the *alt.
rec.* adds *poson* (quantity)) to being.

preservation[362] (for each of the things that are is one inasmuch as it exists), but that the cause of its destruction is the dissolution of the one into many; for each of the things that are will exist [as long as it is] in its own nature, in which alone it is also preserved, but
25 if it is dissolved it perishes. And they were convinced of this on the
124,1 one hand by living things, whose salvation was their remaining in the one and in the same form, and on the other hand [by what they observed] in the case of each of the inanimate things as well. [They saw,] moreover, that the universe (*kosmos*) is preserved because it remains in the one and in the same [form],[363] but that it would be destroyed were it to abandon its identity and unity. Being
5 convinced, then, by this [evidence] that the nature of the One is the cause for each of the things that are, both of its good (*to eu*) and of its being, they assumed for this reason that it is the supreme principle of all the things that are, and said indeed that the Ideas are causes of being for the other things as if they were unities (*henas*) of some kind,[364] and that in this way they are formal (*eidê-tikos*) causes of being for the things that are reduced to and brought under them.

The Platonists also attempted, by using a kind of [method called]
10 'exposition' (*ekthesis*),[365] to reduce all things to the One and to their proper reality;[366] and their procedure in exposition was as follows. Examining particular men, they would look for the similarity in all of them, and finding this to be one and the same in all men inasmuch as they are men, they reduced all men to this unity, and said that men are men by participation in the one, and this one
15 that is over [particular] men they called man-himself; [and] they did the same in turn in the case of horses, dogs, and the other

---

[362] 123,21–2, *tou men einai te kai sôzesthai.* Cf. the expression at 1,6–7 and n. 5 above.

[363] 124,3, *dia tên en tôi heni te kai tôi autôi.* This might be taken as a spatial reference, so that the sense would be: 'because it remains in one and the same place'; but the context suggests that the reference is rather to the interior unity of the universe.

[364] 124,8–10, *hôsper henadas tinas ousas*, which Bertier translates, 'parce qu'elles *sont* des hénades' (op. cit., 43; italics added); but Alexander is expressing a natural reservation about the theory, which clearly suggests that each Idea, as a unity, is immanent in the things that participate in it, thus conferring unity on them. On the Neoplatonic distinction between the Ideas as *monadeis* and *henadeis* see Bertier, 44–6.

[365] 124,9, *ekthesis.* Ross translates as 'setting out', ROTA as 'exposition'. The latter term serves well for the noun, but forms of the verb *ektithesthai* occurring in Alexander's commentary require 'to set out'.

[366] 124,10, *eis tên oikeian ousian.* In light of what follows, this must mean that the proper reality of, e.g. men, is not their reality as individuals, but the common reality that is theirs by their participation in the unity of the Idea, man-himself, so that there are successively higher levels of reality corresponding to higher levels of unity up to the supreme reality (cf. 123,19) and unity of the One.

[animals]. Moreover, setting out in turn both men and dogs and the other animals, they again assumed that [all] these owe the fact that they are animals to a one, and this one they made the cause for their being animals, and what is more, they again made a unity and an Idea and called it animal-itself, and to this unity they 20 reduced animals. In similar fashion, they again took animals and plants and the other bodies, and finding that all these are substances by participation in a one, they assumed an Idea and unity of substance, substance-itself, and under this one [substance] they in turn brought all substances. And in this way, saying that substance and quality are in turn beings by participation in being (*to* 125,1 *on*), and making a being-itself, they reduced all the things that are to this one. And thus, as they proceeded methodically and employed [the method of] exposition, they thought they were reducing all the things that are to the One, i.e. to the principle.[367]

But although it seems that they have established this point at least by the [method of] exposition, and shown as something obvious 5 the fact that all things become one, Aristotle says that the outcome is not as they imagine. For when they set out a number of particulars and, taking a characteristic these things have in common by reference to something, they make that by reference to which those things have their common characteristic and similarity a one and an Idea, the things themselves that have been set forth do not become one for them, e.g. men *qua* men – they will have shown that 'man' itself is something one from the similarity of those 10 [particular] men to one another, but these many men will not be one thing. Consequently, even if one were to grant them all their assumptions, the many things and all things do not become one thing, but, although they are referred to something one, nevertheless they are and remain many. For it has not been proved that the many particular men are man-himself (for this latter is other than these particulars), nor that all beings are being-itself or one-itself, 15 but [only] that both the one and being (*to on*) are something common over them, who are many. Consequently, even if it is granted and conceded to them that these things come to be by reference to a

---

[367] 124,9–125,4. Cf. ps.-Alexander 813,24–9: '. . . to make an exposition, i.e. to set beside [one another] each one among sensible things, such as Plato, Socrates, Alcibiades, Dion, and to say that "man" is the same as Socrates or other than he, then to argue that if it were the same, it would not be in Plato too; therefore, it is other than Socrates, and likewise, for the same reason, than Plato and Alcibiades and all the individuals. But if this is so, there exists a one apart from the many men, and this is man-himself in himself. It is possible to make this collection in the case of horses too, and in that of cows and of all other things.' Bertier points out the banality of this explanation in comparison with the description of *ekthesis* offered in the present text. On the passage from Alexander, see Schmitz, op. cit., II, 128–33; he believes that Alexander misunderstands Aristotle's text.

model, the one-itself, and that there is a one by participation in
which the many things are said to be either specifically or generically identical with one another, not even on this basis do all things
become one; but [although] a one-itself and a unity does come to be

20   according to each similarity of these many things, these things are
not one thing.

126,1   But it is not even possible, Aristotle says, either to prove or to
say that there is a one-itself based on (*kata*) every similarity if the
similarity of the things under consideration is not based on their
species or genus; for the identity and similarity based on the essence
(*ousia*), i.e. the genus and the species, is an Idea,[368] but not one

5   based on an accident. For there are many things that are predicated
in the same way by reason of some similarity they have to one
another, but that do not have any one-itself over them because their
similarity is not [based on] either genus or species. Things that are
predicated negatively are of this sort; for 'not running' is common
to and similar in the subjects of which it is predicated truly, but it
has neither genus nor species, nor is 'not running' an Idea. [And

10   the same is true] again in the case of those who sit or walk or are
dead or dying, [and] in the case of a thousand other things that do
indeed have something in common, but over which it is surely
impossible to assume any one-itself. Fathers, moreover, are all
fathers in virtue of some common relation, but there is not any one
thing, father-himself. Further, it is universally true of triangles
that the interior angles are equal to two right angles, but surely
[this similarity is] not a genus as well. Consequently, it is not

15   possible in all cases to take the one [arrived at] by exposition and,
making this a one-itself, to reduce all things to this, but only in
the case of things of which what is predicated in common and said
universally is either a genus or a species. And from this it is also
clear that the Idea of the Platonists is nothing other than either
genera or species, which are said in common and predicated synonymously of the things of which they are either species or genera.

20   It is therefore so far from being the case that they have reduced
all things to a one, as they imagine they have done, that it is not
even possible to assume the one-over-many on the basis of every
similarity. I believe that in adding the words, 'if we grant all their
assumptions', Aristotle is pointing out that they will not be
permitted, if certain things are predicated in the same way on the

---

[368] 126,4. That is, on the assumption (being conceded to the Platonists) that there
is an Idea corresponding to every similarity found in things. On that assumption,
there will in fact be Ideas of universals based on the essence of things, especially
on their genus; cf. *in Top.* 108,22: 'Of the common predicates, that which is predicated
essentially most of all must be the genus.' But there are universals that are not
genera or species, of which, consequently, there will not be Ideas, as Alexander goes
on to explain.

basis of some characteristic they have in common, thereupon to make that [common] thing one, on the assumption that all the things under it have their being by reference to it as something 25 separated from them. Or else, 'if we grant all their assumptions' could signify that if one were to concede that all things predicated in the same way are so predicated on the basis of their sharing in a particular one, and should [further] concede that there exists a one-over-many of this sort, [still] there will not even be this result in the case of things other than those that are common as genera and species; for, he says, only things that are common and universal 30 in this way seem to signify an Idea. And yet, 'this is impossible in at least some cases' [992b12], for it happens that some of the things predicated in common of particulars cannot be genera of the things of which they are predicated in common; for the things that are said in many ways are of this sort. He must be referring to things said in many ways because of being (*to on*) in particular, which the Platonists, taking it as a kind of common genus of all things what- ever, made an Idea, being-itself and one-itself, and brought all 35 things under it.[369] But if one is not a genus, but is among things said in many ways, it is clear that neither would the things that are have an essential (*ousiôdês*) similarity based on this [one].

992b13 There is also no explanation of how the things that 127,1 come after the numbers . . . [come to exist].

[**Obj. 19**] Aristotle himself adds what the things that come after the numbers are; for they are lines (*mêkos*), planes, and solids. For both the Pythagoreans and Plato, resolving the things that are into these, said that numbers are principles of the things that are, and are the first things; but after numbers they ranked lines, and after 5 lines, planes, then solids, on the ground that these are not numbers. But it is clear that as lines, planes, and solids are ordered by reference to one another, so their principles too will be ordered by reference to one another, for there are, according to the Platonists, principles proper to each of these; for of these things too they posited Ideas, which are then principles of the things coming after numbers. But if the principles of line and plane and solid are length-itself, 10 breadth-itself, and solid-itself, it is difficult to discover in what nature and power these participate according to those who posit the Ideas. For these [i.e. length-itself and the others] are not Ideas, since the Ideas are numbers but these are not numbers; for they hold, in the view of the Platonists, the rank after numbers. But the

---

[369] 126,35. Alexander deals at greater length with the familiar Aristotelian thesis that being is not a genus in his commentary on *Metaphysics* 3, 204,10ff.

short and the long and the narrow and the broad and the deep and
the shallow, the principles [of lines, planes, and solids,] are not
15   numbers either. But neither will they be included among mathematical objects, which the Platonists located between the Ideas
and sensible things; for mathematical objects are [constituted] out
of these, but are not their principles. For mathematical objects are
not principles, and are divisible and many; but these things are
principles and indivisible, and each of them is one.[370] But neither
are these things corruptible, for they are principles and incorrupt-
20   ible. This will therefore be in turn, for the Platonists, a fourth
nature of the things that are, and a fourth class in addition to the
three they posit, which were the Ideas, mathematical objects and
sensible things. For the principles ‹of line and plane and solid›[371]
are different from all of these, for they are not Ideas because they
are not numbers, nor do they belong to the remaining two [classes]
that have just been mentioned; for the Platonists say they are
one,[372] and assign to them the rank [after numbers] spoken of above.
128,1 But it is impossible to say how they exist or to what nature of the
things that are they belong according to the Platonists. For in their
view, the things that are are either Ideas or mathematical objects
or sensible things. But length-itself and plane-itself and solid-itself

[370] 127,18. Reading *hen* for *aei* (Bonitz, comparing 127,24 and 128,6 below).

[371] 127,22. Reading *mêkous kai epipedou kai stereou* for *tôn mathêmatikôn*,
although the apparatus offers no support for this conjecture. *Tôn mathêmatikôn* is
impossible in the present context, especially since *gar* in l. 23 indicates that the
next clause is intended to provide a reason for the present statement, and in that
clause the principles here referred to are distinguished from the three classes Alexander has mentioned: Ideas, mathematical objects, and sensible things. The diffuse
argument of Hayduck's text is expressed so much more clearly in the *alt. rec.* that
it seems useful to append this latter. 'Numbers are first of all things, and their
principles are prior to the principles of length and breadth and solid, for the indefinite
dyad is first, and the Platonists attempted to bring under it the long and short and
the broad and narrow and the deep and shallow, which are the principles of the
things mentioned. Where, then, will length-itself and breadth-itself and solid-itself
be located? For they are not Ideas, but the Ideas are numbers. They will not be
included among the things that are intermediate [i.e. mathematical objects] . . ., nor
among those that are corruptible [i.e. sensible things] . . . The conclusion therefore
is that there is a yet another [and] fourth class of the things that are, in addition
to the Ideas and the intermediates and sensible things: length-itself, breadth-itself,
and solid-itself – if that is not the case, it is difficult to discover in what nature and
power [line and plane and solid] participate according to those who posit the Ideas
. . .' (127). Margherita Isnardi-Parente, who questions the traditional view that Plato
or the early Platonists posited 'ideal magnitudes' (*eidêtikê megethê*) ('*Ta meta tas
ideas*: figures idéales ou premières figures?', *Mathematics and Metaphysics in Aristotle*, Bern 1987, 261–80), says that the terms *automêkos, autoepipedon*, and *auto-
stereon* in this text of Alexander '. . . sont expressions ambiguës, qui pourraient
aussi se référer simplement aux idées des figures géométriques' (263, n. 4). Alexander, however, clearly regards them as principles (*arkhai*) out of which line, plane
and solid are constituted.

[372] i.e. each of them – length-itself, etc. – is a unity, as he explains more clearly
at 128,6 below.

will not be Ideas because, according to the Platonists, the Ideas are numbers, but they said that these things come after numbers. But 5 neither are they intermediates, for according to the Platonists [it is] mathematical objects [that are] intermediates. But mathematical objects were also many, but length-itself and plane-itself and solid-itself are not many. But neither are they among things that are sensible and corruptible, for none of these [latter] is a being in the proper sense. Obviously, then, this becomes, according to the Platonists, a fourth class of the things that are.

992b18 And in general, if we seek for the elements of the 10 things that are without distinguishing the many ways in which things are said [to exist], we cannot find them.

[**Obj. 20**] The argument is as follows. It is impossible to discover any common principles of things that have no common principles; but there are no common principles of the things that are, so that it is also impossible to discover their common principles. That there are no common and identical principles of the things that are is clear from the following: there are no common and identical prin- 15 ciples of things that are said in many ways; but the things that are are said in many ways; therefore, there are not identical principles of the things that are. (Aristotle has stated in many places that being (*to on*) is among the things that are said in many ways.) He is criticizing the Platonists, then, because they were seeking principles of the things that are without having first distinguished things, or articulated the meanings of [the term] 'being' (*to on*). [The attempt is absurd] in other respects, and it is still more absurd to seek, [as] such principles, the same principles out of which these 20 things are [constituted], and these are the matter and the form;[373] for it is principles of this sort that the Platonists assume, the indefinite dyad and the unit. For some of the things that are do not even have principles and elements of this kind in virtue of their own nature, except *per accidens*; for from what matter are 'to make 129,1 something' or 'to be acted on' (*paskhein*)? For even these do have

---

[373] 128,19–21. The point of this statement is that the universal principles of the Platonists, the indefinite dyad and the One, here conveniently identified with Aristotle's matter and form, are, like matter and form, constituent principles, so that the Platonists are seeking, as their universal principles, the same principles which, by assumption, they use to constitute things. But, from the Aristotelian point of view, these are constituent principles in the proper sense only of substances: matter and form are *in* substances, whereas substances are only analogously the matter or substrate of actions and affections, inasmuch as these accidents belong to substances. If, then, the Platonists identify their supposedly universal principles with matter and form, or with their Platonic equivalents, they have not in fact discovered the principles of all things.

matter, [but only] *per accidens*; for because they belong to substances, which have a particular matter, there would be in this
respect a particular matter of things of this kind too, but not *per
se*. Similarly, neither is there a particular matter of the straight,
nor of anything else except substance. For it is on this account that
5   Aristotle says it is impossible to find such elements of these things,
because [elements of this kind] simply do not exist; for it is possible
to find such principles, those that are like elements and are in [a
thing], and from which something is said to be, only of substance;
for only substance is a substrate of the things that are, but the
other things are in substance and are some [modification] of it. It
is therefore foolish either to seek, or to think that one has found,
[common principles] of things that do not have such principles.

10   **992b24** But how could one even learn the elements of all
      things?

[**Obj. 21**] Aristotle shows that even if the elements of the things
that are are common to all things, it is impossible either to learn
or to know them. He adds the reason why it is impossible to learn
the elements of all things, saying: 'for clearly we cannot start by
knowing anything beforehand' [992b25]. His argument is as follows.
15   It is impossible to know any of the things that have principles
unless one knows its principles; for it is impossible to know things
the knowledge of which is through their principles before [one has]
knowledge of their principles. But according to the Platonists, there
are common principles of all the things that are; therefore, it is
impossible to know any of the things that are without having first
learned its principles. But it is surely impossible to have knowledge
of things having principles whose principles it is impossible to learn;
20   but it is impossible to learn the principles of the things that are;
therefore, it is impossible to have knowledge of the things that are.
And that it is impossible to learn the principles of the things that
are he proves in this way. All learning comes from things known
beforehand; for as he said at the beginning of the *Posterior
Analytics*, 'All teaching and all learning that involves the use of
reason comes from pre-existent knowledge' [71a11].[374] For what a
130,1 person is learning because he does not know it he cannot know
before [he learns]; but it is of course necessary to have prior knowledge of certain things by means of which learning [takes place]. At

---

[374] 129,2-3. Alexander has quoted this same text in the same form at 19,24 above.
Paul Moraux records a text in which Philoponus criticizes Alexander for substituting
heureseôs (discovery) for Aristotle's *gnôseôs* (knowledge); see Moraux's comment
on this point (*Le commentaire d'Alexandre d'Aphrodisie aux 'Seconds Analytiques'
d'Aristote*, Berlin 1979, fr. 1 (9)).

any rate, one who is learning to be a geometrician has no prior knowledge, at the time he begins to learn, of any of the things with which the science of geometry deals, but he certainly knows some things that enable him to understand matters through which his instruction [takes place], e.g. greater, less, equal, straight, crooked; but he also has an idea of line and plane and body. Now if all learning comes from a prior knowledge of certain other things, not of the things being learned, one who hopes to learn the principles of the things that are will also need to know certain other things [beforehand]. But this is impossible; for whatever might be taken [as a thing for him] to know [beforehand] will be a being of some sort and under the principles of being (*to on*), but it is impossible to know any of the things that are before having learned its principles. Therefore, either the learner will know beforehand what he is learning, or he will not learn.

Aristotle proves that all learning comes from things known beforehand by taking up [the ways in which] learning [takes place]; for we learn something either by demonstration or by definition or by induction. And even in teaching by demonstration there are certain things known by the learner, things that are other than those being demonstrated; for of this sort are the axioms, which are certain natural notions and immediate premises, such as: 'Things equal to the same things are equal to each other'; or, 'In the case of everything there is either affirmation or negation';[375] or, 'The good is beneficial by its very nature.' And all knowledge by a syllogism is by means of things known beforehand, for [it is] by means of the premises that must be granted and assumed. And teaching by means of definitions also comes about from things known beforehand; for one learning the definition of man – that man is a walking two-footed animal – does not know beforehand that man is these things, but he does know each of them, 'animal', 'walking', and 'two-footed', or he would not learn that man is these things. Similarly, teaching by induction also aims at teaching the universal, but the learner must know the things by means of which induction teaches (these are the particulars). Now if all teaching [takes place] in this way, but those who seek the principles of all the things that are, and say they teach [them], do away with the possibility of the learner's being acquainted with and knowing anything, they do away with both teaching and learning in general. – Aristotle says, '[All learning is by means of premises known beforehand,] either all of them or some of them' [992b31], because in demonstration

5

10

15

20

131,1

5

---

[375] 130,18. This axiom is given more fully in the *alt. rec.*: 'In the case of everything, either the affirmation or the negation is either true or false.' Another definition of axioms is found *in Metaph.* 4, 264,35: 'The axioms are common and indemonstrable principles useful for proving things in all the sciences.' On the axioms, see n. 62.

and the syllogism it is possible for one to know beforehand and to
be acquainted with both the premises, as in definition too he can
be acquainted with and know beforehand all the things from which
the definition is [composed]; and induction is by means of things all
10 [of which] are familiar or known beforehand. Or else [he says,]
'either all of them', as in [the case of] definitions and inductions,
'or some of them', as in [the case of] demonstrations.[376]

922b33 But if the knowledge were innate, [it is surprising that
we are not aware that we possess it].

Having eliminated [the possibility] that there can be learning if
there are common principles and causes of the things that are,
Aristotle now explains that neither is it possible, without teaching,
15 to have an innate knowledge of these [principles],[377] so that in order
to know them there is no need either of teaching or of any things
known beforehand. For the knowledge of the most sovereign things
is the most excellent of the sciences, but the knowledge of the
principles, whichever of them are the principles of all the things
that are, is knowledge of the most sovereign things, for that because
of which something [else] exists is always more sovereign than what
exists because of it; but it is because of the principles that the
20 things after the principles [exist]; therefore, the knowledge of the
principles is the most excellent of the sciences. But that [we] should
132,1 possess the most excellent of the sciences innately and not know
this is against all reason. We are not, however, unaware of the
sense perception that we possess innately, nor that we are able to
walk; but we are unaware that in possessing the principles of the
things that are we possess the knowledge of these things, or that
we know at least the principles of all the things that are, and cannot
5 say [that we possess them] even when we have scrutinized them
and fixed our attention on them. How then would we possess innate
knowledge of these things that we do not know? This [argument]
can also [be used] to refute the doctrine of the Platonists that the
knowledge we possess of the things that are is innate; [they hold]
this because they believe that learning is reminiscence (*anamnêsis*).

---

[376] 131,11. Because one does not always need prior knowledge of the minor premise,
which is sometimes known simultaneously with the conclusion (Aristotle, *An. Post.*
71a17ff). Thus Alexander says above (l. 7) only that it is possible to know both
premises beforehand.
[377] 131,14. This is what Alexander says, but he must obviously intend *khôris
didaskalias* as an explanation of *sumphuton*, since knowledge that results from
teaching is not innate. The requisite sense can be brought out by translating, 'that
it is impossible to have innate knowledge of these principles – [i.e. knowledge that
exists in us] without teaching'.

993a2 Again, how will one know from what principles things are, and how will this be clear? This point too presents a   10
difficulty.

[**Obj. 22**] Even if the principles of all things are common and identical, how will one know that they are these particular ones and that the things that are are from these, if he does not have prior knowledge of certain things by means of which he will be able to know and to prove that the principles are these? For why will he know that they are these particular principles rather than these [others], if he does not have principles for recognizing what he is   15
seeking? For certainly not everyone will agree without controversy that [the principles] are these particular ones; but just as people disagree about whether the syllable *za* should be written *za* or *sda*, so there would surely be a controversy about the principles. (In   133,1
ancient times each of these letters, [*zeta, xi,* and *psi,*] used to be written with two letters, and for this reason they were called 'double letters' of the alphabet; and *zeta* [was written] with *sd*, *xi* with *ks*, and *psi* with *ps*.) For if people were to dispute [about the form of letters], one could investigate them[378] and recognize [the correct form] through either definition or syllogism or induction, all of   5
which (as was said above) prove by means of things known beforehand.

It seems likely that Aristotle is saying that the problem (*aporia*) stated by Plato in the *Meno* [80E] can be raised as a difficulty against those who posit certain common and identical principles of all the things that are. For they are forced to say that the principles can be taught (for [if we knew them] we would certainly not be   10
unaware that we possess the most excellent of all the sciences, that which is knowledge of all the things that are); but because one who is ignorant of the principles of the things that are is incapable of knowing any of the things that are, those who are learning principles of this kind would not have prior knowledge of any of the things that are. But if this is the case, [the learners] would not even be able to recognize the principles of being (*to on*), that scl. they are [the principles] of being, even if these principles were to be discovered, because such recognition comes about by means of   15
some pre-existent knowledge. But it is impossible for one who does not yet possess the principles of being to have this knowledge,

---

[378] 133,4. Alexander says only *auta*, and the neuter seems to mandate a reference to *grammatôn* (letters) (l. 2). But this may be another instance of loose reference of a neuter plural to a feminine antecedent, so that *auta* might possibly refer to *tôn arkhôn* (the principles) (l. 1), especially since the question of the correct formation of a letter can scarcely be settled by appeal to definition or syllogism. But the whole sentence is imprecise, and seems to be an attempt to bring the discussion back to the necessity of prior knowledge.

because they are also the principles of these things [known before-
hand], at least if the latter too belong to the things that are. The
words, 'from what principles things are', probably point to the principles themselves, the kind of common principles of all things that
the Platonists were seeking; for they were seeking the matter and
the form.

20   **993a7** Again, how would one have[379] the things of which there
        is sense perception if he does not have the sense power?

[**Obj. 23**] This too Aristotle says [as proof that] there are not identical principles and elements of all things. For if there should be
certain common principles of all the things that are, one who has
learned these principles would be able to know, through them, all
25   the things that are. For just as one who knows all the letters and
the elements [of sounds] knows too all the sounds composed from
them, so it follows that if one knows the principles of the things
that are he will also know, through them, all the things that are
[constituted] from them; but if that is so, one who knows these
principles will be able to know sensible things as well, for they too
are from these principles, at least if they exist. How then will one
who does not have the sense power (*aisthêsis*) know sensible things?
30   For sensible things are known by sense perception, and in no other
way.[380] But it follows that if one knows the principles of sensible
things, he knows these things through those principles; but one
134,1   who knows the common principles of all the things that are will
know the principles [of sensible things] even if he does not have
the sense power (for certainly the principles of the things that are
are not perceptible). For as he knows things that are not sensible
through these principles, so he will know sensible things too
through them, if they[381] are likewise principles of sensible things
5   as well. For just as all composite sounds of which the elements are

---

[379] 133,21. The lemma has *ekhoi* for the *gnoiê* of our text of *Metaphysics*.

[380] 133,29–30. The question is oddly placed here, since Alexander has already
given his answer to the problem, an answer he then repeats after stating the
question. According to Ross, Aristotle's own argument is a relatively simple one: if
all things are constituted out of the same elements, all sensible objects would be
equally perceptible to a single sense power, so that a blind man e.g. would perceive
colours along with sounds (*Metaphysics* I, 211 ad 8–10). But Alexander takes a
different line: he seems to assume that the knower has no sensory apparatus whatever, but will know sensible objects if these latter have the same principles as all
other things, and if these principles can be known – postulates, as he said before,
of the Platonists. Thus a person deprived of all sense powers will know sensible
objects through knowledge of their principles – an argument that does find some
support in Aristotle's statement, 'And yet he ought to know [sensible things] if the
elements of all things are the same' (993a8).

[381] 134,4. Reading *ekeinai* for *ekeina* (Bonitz).

the same are composed from the same elements, so all the things that are will be known from the same elements,[382] if the elements of all of them are the same.

Aristotle would not be contradicting himself in saying, on the one hand, that he is seeking the principles of being *qua* being, while proving by these arguments, on the other hand, that the principles cannot be known; for he will show that there simply are not any common principles of the things that are, as those who attempt to reduce all things to the One because of their common similarities think [there are]. But the principles of being *qua* being that he is seeking *are* common principles of all things; but the principles of substance, since they are not principles in the same way as the other things that exist in addition to substance, become in a sense principles of these latter things as well, because each of the other things that are has its being from substance.

10

---

[382] 134,6. Throughout this passage, *ek tôn autôn stoikheiôn* has meant '[constituted] from the same elements'; but here *ek* must have the sense of *apo* (from), as it has e.g. at 2,2; 5,27; 15,6.11.23. *Estai gnôrizomena* (will be known) is an echo of Aristotle's *gnoiê* (*Metaph.* 993a8), as Alexander's *sunthetoi phônai* (composite sounds) derives from the next line of Aristotle's text; so that in this concluding sentence Alexander is attempting to bring his commentary more directly into line with Aristotle's argument.

CHAPTER 10

134,15   **993a11** [It is evident,] then, that all philosophers seem to be seeking the causes named in the *Physics*.

In the lectures [entitled] the *Physics*, Aristotle reduced all the causes to four kinds. And wishing to confirm that classification [in this treatise] too, he proceeded to state the opinions of the earlier [philosophers] who had spoken[383] about the causes. [These opinions]
20   he examined in detail lest perchance anyone was seeking some other kind of cause; and he found that all those who had spoken about causes mentioned [as] cause some of the causes named [in the *Physics*]. Some of them mentioned one of the causes, as those who assigned the material cause, others two, others three; and of these latter some assumed the efficient cause in addition to the
135,1   matter, as Anaxagoras and Empedocles, others the form, as those who [posited] the Ideas, others even touched on both of these in some manner, the efficient and the formal cause, as he will say about Empedocles. [Thus they mentioned the causes,] except that certainly none of them was seeking or assumed some other kind of cause apart from these [four] kinds, although all of them spoke
5   obscurely about the causes and not articulately. Plato might indeed be found to have mentioned the four causes and Empedocles three of them, as Aristotle will say, but not clearly nor with proper distinctions. The reason he gives for their having spoken inarticulately about the causes, even while contributing something to this inquiry, is that none of the thinkers before Aristotle had as yet gained any precise knowledge of philosophical matters, but, as those
10   who lisp pronounce their words [inarticulately], so too those before him spoke [inarticulately] about philosophy.

[As evidence] that they did not say these things distinctly he mentions Empedocles, who said that bone is bone by reference to its formula[384] but not by reference to its matter; for according to him the matter is common to the other things as well (for it is the four elements), but he says that bone comes to be in the qualitative and quantitative blending (*krasis*) of these elements. His words are:

---

[383] 134,19. Reading *tôn proterôn* (LF) *aitiôn eirêkotôn* (Bonitz).

[384] 135,12. *Logos* in the text of Aristotle (*Metaph.* 933a17,20) probably means 'ratio' or 'proportion': that is, the proportion of earth, water, and fire contained in the mixture that is bone. But Alexander's subsequent discussion indicates that he interprets *logos* as formula = definition; and in quoting Empedocles he omits the reference to *harmonia*.

The kindly earth received in its broad funnels two parts of gleaming   15
Nestis out of the eight, and four of Hephaistos. So arose white bones
[divinely fitted together by the cement of proportion].[385]

But if, according to him, bones owe the fact that they are bone to
their formula, i.e. to their form and essence (for this is what the
formula is), it is clear that flesh too, and sinew, and each of the   20
other things that are, such as stone [or] wood, has its being by
reference to its formula and form; for it is either in all cases or in
none that the form and the formula are responsible for each thing's
being what it is.[386] For it is because of the formula and the form
that there is a difference among the things that are, and that one
of them is this particular thing, flesh, another this particular thing,
bone, and another this other particular thing, since the matter at
least is, according to him, the same for all the things that are, as
we have stated; for the four elements were his material principle.   25
Empedocles would therefore have agreed completely that this is the
way these things are, and that the form is responsible for each
thing's being the particular thing that it is, if [only] someone had
led him on by argument, pointing out that each thing is in this way.
Speaking for himself, however, he has made no clear determination   136,1
about the subject, nor has he stated matters scientifically, because
he did not speak in the same way about all the things that are
similar.

993a24 We have already expressed our opinion about matters
of this sort.

Perhaps Aristotle says, 'about these matters',[387] with the implication that he has already discussed them, because he spoke [about
them] in an earlier passage too when speaking about Anaxagoras   5
and correcting his opinion, [saying] that although Anaxagoras
would[388] have concurred with another who said these things, he

---

[385] 135, 15–18. Fr. 96 DK I, 346; translation of John Burnet, *EGP*, reprint of the
fourth edition (N.Y. 1957), 218. Alexander quotes only the first three lines of the
fragment.

[386] 135,21, *to eidos kai ho logos aitios tou hekastou einai ho estin*, which corresponds
to Jaeger's text, *anankaion kai sarkas kai tôn allôn hekaston einai ‹dia› ton logon*
(*Metaph.* 933a19–20). Ross, however, omits *dia*, inserted by Jaeger, so that the sense
is: 'that flesh and each of the other things should *be* its *logos*.' Owens thinks that
Alexander (and Jaeger) have missed Aristotle's meaning; his own translation of
Aristotle's text emphasizes the existential sense of *einai* (op. cit., 195, n. 116).

[387] 136,4. The lemma has *peri men oun tôn toioutôn*, but the commentary shows
that Alexander read *peri men oun toutôn*, the reading of our text of *Metaphysics*.

[388] 136,6. Reading *an* for *oun* (Bonitz); cf. *Metaph.* 989a32.

himself did not say anything clearly about them,[389] as Empedocles, about whom he spoke just now, also did not. In addition, he announces that he will raise certain difficulties pertaining to the discussion about the principles, and says that as a result of having stated these, and of having been puzzled in the right way, we shall
10 be better prepared to solve the difficulties that will occur later on; for the difficulties about the principles, and their solutions, become starting-points for solving the difficulties that [come] after them. And he is speaking about the difficulties raised in book Beta (3); and for this reason one might think, so far as [he can judge] from what is said here, that Beta is the sequel to this book. [This] is not, however, [the case,] but in Alpha Elatton (2) too he does in fact
15 speak about the difficulties that he here proposed [to discuss]. For when he says, 'Let us return again to the difficulties one might raise in regard to these same matters' [993a25], [he means] the questions and difficulties about the principles and the causes [that] he also raises in [Book] 2, [the book] that follows this one.

---

[389] 136,4–7. This remark is perhaps intended to correct what Alexander has said above (135,25–8) about Empedocles, for the text of *Metaphysics* to which he here refers (989a30f) does in fact deal with Anaxagoras. (For Alexander's commentary on that text, see 68,6–69,1 above). In referring Aristotle's remark to Empedocles rather than to Anaxagoras, he might have had in mind *Metaph.* 985a4–10, where Aristotle says that Empedocles, though lisping, intended in fact to make *philia* and *neikos* the causes of good and evil respectively. (For Alexander's commentary on that text, see 35,19ff above.)

Appendix
The Commentators*

The 15,000 pages of the Ancient Greek Commentaries on Aristotle are the largest corpus of Ancient Greek philosophy that has not been translated into English or other modern European languages. The standard edition (*Commentaria in Aristotelem Graeca*, or *CAG*) was produced by Hermann Diels as general editor under the auspices of the Prussian Academy in Berlin. Arrangements have now been made to translate at least a large proportion of this corpus, along with some other Greek and Latin commentaries not included in the Berlin edition, and some closely related non-commentary works by the commentators.

The works are not just commentaries on Aristotle, although they are invaluable in that capacity too. One of the ways of doing philosophy between AD 200 and 600, when the most important items were produced, was by writing commentaries. The works therefore represent the thought of the Peripatetic and Neoplatonist schools, as well as expounding Aristotle. Furthermore, they embed fragments from all periods of Ancient Greek philosophical thought: this is how many of the Presocratic fragments were assembled, for example. Thus they provide a panorama of every period of Ancient Greek philosophy.

The philosophy of the period from AD 200 to 600 has not yet been intensively explored by philosophers in English-speaking countries, yet it is full of interest for physics, metaphysics, logic, psychology, ethics and religion. The contrast with the study of the Presocratics is striking. Initially the incomplete Presocratic fragments might well have seemed less promising, but their interest is now widely known, thanks to the philological and philosophical effort that has been concentrated upon them. The incomparably vaster corpus which preserved so many of those fragments offers at least as much interest, but is still relatively little known.

The commentaries represent a missing link in the history of philosophy: the Latin-speaking Middle Ages obtained their knowledge of Aristotle at least partly through the medium of the commentaries. Without an appreciation of this, mediaeval interpre-

* Reprinted from the Editor's General Introduction to the series in Christian Wildberg, *Philoponus Against Aristotle on the Eternity of the World*, London and Ithaca N.Y., 1987.

tations of Aristotle will not be understood. Again, the ancient commentaries are the unsuspected source of ideas which have been thought, wrongly, to originate in the later mediaeval period. It has been supposed, for example, that Bonaventure in the thirteenth century invented the ingenious arguments based on the concept of infinity which attempt to prove the Christian view that the universe had a beginning. In fact, Bonaventure is merely repeating arguments devised by the commentator Philoponus 700 years earlier and preserved in the meantime by the Arabs. Bonaventure even uses Philoponus' original examples. Again, the introduction of impetus theory into dynamics, which has been called a scientific revolution, has been held to be an independent invention of the Latin West, even if it was earlier discovered by the Arabs or their predecessors. But recent work has traced a plausible route by which it could have passed from Philoponus, via the Arabs, to the West.

The new availability of the commentaries in the sixteenth century, thanks to printing and to fresh Latin translations, helped to fuel the Renaissance break from Aristotelian science. For the commentators record not only Aristotle's theories, but also rival ones, while Philoponus as a Christian devises rival theories of his own and accordingly is mentioned in Galileo's early works more frequently than Plato.[1]

It is not only for their philosophy that the works are of interest. Historians will find information about the history of schools, their methods of teaching and writing and the practices of an oral tradition.[2] Linguists will find the indexes and translations an aid for studying the development of word meanings, almost wholly uncharted in Liddell and Scott's *Lexicon*, and for checking shifts in grammatical usage.

[1] See Fritz Zimmermann, 'Philoponus' impetus theory in the Arabic tradition'; Charles Schmitt, 'Philoponus' commentary on Aristotle's *Physics* in the sixteenth century', and Richard Sorabji, 'John Philoponus', in Richard Sorabji (ed.), *Philoponus and the Rejection of Aristotelian Science* (London and Ithaca, N.Y. 1987).

[2] See e.g. Karl Praechter, 'Die griechischen Aristoteleskommentare', *Byzantinische Zeitschrift* 18 (1909), 516–38; M. Plezia, *de Commentariis Isagogicis* (Cracow 1947); M. Richard, '*Apo Phônês*', *Byzantion* 20 (1950), 191–222; É. Evrard, *L'Ecole d'Olympiodore et la composition du commentaire a la physique de Jean Philopon*, Diss. (Liège 1957); L.G. Westerink, *Anonymous Prolegomena to Platonic Philosophy* (Amsterdam 1962) (new revised edition, translated into French, Collection Budé, forthcoming); A.-J. Festugière, 'Modes de composition des commentaires de Proclus', *Museum Helveticum* 20 (1963), 77–100, repr. in his *Études* (1971), 551–74; P. Hadot, 'Les divisions des parties de la philosophie dans l'antiquité', *Museum Helveticum* 36 (1979), 201–23; I. Hadot, 'La division néoplatonicienne des écrits d'Aristote', in J. Wiesner (ed.), *Aristoteles Werk und Wirkung* (Paul Moraux gewidmet), vol. 2 (Berlin 1986); I. Hadot, 'Les introductions aux commentaires exégétiques chez les auteurs néoplatoniciens et les auteurs chrétiens', in M. Tardieu (ed.), *Les règles de l'interprétation* (Paris 1987), 99–119. These topics are treated, and a bibliography supplied, in R. Sorabji (ed.), *Aristotle Transformed* (London and Ithaca, N.Y. 1989), which includes several of the articles mentioned above.

Given the wide range of interests to which the volumes will appeal, the aim is to produce readable translations, and to avoid so far as possible presupposing any knowledge of Greek. Footnotes will explain points of meaning, give cross-references to other works, and suggest alternative interpretations of the text where the translator does not have a clear preference. The introduction to each volume will include an explanation why the work was chosen for translation: none will be chosen simply because it is there. Two of the Greek texts are currently being re-edited – those of Simplicius *in Physica* and *in de Caelo* – and new readings will be exploited by translators as they become available. Each volume will also contain a list of proposed emendations to the standard text. Indexes will be of more uniform extent as between volumes than in the case with the Berlin edition, and there will be three of them: an English-Greek glossary, a Greek-English index, and a subject index.

The commentaries fall into three main groups. The first group is by authors in the Aristotelian tradition up to the fourth century AD This includes the earliest extant commentary, that by Aspasius in the first half of the second century AD on the *Nicomachean Ethics*. The anonymous commentary on Books 2, 3, 4 and 5 of the *Nichomachean Ethics*, in *CAG* vol. 20, may be partly or wholly by Adrastus, a generation later.[3] The commentaries by Alexander of Aphrodisias (appointed to his chair between AD 198 and 209) represent the fullest flowering of the Aristotelian tradition. To his successors Alexander was The Commentator *par excellence*. To give but one example (not from a commentary) of his skill at defending and elaborating Aristotle's views, one might refer to his defence of Aristotle's claim that space is finite against the objection that an edge of space is conceptually problematic.[4] Themistius (*fl.* late 340s to 384 or 385) saw himself as the inventor of paraphrase, wrongly thinking that the job of commentary was completed.[5] In fact, the Neoplatonists were to introduce new dimensions into commentary. Themistius' own relation to the Neoplatonist as opposed to the Aristotelian tradition is a matter of controversy,[6] but it would be

[3] Anthony Kenny, *The Aristotelian Ethics* (Oxford 1978), 37, n. 3; Paul Moraux, *Der Aristotelismus bei den Griechen*, vol. 2 (Berlin 1984) 323–30.

[4] Alexander, *Quaestiones* 3.12, discussed in my *Matter, Space and Motion* (London and Ithaca, N.Y. 1988). For Alexander see R. W. Sharples, 'Alexander of Aphrodisias: scholasticism and innovation', in W. Haase (ed.), *Aufstieg und Niedergang der römischen Welt*, part 2 *Principat*, vol. 36.2, *Philosophie und Wissenschaften* (1987) 1176–243.

[5] Themistius *in An. Post.* 1.2–12. See H. J. Blumenthal, 'Photius on Themistius (Cod. 74): did Themistius write commentaries on Aristotle?', *Hermes* 107 (1979), 168–82.

[6] For different views, see H. J. Blumenthal, 'Themistius, the last Peripatetic commentator on Aristotle?', in Glen W. Bowersock, Walter Burkert, Michael C. J. Putnam, *Arktouros*, Hellenic Studies Presented to Bernard M. W. Knox (Berlin and

agreed that his commentaries show far less bias than the full-blown Neoplatonist ones. They are also far more informative than the designation 'paraphrase' might suggest, and it has been estimated that Philoponus' *Physics* commentary draws silently on Themistius six hundred times.[7] The pseudo-Alexandrian commentary on *Metaphysics* 6–14, of unknown authorship, has been placed by some in the same group of commentaries as being earlier than the fifth century.[8]

By far the largest group of extant commentaries is that of the Neoplatonists up to the sixth century AD. Nearly all the major Neoplatonists, apart from Plotinus (the founder of Neoplatonism), wrote commentaries on Aristotle, although those of Iamblichus (*c.* 250 – *c.* 325) survive only in fragments, and those of three Athenians, Plutarchus (died 432), his pupil Proclus (410–485) and the Athenian Damascius (*c.* 462 – after 538), are lost.[9] As a result of these losses, most of the extant Neoplatonist commentaries come from the late fifth and the sixth centuries and a good proportion from Alexandria. There are commentaries by Plotinus' disciple and editor Porphyry (232–309), by Iamblichus' pupil Dexippus (*c.* 330), by Proclus' teacher Syrianus (died *c.* 437), by Proclus' pupil Ammonius (435/455–517/526), by Ammonius' three pupils Philoponus (*c.* 490 to 570s). Simplicius (wrote after 532, probably after 538) and Asclepius (sixth century), by Ammonius' next but one successor Olympiodorus (495/505 – after 565), by Elias (*fl.* 541?), by David (second half of the sixth century, or beginning of the seventh) and by Stephanus (took the chair in Constantinople *c.* 610).

N.Y. 1979), 391–400; E. P. Mahoney, 'Themistius and the agent intellect in James of Viterbo and other thirteenth-century philosophers: (Saint Thomas Aquinas, Siger of Brabant and Henry Bate)', *Augustiniana* 23 (1973), 422–67, at 428–31; id., 'Neoplatonism, the Greek commentators and Renaissance Aristotelianism', in D. J. O'Meara (ed.), *Neoplatonism and Christian Thought* (Albany N.Y. 1982), 169–77 and 264–82, esp. n. 1, 264–6; Robert Todd, introduction to translation of Themistius *in DA 3, 4–8*, forthcoming in a collection of translations by Frederick Schroeder and Robert Todd of material in the commentators relating to the intellect.

[7] H. Vitelli, *CAG* 17, p. 992, s.v. Themistius.

[8] The similarities to Syrianus (died *c.* 437) have suggested to some that it predates Syrianus (most recently Leonardo Tarán, review of Paul Moraux, *Der Aristotelismus*, vol. 1, in *Gnomon* 46 (1981), 721–50 at 750), to others that it draws on him (most recently P. Thillet, in the Budé edition of Alexander *de Fato*, p. lvii). Praechter ascribed it to Michael of Ephesus (eleventh or twelfth century), in his review of *CAG* 22.2, in *Göttingische Gelehrte Anzeigen* 168 (1906), 861–907.

[9] The Iamblichus fragments are collected in Greek by Bent Dalsgaard Larsen, *Jamblique de Chalcis, Exégète et Philosophe* (Aarhus 1972), vol. 2. Most are taken from Simplicius, and will accordingly be translated in due course. The evidence on Damascius' commentaries is given in L. G. Westerink, *The Greek Commentaries on Plato's Phaedo*, vol. 2., Damascius (Amsterdam 1977), 11–12; on Proclus' in L. G. Westerink, *Anonymous Prolegomena to Platonic Philosophy* (Amsterdam 1962), xii, n. 22; on Plutarchus' in H. M. Blumenthal, 'Neoplatonic elements in the de Anima commentaries', *Phronesis* 21 (1976), 75.

Further, a commentary on the *Nicomachen Ethics* has been ascribed speculatively to Ammonius' brother Heliodorus, and there is a commentary by Simplicius' colleague Priscian of Lydia on Aristotle's successor Theophrastus. Of these commentators some of the last were Christians (Philoponus, Elias, David and Stephanus), but they were Christians writing in the Neoplatonist tradition, as was also Boethius who produced a number of commentaries in Latin before his death in 525 or 526.

The third group comes from a much later period in Byzantium. The Berlin edition includes only three out of more than a dozen commentators described in Hunger's *Byzantinisches Handbuch*.[10] The two most important are Eustratius (1050/1060 – c. 1120), and Michael of Ephesus. It has been suggested that these two belong to a circle organised by the princess Anna Comnena in the twelfth century, and accordingly the completion of Michael's commentaries has been redated from 1040 to 1138.[11] His commentaries include areas where gaps had been left. Not all of these gap-fillers are extant, but we have commentaries on the neglected biological works, on the *Sophistici Elenchi*, and a small fragment of one on the *Politics*. The lost *Rhetoric* commentary had a few antecedents, but the *Rhetoric* too had been comparatively neglected. Another product of this period may have been the composite commentary on the *Nicomachean Ethics* (*CAG* 20) by various hands, including Eustratius and Michael, along with some earlier commentators, and an improvisation for Book 7. Whereas Michael follows Alexander and the conventional Aristotelian tradition, Eustratius' commentary introduces Platonist, Christian and anti-Islamic elements.[12]

The composite commentary was to be translated into Latin in the next century by Robert Grosseteste in England. But Latin translations of various logical commentaries were made from the Greek still earlier by James of Venice (*fl. c.* 1130), a contemporary of

[10] Herbert Hunger, *Die hochsprachliche profane Literatur der Byzantiner*, vol. 1 (= *Byzantinisches Handbuch*, part 5, vol. 1) (Munich 1978), 25–41. See also B. N. Tatakis, *La Philosophie Byzantine* (Paris 1949).

[11] R. Browning, 'An unpublished funeral oration on Anna Comnena', *Proceedings of the Cambridge Philological Society* ns. 8 (1962), 1–12, esp. 6–7.

[12] R. Browning, op. cit. H. D. P. Mercken, *The Greek Commentaries of the Nicomachean Ethics of Aristotle in the Latin Translation of Grosseteste*, Corpus Latinum Commentariorum in Aristotelem Graecorum VII (Leiden 1973), ch. 1, 'The compilation of Greek commentaries on Aristotle's Nicomachean Ethics'. Sten Ebbesen, 'Anonymi Aurelianensis I Commentarium in *Sophisticos Elenchos*', *Cahiers de l'Institut Moyen Age Grecque et Latin* 34 (1979), 'Boethius, Jacobus Veneticus, Michael Ephesius and "Alexander" ', pp. v-xiii; id., *Commentators and Commentaries on Aristotle's Sophistici Elenchi*, 3 parts, *Corpus Latinum Commentariorum in Aristotelem Graecorum*, vol. 7 (Leiden 1981); A. Preus, *Aristotle and Michael of Ephesus on the Movement and Progression of Animals* (Hildesheim 1981), introduction.

Appendix

Michael of Ephesus, who may have known him in Constantinople. And later in that century other commentaries and works by commentators were being translated from Arabic versions by Gerard of Cremona (died 1187).[13] So the twelfth century resumed the transmission which had been interrupted at Boethius' death in the sixth century.

The Neoplatonist commentaries of the main group were initiated by Porphyry. His master Plotinus had discussed Aristotle, but in a very independent way, devoting three whole treatises (*Enneads* 6.1–3) to attacking Aristotle's classification of the things in the universe into categories. These categories took no account of Plato's world of Ideas, were inferior to Plato's classifications in the *Sophist* and could anyhow be collapsed, some of them into others. Porphyry replied that Aristotle's categories could apply perfectly well to the world of intelligibles and he took them as in general defensible.[14] He wrote two commentaries on the *Categories*, one lost, and an introduction to it, the *Isagôgê*, as well as commentaries, now lost, on a number of other Aristotelian works. This proved decisive in making Aristotle a necessary subject for Neoplatonist lectures and commentary. Proclus, who was an exceptionally quick student, is said to have taken two years over his Aristotle studies, which were called the Lesser Mysteries, and which preceded the Greater Mysteries of Plato.[15] By the time of Ammonius, the commentaries reflect a teaching curriculum which begins with Porphyry's *Isagôgê* and Aristotle's *Categories*, and is explicitly said to have as its final goal a (mystical) ascent to the supreme Neoplatonist deity, the One.[16] The curriculum would have progressed from Aristotle to Plato, and would have culminated in Plato's *Timaeus* and *Parmenides*. The latter was read as being about the One, and both works

[13] For Grosseteste, see Mercken as in n. 12. For James of Venice, see Ebbesen as in n. 12, and L. Minio-Paluello, 'Jacobus Veneticus Grecus', *Traditio* 8 (1952), 265–304; id., 'Giacomo Veneto e l'Aristotelismo Latino', in Pertusi (ed.), *Venezia e l'Oriente fra tardo Medioevo e Rinascimento* (Florence 1966), 53–74, both reprinted in his *Opuscula* (1972). For Gerard of Cremona, see M. Steinschneider, *Die europäischen Übersetzungen aus dem arabischen bis Mitte des 17. Jahrhunderts* (repr. Graz 1956); E. Gilson, *History of Christian Philosophy in the Middle Ages* (London 1955), 235–6 and more generally 181–246. For the translators in general, see Bernard G. Dod, 'Aristoteles Latinus', in N. Kretzmann, A. Kenny, J. Pinborg (eds), *The Cambridge History of Latin Medieval Philosophy* (Cambridge 1982).

[14] See P. Hadot, 'L'harmonie des philosophies de Plotin et d'Aristote selon Porphyre dans le commentaire de Dexippe sur les Catégories', in *Plotino e il neoplatonismo in Oriente e in Occidente* (Rome 1974), 31–47; A. C. Lloyd, 'Neoplatonic logic and Aristotelian logic', *Phronesis* 1 (1955–6), 58–79 and 146–60.

[15] Marinus, *Life of Proclus* ch. 13, 157, 41 (Boissonade).

[16] The introductions to the *Isagôgê* by Ammonius, Elias and David, and to the *Categories* by Ammonius, Simplicius, Philoponus, Olympiodorus and Elias are discussed by L. G. Westerink, *Anonymous Prolegomena* and I. Hadot. 'Les Introductions', see n. 2 above.

were established in this place in the curriculum at least by the time of Iamblichus, if not earlier.[17]

Before Porphyry, it had been undecided how far a Platonist should accept Aristotle's scheme of categories. But now the proposition began to gain force that there was a harmony between Plato and Aristotle on most things.[18] Not for the only time in the history of philosophy, a perfectly crazy proposition proved philosophically fruitful. The views of Plato and of Aristotle had both to be transmuted into a new Neoplatonist philosophy in order to exhibit the supposed harmony. Iamblichus denied that Aristotle contradicted Plato on the theory of Ideas.[19] This was too much for Syrianus and his pupil Proclus. While accepting harmony in many areas,[20] they could see that there was disagreement on this issue and also on the issue of whether God was causally responsible for the existence of the ordered physical cosmos, which Aristotle denied. But even on these issues, Proclus' pupil Ammonius was to claim harmony, and, though the debate was not clear cut,[21] his claim was on the whole to prevail. Aristotle, he maintained, accepted Plato's Ideas,[22] at least in the form of principles (*logoi*) in the divine intellect, and these principles were in turn causally responsible for the beginningless existence of the physical unvierse. Ammonius wrote a whole book to show that Aristotle's God was thus an efficient cause, and though the book is lost, some of its principal arguments are preserved by Simplicius.[23] This tradition helped to make it possible for Aquinas to claim Aristotle's God as a Creator, albeit not in the

[17] Proclus *in Alcibiadem 1*, p. 11 (Creuzer); Westerink, *Anonymous Prolegomena*, ch. 26, 12f. For the Neoplatonist curriculum see Westerink, Festugière, P. Hadot and I. Hadot in n. 2.

[18] See e.g. P. Hadot (1974), as in n. 14 above; H. J. Blumenthal, 'Neoplatonic elements in the de Anima commentaries', *Phronesis* 21 (1976), 64–87; H. A. Davidson, 'The principle that a finite body can contain only finite power', in S. Stein and R. Loewe (eds), *Studies in Jewish Religious and Intellectual History presented to A. Altmann* (Alabama 1979), 75–92; Carlos Steel, 'Proclus et Aristote', Proceedings of the Congrès Proclus held in Paris 1985, J. Pépin and H. D. Saffrey (eds), *Proclus, lecteur et interprète des anciens* (Paris 1987), 213–25; Koenraad Verrycken, *God en Wereld in de Wijsbegeerte van Ioannes Philoponus*, Ph.D. Diss. (Louvain 1985).

[19] Iamblichus ap. Elian *in Cat*. 123, 1–3.

[20] Syrianus *in Metaph*. 80.4–7; Proclus *in Tim*, 1.6, 21–7, 16.

[21] Asclepius sometimes accepts Syranius' interpretation (*in Metaph*, 433,9–436,6); which is, however, qualified, since Syrianus thinks Aristotle is really committed willy-nilly to much of Plato's view (*in Metaph*, 117,25–118,11; ap. Asclepium *in Metaph*, 433,16, 450,22); Philoponus repents of his early claim that Plato is not the target of Aristotle's attack, and accepts that Plato is rightly attacked for treating ideas as independent entities outside the divine Intellect (*in DA* 37,18–31; *in Phys*, 225,4–226,11, *contra Procl.*, 26,24–32,13; *in An. Post*. 242,14–243,25).

[22] Asclepius *in Metaph* from the voice of (i.e. from the lectures of) Ammonius 69, 17–21; 71,28; cf. Zacharius *Ammonius, Patrologia Graeca* vol. 85, col. 952 (Colonna).

[23] Simplicius *in Phys*, 1361,11–1363,12. See H. A. Davidson; Carlos Steel; Koenraad Verrycken in n. 18 above.

sense of giving the universe a beginning, but in the sense of being causally responsible for its beginningless existence.[24] Thus what started as a desire to harmonise Aristotle with Plato finished by making Aristotle safe for Christianity. In Simplicius, who goes further than anyone,[25] it is a formally stated duty of the commentator to display the harmony of Plato and Aristotle in most things.[26] Philoponus, who with his independent mind had thought better of his earlier belief in harmony, is castigated by Simplicius for neglecting this duty.[27]

The idea of harmony was extended beyond Plato and Aristotle to Plato and the Presocratics. Plato's pupils Speusippus and Xenocrates saw Plato as being in the Pythagorean tradition.[28] From the third to first centuries BC, pseudo-Pythagorean writings present Platonic and Aristotelian doctrines as if they were the ideas of Pythagoras and his pupils,[29] and these forgeries were later taken by the Neoplatonists as genuine. Plotinus saw the Presocratics as precursors of his own views,[30] but Iamblichus went far beyond him by writing ten volumes on Pythagorean philosophy.[31] Thereafter Proclus sought to unify the whole of Greek philosophy by presenting it as a continuous clarification of divine revelation,[32] and Simplicius argued for the same general unity in order to rebut Christian charges of contradictions in pagan philosophy.[33]

Later Neoplatonist commentaries tend to reflect their origin in a teaching curriculum:[34] from the time of Philoponus, the discussion is often divided up into lectures, which are subdivided into studies of doctrine and of text. A general account of Aristotle's philosophy is prefixed to the *Categories* commentaries and divided, according to a formula of Proclus,[35] into ten questions. It is here that commentators explain the eventual purpose of studying Aristotle

[24] See Richard Sorabji, *Matter, Space and Motion* (London and Ithaca N.Y. 1988), ch. 15.

[25] See e.g. H. J. Blumenthal in n. 18 above.

[26] Simplicius *in Cat.* 7, 23–32.

[27] Simplicius *in Cael.* 84,11–14; 159,2–9. On Philoponus' *volte face* see n. 21 above.

[28] See e.g. Walter Burkert, *Weisheit und Wissenschaft* (Nürnberg 1962), translated as *Lore and Science in Ancient Pythagoreanism* (Cambridge Mass. 1972), 83–96.

[29] See Holger Thesleff, *An Introduction to the Pythagorean writings of the Hellenistic Period* (Åbo 1961); Thomas Alexander Szlezák, *Pseudo-Archytas über die Kategorien*, Peripatoi vol. 4 (Berlin and New York 1972).

[30] Plotinus e.g. 4.8.1; 5.1.8 (10–27); 5.1.9.

[31] See Dominic O'Meara, *Pythagoras Revived: Mathematics and Philosophy in late Antiquity*, forthcoming.

[32] See Christian Guérard, 'Parménide d'Elée selon les Neoplatoniciens', forthcoming.

[33] Simplicius *in Phys.* 28,32–29,5; 640,12–18. Such thinkers as Epicurus and the Sceptics, however, were not subject to harmonisation.

[34] See the literature in n. 2 above.

[35] ap. Elian *in Cat.* 107,24–6.

(ascent to the One) and state (if they do) the requirement of displaying the harmony of Plato and Aristotle. After the ten-point introduction to Aristotle, the *Categories* is given a six-point introduction, whose antecedents go back earlier than Neoplatonism, and which requires the commentator to find a unitary theme or scope (*skopos*) for the treatise. The arrangements for late commentaries on Plato are similar. Since the Plato commentaries form part of a single curriculum they should be studied alongside those on Aristotle. Here the situation is easier, not only because the extant corpus is very much smaller, but also because it has been comparatively well served by French and English translators.[36]

Given the theological motive of the curriculum and the pressure to harmonise Plato with Aristotle, it can be seen how these commentaries are a major source for Neoplatonist ideas. This in turn means that it is not safe to extract from them the fragments of the Presocratics, or of other authors, without making allowance for the Neoplatonist background against which the fragments were originally selected for discussion. For different reasons, analogous warnings apply to fragments preserved by the pre-Neoplatonist commentator Alexander.[37] It will be another advantage of the present translations that they will make it easier to check the distorting effect of a commentator's background.

Although the Neoplatonist commentators conflate the views of Aristotle with those of Neoplatonism, Philoponus alludes to a certain convention when he quotes Plutarchus expressing disapproval of Alexander for expounding his own philosophical doctrines in a commentary on Aristotle.[38] But this does not stop Philoponus from later inserting into his own commentaries on the *Physics* and *Meteorology* his arguments in favour of the Christian view of Creation. Of course, the commentators also wrote independent works of their own, in which their views are expressed independently of the exegesis of Aristotle. Some of these independent works will be included in the present series of translations.

The distorting Neoplatonist context does not prevent the commentaries from being incomparable guides to Aristotle. The intro-

---

[36] English: Calcidius *in Tim.* (parts by van Winder; den Boeft); Iamblichus fragments (Dillon); Proclus *in Tim.* (Thomas Taylor). Proclus *in Parm.* (Dillon); Proclus *in Parm.*, end of 7th book, from the Latin (Kilbansky, Labowsky, Anscombe); Proclus *in Alcib. 1* (O'Neill); Olympiodorus and Damascius *in Phaedonem* (Westerink); Damascius *in Philebum* (Westerink); *Anonymous Prolegomena to Platonic Philosophy* (Westerink). See also extracts in Thomas Taylor, *The Works of Plato*, 5 vols. (1804). French: Proclus *in Tim.* and *in Rempublican* (Festugière); *in Parm.* (Chaignet); Anon. *in Parm.* (P. Hadot). Damascius *in Parm.* (Chaignet).

[37] For Alexander's treatment of the Stoics, see Robert B. Todd, *Alexander of Aphrodisias on Stoic Physics* (Leiden 1976), 24–9.

[38] Philoponus *in DA* 21,20–3.

ductions to Aristotle's philosophy insist that commentators must have a minutely detailed knowledge of the entire Aristotelian corpus, and this they certainly have. Commentators are also enjoined neither to accept nor reject what Aristotle says too readily, but to consider it in depth and without partiality. The commentaries draw one's attention to hundreds of phrases, sentences and ideas in Aristotle, which one could easily have passed over, however often one read him. The scholar who makes the right allowance for the distorting context will learn far more about Aristotle than he would be likely to on his own.

The relations of Neoplatonist commentators to the Christians were subtle. Porphyry wrote a treatise explicitly against the Christians in 15 books, but an order to burn it was issued in 448, and later Neoplatonists were more circumspect. Among the last commentators in the main group, we have noted several Christians. Of these the most important were Boethius and Philoponus. It was Boethius' programme to transmit Greek learning to Latin-speakers. By the time of his premature death by execution, he had provided Latin translations of Aristotle's logical works, together with commentaries in Latin but in the Neoplatonist style on Porphyry's *Isagôgê* and on Aristotle's *Categories* and *de Interpretatione*, and interpretations of the *Prior* and *Posterior Analytics, Topics* and *Sophistici Elenchi*. The interruption of his work meant that knowledge of Aristotle among Latin-speakers was confined for many centuries to the logical works. Philoponus is important both for his proofs of the Creation and for his progressive replacement of Aristotelian science with rival theories, which were taken up at first by the Arabs and came fully into their own in the West only in the sixteenth century.

Recent work has rejected the idea that in Alexandria the Neoplatonists compromised with Christian monotheism by collapsing the distinction between their two highest deities, the One and the Intellect. Simplicius (who left Alexandria for Athens) and the Alexandrians Ammonius and Asclepius appear to have acknowledged their beliefs quite openly, as later did the Alexandrian Olympiodorus, despite the presence of Christian students in their classes.[39]

The teaching of Simplicius in Athens and that of the whole pagan Neoplatonist school there was stopped by the Christian Emperor Justinian in 529. This was the very year in which the Christian Philoponus in Alexandria issued his proofs of Creation against the

---

[39] For Simplicius, see I. Hadot, *Le Problème du Néoplatonisme Alexandrin: Hiéroclès et Simplicius* (Paris 1978); for Ammonius and Asclepius, Koenraad Verrycken, *God en Wereld in de Wijsbegeerte van Ioannes Philoponus*, Ph.D. Diss. (Louvain 1985); for Olympiodorus, L. G. Westerink, *Anonymous Prolegomena to Platonic Philosophy* (Amsterdam 1962).

earlier Athenian Neoplatonist Proclus. Archaeological evidence has been offered that, after their temporary stay in Ctesiphon (in present-day Iraq), the Athenian Neoplatonists did not return to their house in Athens, and further evidence has been offered that Simplicius went to Ḥarrān (Carrhae), in present-day Turkey near the Iraq border.[40] Wherever he went, his commentaries are a treasure house of information about the preceding thousand years of Greek philosophy, information which he painstakingly recorded after the closure in Athens, and which would otherwise have been lost. He had every reason to feel bitter about Christianity, and in fact he sees it and Philoponus, its representative, as irreverent. They deny the divinity of the heavens and prefer the physical relics of dead martyrs.[41] His own commentaries by contrast culminate in devout prayers.

Two collections of articles by various hands are now available, making the work of the commentators better known.[42] The first is devoted to Philoponus; the second is about the commentators in general, and goes into greater detail on some of the issues briefly mentioned here.[43]

[40] Alison Frantz, 'Pagan philosophers in Christian Athens', *Proceedings of the American Philosophical Society* 119 (1975), 29–38; M. Tardieu, 'Témoins orientaux du *Premier Alcibiade* à Ḥarrān et à Nag 'Hammādi', *Journal Asiatique* 274 (1986); id., 'Les calendriers en usage à Harrān d'après les sources arabes et le commentaire de Simplicius à la *Physique* d'Aristote', in I. Hadot (ed.), *Simplicius, sa vie, son oeuvre, sa survie* (Berlin 1987), 40–57; *Coutumes nautiques mésopotamiennes chez Simplicius*, in preparation. The opposing view that Simplicius returned to Athens is most fully argued by Alan Cameron, 'The last days of the Academy at Athens', *Proceedings of the Cambridge Philological Society* 195, n.s. 15 (1969), 7–29.

[41] Simplicius *in Cael*, 26,4–7; 70,16–18; 90,1–18; 370,29–371,4. See on his whole attitude Philippe Hoffmann, 'Simplicius' polemics', in Richard Sorabji (ed.), *Philoponus and the Rejection of Aristotelian Science* (London and Ithaca, N.Y. 1987).

[42] Richard Sorabji (ed.), *Philoponus and the Rejection of Aristotelian Science* (London and Ithaca, N.Y. 1987); *Aristotle Transformed* (London and Ithaca, N.Y. 1989).

[43] The lists of texts and previous translations of the commentaries included in Wildberg, *Philoponus Against Aristotle on the Eternity of the World* (pp. 12ff.) are not included here. The list of translations should be augmented by: F. L. S. Bridgman, Heliodorus (?) in *Ethica Nicomachea*, London 1807.

I am grateful for comments to Henry Blumenthal, Victor Caston, I. Hadot, Paul Mercken, Alain Segonds, Robert Sharples, Robert Todd, L. G. Westerink and Christian Wildberg.

Select Bibliography

This Bibliography is restricted, with a few exceptions, to works cited in the footnotes, since the exhaustive bibliography in R.W. Sharples' encyclopaedic article, 'Alexander of Aphrodisias: scholasticism and innovation' (see Secondary sources: individual authors) makes a more complete listing unnecessary. This article is also the best account of Alexander presently available in any language. Paul Moraux, the doyen of Alexander studies in the present century, intended to devote the third and final volume of his monumental work, *Der Aristotelismus bei den Griechen*, entirely to a study of Alexander, but was prevented from completing it by his untimely death. The work is now being completed by various hands. There is a general account of Alexander in the introduction of a recent work: Robert B. Todd, *Alexander of Aphrodisias on Stoic Physics* (see Primary sources), 1–20; and a general survey in Italian in Pierluigi Donini, *Le scuole, l'anima, l'impero* (see Secondary sources: individual authors), 220–48. Philip Merlan included a section on Alexander in his contribution to *The Cambridge History of Later Greek and Early Medieval Philosophy*, edited by A.H. Armstrong, Cambridge 1967, 117–23; this lays emphasis on the place of Alexander in the development of Greek metaphysical thinking. See also G. Movia, *Alessandro di Afrodisia tra naturalismo e misticismo*, Padua, 1970. Discussion of the commentary on the *Metaphysics* as a whole has centred on the question of the authorship of the later books in their present form and their relation to Alexander's original commentary, a topic which does not directly concern us here.

1. Primary sources

Alexandri Aphrodisiensis in Aristotelis Metaphysica Commentaria (*CAG* 1), ed. Michael Hayduck, Berlin 1891.

Alexandri in Aristotelis Analyticorum Priorum Librum I Commentarium (*CAG* 2,1), ed. Maximilian Wallies, Berlin 1883.

Alexandri Aphrodisiensis in Aristotelis Topicorum Libros Octo Commentaria (*CAG* 2,2), ed. Maximilian Wallies, Berlin 1891.

Alexandri in Librum De sensu Commentarium (*CAG* 3,1), ed. Paul Wendland, Berlin 1901.

Alexandri in Aristotelis Meteorologicorum Libros Commentaria (*CAG* 3,2), ed. Michael Hayduck, Berlin 1899.

Alexandri Aphrodisiensis praeter Commentaria Scripta Minora (*Supplementum Aristotelicum* 2,1): *De Anima Liber cum Mantissa*, ed. Ivo Bruns, Berlin 1887.

Alexandri Aphrodisiensis praeter Commentaria Scripta Minora (*Supplementum Aristotelicum* 2,2): *Quaestiones; De Fato; De Mixtione*, ed. Ivo Bruns, Berlin 1882.

'Il *De Ideis* di Aristotele (= Alexander *in Metaphysica* 79,3–88,2): edizione critica del testo a cura di Dieter Harlfinger', Walter Leszl, *Il 'De Ideis' di Aristotele e la teoria platonica delle Idee*, Florence 1975, 22–39.

Alexander of Aphrodisias on Stoic Physics. A study of the *de Mixtione* with preliminary essays, text, translation and commentary by Robert B. Todd (Philosophia Antiqua 28), Leiden 1976.

Le commentaire d'Alexandre d'Aphrodise aux 'Seconds Analytiques' d'Aristote, by Paul Moraux (Peripatoi 13), Berlin 1979.

Alexander of Aphrodisias On Fate. Text, translation and commentary by R.W. Sharples, London 1983.

A.A. Long and D.N. Sedley, *The Hellenistic Philosophers,* vol. 1: *Translations of the principal sources with philosophical commentary,* Cambridge 1987 (contains translation of passages from various works of Alexander; see p. 492 for a list).

The Complete Works of Aristotle. The Revised Oxford Translation, ed. Jonathan Barnes, 2 vols, Princeton 1984.

Aristotelis Metaphysica, recognovit W. Jaeger, Oxford 1957; reprinted 1969.

Aristotle's Metaphysics. A revised text with introduction and commentary by W.D. Ross, 2 vols, Oxford 1924; reprinted 1948.

The Works of Aristotle Translated into English, vol. 8: *Metaphysica,* translated by W.D. Ross, 2nd ed. Oxford 1928; reprinted 1948.

Aristotelis Fragmenta Selecta, recognovit W.D. Ross, Oxford 1955; reprinted 1970.

The Works of Aristotle Translated into English, vol. 12: *Select Fragments,* translated by David Ross, Oxford 1952.

Aristotle's *De Motu Animalium.* Text with translation, commentary, and interpretive essays by Martha Craven Nussbaum, Princeton 1978.

J.L. Ackrill, *Aristotle's Categories and De interpretatione,* Oxford 1963.

Julia Annas, *Aristotle's Metaphysics, Books M and N,* Oxford 1976.

Christopher Kirwan, *Aristotle's Metaphysics, Books Gamma, Delta, Epsilon,* Oxford 1971.

C.J.F. Williams, *Aristotle's De Generatione et Corruptione,* Oxford 1982.

Hermann Diels, *Doxographi Graeci,* 4th ed. Berlin 1965; reprinted 1976.

2.1. Secondary sources: collected works

Aristote et les problèmes de méthode (Symposium Aristotelicum, 1960), Louvain 1961.

Aristoteles Werk und Wirkung (Paul Moraux gewidmet), vol. 1: *Aristoteles und seine Schule,* ed. Jürgen Wiesner, Berlin 1985.

Aristotelica. Mélanges offerts à Marcel de Corte, Bruxelles 1985.

Aristotle on Mind and the Senses (7th Symposium Aristotelicum), ed. G.E.R. Lloyd & G.E.L. Owen, Cambridge 1978.

Aristotle Transformed, ed. Richard Sorabji, London and Ithaca N.Y. 1989.

Aufstieg und Niedergang der römischen Welt, Part 2: *Principat,* vol. 36,2: *Philosophie und Wissenschaften,* ed. Wolfgang Haase, Berlin 1987.

Autour d'Aristote. Recueil d'études de philosophie ancienne et médiévale offert à Monseigneur A. Mansion, Louvain 1955.

Beiträge zur alten Geschichte und deren Nachleben. Festschrift für Franz Altheim, ed. Ruth Stiehl & Hans Erich Stier, 2 vols, Berlin 1969.

The Harry Austryn Wolfson Jubilee Volume, ed. Saul Lieberman, 3 vols, Jerusalem 1965.

Language and Logos. Studies in ancient philosophy presented to G.E.L. Owen, ed. Malcolm Schofield & Martha Craven Nussbaum, London and N.Y. 1982.

Mathematics and Metaphysics in Aristotle (Symposium Aristotelicum 10, 1984), ed. Andreas Graeser, Bern 1987.

Mélanges d'études anciennes offerts à M. Lebel, ed. J.-B. Caron, Québec 1979.

Oxford Studies in Ancient Philosophy, vol. 2, ed. Julia Annas, 1984.

Oxford Studies in Ancient Philosophy, vol. 4: *Festschrift for J.L. Ackrill*, ed. Michael Wood, 1986.

Philoponus and the Rejection of Aristotelian Science, ed. Richard Sorabji, London and Ithaca N.Y. 1987.

Problems in Stoicism, ed. A.A. Long, London 1971.

Proceedings of the World Congress on Aristotle II, Athens 1981.

Simplicius: sa vie, son oeuvre, sa survie. Actes du Colloque International de Paris (Peripatoi 15), ed. Ilsetraut Hadot, Berlin 1987.

Les Stoïciens et leur logique. Actes du Colloque de Chantilly, 1976, Paris 1976.

Studies in Aristotle (Studies in Philosophy and the History of Philosophy, 9), ed. Dominic O'Meara, Washington D.C. 1981.

Studies in Plato's Metaphysics, ed. R.E. Allen, N.Y. 1965.

Theophrastus of Eresus: on his life and work, ed. William W. Fortenbaugh, with Pamela M. Huby & Anthony A. Long, New Brunswick N.J. 1985.

Untersuchungen zur Eudemischen Ethik (Peripatoi 1), ed. Paul Moraux & Dieter Harlfinger, Berlin 1971.

2.2. Secondary sources: individual authors

Annas, Julia, 'Forms and first principles', *Phronesis* 19, 1974, 257–83.

Arpe, Curt, 'Das Argument *Tritos anthrôpos*', *Hermes* 76, 1941, 171–207.

Aubenque, Pierre, *Le problème de l'être chez Aristote*, 2nd ed., Paris 1966.

Balleriaux, Omer, 'En relisant le début de la *Métaphysique*', *Aristotelica*, Bruxelles 1985, 41–64.

Barford, Robert, 'A proof from the *Peri Ideôn* revisited', *Phronesis* 21, 1976, 198–218.

Barker, Andrew, *Greek Musical Writings* I, Cambridge 1984.

Bertier, Janine, 'Une hénadologie liée au Stoïcisme tardif', *Les Stoïciens et leur logique*, 41–57.

———, 'Les preuves de la réalité des nombres et la théorie des idées d'après Métaphysique N2, 1090a2–3, 1090b5', *Mathematics and Metaphysics in Aristotle*, 281–309.

Brunschwig, Jacques, '*EE* I 8, 1218a15–32 et le *Peri Tagathou*', *Untersuchungen zur Eudemischen Ethik*, 197–222.

Burkert, Walter, *Lore and Science in Ancient Pythagoreanism*, English translation by E. Minar, Harvard 1972.

Calvetti, Gianmaria, 'Eudoro di Alessandria: medioplatonismo et neopitagorismo nel I secolo A.C.', *Rivista di Filosofia Neoscolastica* 69, 1977, 3–19.

Chailley, Jacques, *La musique grecque antique*, Paris 1979.

Cherniss, Harold, *Aristotle's Criticism of Plato and the Academy* I, Baltimore 1944.

De Vogel, C.J., 'La méthode d'Aristote en métaphysique d' après *Métaphysique* A 1–2', *Aristote et les Problèmes de Méthode*, 147–70.

Dillon, John, *The Middle Platonists*, London and Ithaca N.Y. 1977.

Doering, K., 'Über den Sophisten Polyxenos', *Hermes* 100, 1972, 29–42.

Donini, Pierluigi, *Le scuole, l'anima, l'impero: la filosofia antica da Antioco a Plotino*, Turin 1982.

Dörrie, Heinrich, 'Der Platoniker Eudoros von Alexandreia', *Hermes* 79, 1944, 25–38; reprinted in his *Platonica Minora*, München 1976, 297–309.

Düring, Ingemar, *Aristoteles. Darstellung und Interpretation seines Denkens*, Heidelberg 1966.

Fine, Gail, 'Aristotle and the more accurate arguments', *Language and Logos*, 155–77.

————, 'Immanence', *Oxford Studies in Ancient Philosophy* IV, 87–96.

————, 'The One over Many', *Philosophical Review* 89, 1980, 197–240.

Fortenbaugh, William, 'Theophrastus on Emotion', *Theophrastus of Eresus*, 209–29.

Frank, D.H., *The Arguments from the Sciences in Aristotle's 'Peri Ideôn'*, Bern and Frankfurt a.M. 1984.

————, 'A Disproof in the *Peri Ideôn*', *Southern Journal of Philosophy* 22, 1984, 49–59.

Frohn-Villeneuve, Winnie, *Alexander of Aphrodisias as a Source for the Presocratics*, Ph.D. dissertation (unpublished), University of Laval, Québec.

————, 'Space, time, and change: Alexander's interpretation of Melissus', *Mélanges d'études anciennes offerts à M. Lebel*, 173–86.

Furley, David J., *The Greek Cosmologists* I, Cambridge 1987.

————, *Two Studies in the Greek Atomists*, Princeton 1967.

Gaiser, Konrad, *Platons ungeschriebene Lehre*, 2nd ed., Stuttgart 1968.

Genequand, Charles, 'L'objet de la métaphysique selon Alexandre d'Aphrodisie', *Museum Helveticum* 36, 1979, 48–57.

————, 'Quelques aspects de l'idée de la nature d'Aristote à al-Ghazali', *Revue de Théologie et de Philosophie* 116, 1984, 105–29.

Gottschalk, H.B., 'Aristotelian philosophy in the Roman world', *Aufstieg und Niedergang der römischen Welt* 36,2, 1079–174.

Graeser, Andreas, 'Der "Dritte Mensch" des Polyxenos', *Museum Helveticum* 31, 1974, 140–3.

Guthrie, W.K.C., *A History of Greek Philosophy*, vol. 2: *The Presocratic Tradition from Parmenides to Democritus*, Cambridge 1965.

Hadot, Ilsetraut, 'Recherches sur les fragments du commentaire de Simplicius sur la *Métaphysique* d'Aristote', *Simplicius, sa vie, son oeuvre, sa survie*, 225–45.

Happ, Heinz, *Hyle*, Berlin 1971.

Isnardi Parente, M., 'Per l'interpretazione della dottrina delle idee nella prima Accademia platonica', *Annali dell'Istituto Italiano per gli studi storici* 1, 1967/68, 9–33.

————, 'Ta Meta tas Ideas: Figures idéales ou premières figures?' *Mathematics and Metaphysics in Aristotle*, 260–80.

Jaeger, Werner, 'We say in the Phaedo', *Harry Austryn Wolfson Jubilee Volume*, English Section, vol. 1, Jerusalem 1965, 407–21.

Kosman, L.A., 'Substance, being, and *energeia*', *Oxford Studies in Ancient Philosophy* II, 121–49.

Krämer, Hans, *Arete bei Platon und Aristoteles*, Heidelberg 1959.

Leszl, Walter, *Il 'De Ideis' di Aristotele e la teoria platonica delle Idee*, Florence 1975.

Mansion, Suzanne, 'La critique de la théorie des Idées dans le *Peri Ideôn* d'Aristote', *Revue Philosophique de Louvain* 47, 1949, 169–202; reprinted in her *Études Aristoteliciennes*, Louvain 1984.

Merlan, Philip, 'Metaphysik: Name und Gegestand', *Journal of Hellenic Studies* 77, 1957, 87–92; reprinted in his *Kleine Schriften*, Hildesheim 1976, 189–94.

_____, *Monopsychism, Mysticism, Metaconsciousness*, The Hague 1963.

_____, 'Nochmals: War Aristoteles je Anhänger der Ideenlehre? Jaegers letztes Wort', *Archiv für Geschichte der Philosophie* 52, 1970, 35–9.

Moraux, Paul, *Alexandre d'Aphrodise, Exégète de la Noétique d'Aristote*, Liège 1942.

_____, *Der Aristotelismus bei den Griechen*, vol. 2: *Der Aristotelismus im I. und II. Jh. n. Chr.* (Peripatoi 6), Berlin 1984.

_____, 'Eine Korrektur des Mittelplatonikers Eudoros zum Text der Metaphysik des Aristoteles', *Beiträge zur alten Geschichte und deren Nachleben*, vol. 2, 492–504.

Mueller, Ian, 'Aristotle's doctrine of abstraction in some Aristotelian commentators and Neoplatonists', in R. Sorabji (ed.), *Aristotle Transformed*, London and Ithaca N.Y. 1989.

Mugler, Charles, *Dictionnaire Historique de la Terminologie Géometrique des Grecs*, Paris 1958.

Napolitano, Linda, 'Il platonismo di Eudoro: tradizione protoaccademica e medioplatonismo Alessandrino', *Museum Patavinum* 3, 1985, 27–49.

Narcy, Michel, 'L'homonymie entre Aristote et ses commentateurs néo-platoniciens', *Études Philosophiques*, 1981, 35–52.

Nussbaum, Martha, 'The Stoics on the extirpation of the passions', *Apeiron* 20, 1987, 129–77.

O'Brien, D., *Theories of Weight in the Ancient World*, I: *Democritus, Weight and Size* (Philosophia Antiqua 37), Leiden 1981.

Owen, G.E.L., 'A proof in the *Peri Ideôn*', *Journal of Hellenic Studies* 77, 1957, 103–11; reprinted in *Studies in Plato's Metaphysics*, 293–312, and again in his *Logic, Science, and Dialectic: collected papers in Greek philosophy*, ed. Martha Nussbaum, London and Ithaca N.Y. 1986, 165–79.

Owens, Joseph, *The Doctrine of Being in the Aristotelian Metaphysics*, 3rd ed., Toronto 1978.

Penner, Terry, *The Ascent from Nominalism*, Dordrecht 1987.

Philip, J.A., *Pythagoras and Early Pythagoreanism*, Toronto 1966.

Preus, Anthony, 'Michael of Ephesus on Aristotle *IA* and *MA*', *Proceedings of the World Congress on Aristotle* II, Athens 1981, 21–30.

Raven, J.E., *Pythagoreans and Eleatics*, Amsterdam 1966.

Reale, Giovanni, *The Concept of First Philosophy and the Unity of the Metaphysics of Aristotle*, ed. and tr. John R. Catan, Albany N.Y. 1980.

Regenbogen, O., 'Theophrastos', *Pauly-Wissowa Realencyclopädie*, Suppl. 7, 1950, 1354–562.

Richard, Marie-Dominique, *L'Enseignement Oral de Platon*, Paris 1986.

Robin, Léon, *La Theorie Platonicienne des Idées et des Nombres d'après Aristote*, Paris 1908; reprinted Hildesheim 1963.

Rowe, C.J., 'The proof from relatives in the *Peri Ideôn*: further reconsideration', *Phronesis* 24, 1979, 270–81.

Sandbach, F.H., '*Ennoia* and *prolêpsis* in the Stoic theory of knowledge', in A.A. Long (ed.), *Problems in Stoicism*, London 1971, 22–37.

Schavernoch, Hans, *Die Harmonie der Sphären*, Freiburg i. Sw. 1981.

Schmitz, Hermann, *Die Ideenlehre des Aristoteles*, 2 vols, Bonn 1985.

Sharples, R.W., 'Alexander of Aphrodisias: scholasticism and innovation', *Aufstieg und Niedergang der römischen Welt* 36,2, 1177–243.

Spoerri, Walter, 'Inkommensurabilität, Automaten und philosophisches Staunen im Alpha der *Metaphysik*', *Aristoteles Werk und Wirkung*, vol. 1, 239–72.

Steinmetz, Peter, 'Theophrasts Physik und ihr Verhältnis zu den *Phusikôn doxai*', *Die Physik des Theophrastos von Eresos*, Bad Homburg 1964, 334–51.

Stenzl, Julius, *Zahl und Gestalt bei Platon und Aristoteles*, 3rd ed., Bad Homburg 1959.

Todd, Robert B., 'Lexicographical notes on Alexander of Aphrodisias' philosophical terminology', *Glotta* 52, 1974, 207–15.

————, 'The Stoic common notions: a re-examination and reinterpretation', *Symbolae Osloenses* 48, 1973, 47–75.

Tweedale, Martin M., 'Alexander of Aphrodisias' views on universals', *Phronesis* 29, 1984, 279–303.

Verbeke, Gérard, 'Aristotle's Metaphysics viewed by the ancient commentators', in D.J. O'Meara (ed.), *Studies in Aristotle*, Washington D.C. 1981, 107–27.

von Fritz, Kurt, 'Die Ideenlehre des Eudoxos von Knidos und ihr Verhältnis zur platonischen Ideenlehre', *Philologus* 62, 1926/27, 1–26; repr. in his *Schriften zur griechischen Logik*, vol. 1, Stuttgart 1978, 147–70.

Wilpert, Paul, 'Neue Fragmente aus *Peri Tagathou*', *Hermes* 76, 1951, 225–50.

————, 'Reste verlorener Aristotelesschriften bei Alexander von Aphrodisias', *Hermes* 75, 1940, 369–94.

————, *Zwei aristotelische Frühschriften über die Ideenlehre*, Regensburg 1949.

Winnington-Ingram, Reginald, *Mode in Ancient Greek Music*, Cambridge 1936; reprinted Amsterdam 1968.

Zimmermann, Fritz, 'Philoponus' impetus theory in the Arabic tradition', in R. Sorabji (ed.), *Philoponus and the Rejection of Aristotelian Science*, London and Ithaca N.Y. 1987, 121–9.

Indexes

English–Greek Glossary

The Glossary lists key terms in the English Translation, and supplies the Greek words which they represent. It is also an aid to locating terms in the Greek–English Index. (n) = noun; (v) = verb; (a) = adjective.

abstraction: *aphairesis*
absurd: *atopos*
  absurdity: *atopia*
accident: *to huparkhon, pathos, to sumbebêkos*
account (n): *historia, logos*
act (v): *prassein*
  acted on, be: *paskhein*
  action: *praxis*
active: *poiêtikos*
activity: *energeia*
actuality: *energeia*
  in actuality: *energeiai*
ad infinitum: *eis apeiron*
addition (math.): *epithesis, prosthesis*
adequate: *hikanos*
affected, be: *paskhein*
  affection: *pathos*
affirm: *kataphaskein*
  affirmation: *kataphasis*
  affirmative: *kataphatikos*
aggregate (v): *sunkrinein*
  aggregation: *sunkrisis*
air: *aêr*
alteration: *alloiôsis*
analogous: *analogos*
animal, animate being: *zôion*
answer (n): *apodosis, apokrisis*
appetite, object of: *to orekton*
apprehension: *antilêpsis*
argument: *epikheirêsis, logos, sullogismos*
arithmetic: *hê arithmêtikê*
  arithmetical: *arithmêtikos*
arrangement: *taxis*
art: *tekhnê*
  artefact: *to tekhnêton*
  artisan: *tekhnitês*
assert truly: *alêtheuein*
  assertion: *logos*
assume: *hupotithesthai*
  assumption: *hupolêpsis*
astronomy: *astrologia, hê astrologikê*
atoms: *hai atomoi*
attribute (n): *pathos, to sumbebêkos*

axiom: *axiôma*

be: *einai, tunkhanein*
beauty: *to kalon, kallos*
become: *gignesthai*
  becoming: *genesis, to gignesthai*
beginning: *arkhê*
being (n): *to einai, to on, ousia*
belong (to): *huparkhein* (+ Dat.)
blending: *krasis*
body: *sôma*
bone: *ostoun*
breadth: *platos*
  broad: *platus*
  the broad: *to platu*
bring in: *eisagein*
bring under: *hupagein*
by itself: *idiai*
  nature: *phusei*
  one's own power: *automatôs*

cause (n): *aitia, aition*
  efficient: *poiêtikê*
  final: *hou heneka, telikê*
  formal: *kata to eidos, eidêtikê*
  imparting motion: *kinêtikê*
  material: *kata tên hulên, hulikê*
celestial system: *ouranos*
certitude: *pistis*
chance (n): *tukhê*
change (n): *metabolê*
  change (v): *metaballein*
choice (n): *proairesis*
  choose: *haireisthai*
  chosen, to be chosen: *hairetos*
class (n): *eidos, genos*
clear (a): *dêlos, saphês*
  make clear: *dêloun*
coarse: *pakhus*
cold (a): *psukhros*
  cold (n): *to psukhron, psukhrotês*
colour: *khrôma*
combination: *sunkrisis, sunthesis, to suntheton*
  combine: *sunkrinein, suntithenai*

199

combined: *sunkeimenos*
come to be, into being: *gignesthai*
coming-to-be (n): *genesis*
commensurable: *summetros*
commingling: *mixis*
common, commonplace: *koinos*
common conceptions, notions:
koinai prolêpseis, ennoiai
common thing: *to koinon*
community (abstract): *koinônia*
comparable: *analogos*
complete: *teleios*
composite (a): *sunthetos*
composite (n): *to suntheton*
compound (n): *sunkrima*
comprehension: *perilêpsis*
comprehensively: *perilêptikôs*
conception: *prolêpsis*
conclude (syllogism): *sullogizesthai*
conclusion (syllogism): *sumperasma*
concordance, concordant interval:
harmonia
condensation: *puknôsis*
confidence, have: *pisteuein*
confirm: *bebaioun*
consequences: *ta akoloutha*
contemplate: *theôrein*
continuous: *sunekhês*
contradictory: *antiphatikos*
contraries, the: *ta enantia*
contrary to nature: *para phusin*
convertible, be: *antistrephein*
copy (n): *eikôn*
copy (v): *eikazein*
corporeal: *sômatikos*
correspond: *antistrephein*
counter-earth: *antikhthôn*

daring (n): *tolma*
decision: *krisis*
deep: *bathus*
depth: *bathos*
defect: *elleipsis*
define: *horizesthai*
definition: *horismos, horos*
definitory formula: *logos*
deliberation, act of: *to bouleuesthai*
demonstration: *apodeixis*
demonstrate: *apodeiknunai*
capable of demonstrating:
apodeiktikos
dense, the: *to puknon*
deny: *apophaskein*
depth: *bathos*
desire (n): *ephesis, epithumia, orexis*
desire (v): *ephiesthai*
object of desire: *to orekton*
destroy: *anairein*

be destroyed: *phtheiresthai*
destruction: *phthora*
determinate: *hôrismenos*
diagonal (n): *diametros*
dialectic: *hê dialektikê*
differ: *diapherein*
difference: *diaphora*
different: *allos, heteros*
differentia: *diaphora*
differentiation: *diarthrôsis*
difficult: *khalepos*
difficulty: *aporia*
discovery: *heuresis*
dissimilar: *anomoeidês*
dissolution: *dialusis*
distinguish: *diairein*
distinction: *diairesis*
without distinctions: *adioristôs*
divine: *theios*
the divine: *to theion*
divisible: *diairetos*
division: *diairesis*
do: *prassein*
things to be done: *ta prakta*
do away with: *anairein*
double, the: *to diplasion*
dry: *xêros*
dryness: *to xêron, xerotês*
due season: *kairos*
duplicative: *duopoios*
dyad: *duas*
indefinite dyad: *aoristos duas*

eager, be: *spoudazein*
earth: *gê*
effect: *to aitiaton*
efficient cause: *aitia poiêtikê*
element: *stoikheion*
end (n): *telos*
enmattered: *enulos*
entity: *phusis*
equal: *isos*
be equal (math.): *ison dunasthai*
equality: *to ison, isotês*
essence: *to ti ên einai, ousia*
essential: *ousiôdês*
essentially: *en tôi ti esti*
establish: *kataskeuazein, sunistanai*
estimable: *timios*
eternal: *aidios*
eternity: *to aidion*
even (math.): *artios*
evident: *enargês*
evil (a): *kakos*
evil (n): *to kakon*
evil things: *ta kaka*
exact: *akribês*
exactness: *akribeia*

excess: *huperokhê*
exhalation: *anathumiasis*
exist: *einai, huparkhein*
  exist before: *proüparkhein*
  existence: *huparxis*
experience (n): *empeiria*
  men of experience: *hoi empeiroi*
experimentation: *peira*
explain: *apodidonai, exêgeisthai*
explicate: *ektithesthai*
exposition: *ekthesis*

factor (math.): *metron*
false: *pseudês*
few: *oligos*
  the few: *to oligon*
  fewness: *oligotês*
figure (of syllogism): *skhêma*
fire: *pur*
first: *prôtos*
  the things that are first: *ta prôta*
flux: *rhusis*
force (v): *anankazein*
  forced: *biaios*
foresight: *pronoia*
form: *eidos*
  the Forms (Platonic): *ta eidê*
  confer, give, a form: *eidopoiein*
  formal: *eidêtikos*
  formal cause: *aitia kata to eidos, eidêtikê*
formula: *logos*
free (a): *eleutheros*
friendship: *philia*
full: *plêrês*
  the full: *to plêres*
function (n): *ergon*

generate: *gennan*
  generated: *genêtos*
  generation: *genesis*
generically dissimilar: *anomogenês*
genus: *genos*
geometry: *geômetria*
goal: *skopos*
god: *theos*
good (a): *agathos*
  the Good: *to agathon, to eu*
  the Good itself: *to autoagathon*
  particular goods: *ta agatha*
great, the: *to megas*

half, the: *to hêmisu*
harmony: *harmonia* (Pythagoreans), *sumphônia*
having (n): *hexis*
hearth: *hestia*
heat (n): *to thermon, thermotês*

heat (v): *thermainein*
heaven(s): *ouranos*
  heavenly: *ouranios*
heavy: *barus*
  heaviness: *barutês*
homonymous: *homônumos*
hot: *thermos*
human: *anthrôpinos*

idea: *ennoia, idea* (Platonic)
ideal: *eidêtikos*
identical: *tautos*
  identity: *tautotês*
ignorance: *agnoia*
  be ignorant: *agnoein*
image: *phantasma*
imagination, imagining: *phantasia*
imitate: *mimeisthai*
  imitation: *mimêsis*
immediate (premise): *amesos*
immobile: *akinêtos*
  immobility: *to akinêton, akinêsia*
immutable: *akinêtos*
  immutability: *to akinêton*
impassible: *apathês*
imperfect: *atelês*
impossible: *adunatos*
impression: *tupos*
in a fixed order: *tetagmenôs*
in accordance with nature: *kata phusin*
in actuality: *energeiai*
in an invalid way: *asullogistôs*
in an orderly way: *tetagmenôs*
in itself: *kath' hauto*
in the primary, proper, sense: *kuriôs*
inanimate: *apsukhos*
inclination, internal: *rhopê*
incomplete: *atelês*
incomposite: *asunthetos*
incorporeal: *asômatikos*
incorrupt: *aphthartos*
indefinite: *aoristos*
  indefinite dyad: *aoristos duas*
  the indefinite: *to aoriston*
  indefiniteness: *aoristia*
indemonstrable: *anapodeiktos*
independently: *kath' hauto*
individuals: *ta atoma, ta kath' hekasta*
indivisible: *adiairetos, atomos*
induction: *epagôgê*
inequality: *anisotês*
inference: *metabasis*
infinite: *apeiros*
  infinity: *to apeiron, apeiria*
injustice: *adikia*
innate: *sumphutos*
intellect: *nous*

intelligent: *phronimos*
intelligible: *noêtos*
intention: *boulêma, boulêsis*
intermediate: *metaxu*
intermediates: *ta metaxu*
internal inclination: *rhopê*
interval: *apostasis*
irrational: *alogos*

judgment: *hupolêpsis*
justice: *dikaiosunê*

kind (n): *eidos, genos*
know: *eidenai, gignôskein, gnôrizein,*
epistasthai
knowable: *epistêtos, gnôrimos,*
gnôstos
knowledge: *gnôsis*
scientific knowledge: *epistêmê*

last (a): *eskhatos, hustatos*
learn: *manthanein*
learning: *mathêsis*
lecture: *akroasis*
leisure: *skholê*
have leisure: *skholazein*
length: *mêkos*
letter (of alphabet): *gramma*
light (a): *kouphos*
lightness: *kouphotês*
like (a): *homoios*
be made like: *homoiousthai*
likeness (concrete): *eikôn*
likeness (abstract): *homoiotês*
limit: *peras*
limited: *hôrismenos, peperasmenos*
line: *grammê, mêkos*
long: *makros*
love (n): *erôs*
lover of wisdom: *philosophos*

magnitude: *megethos*
make: *poiein*
making (n): *poiêsis*
man: *anthrôpos*
man-himself: *autoanthrôpos*
the third man: *ho tritos anthrôpos*
many: *polla*
the many (concrete): *ta polla*
the many (abstract): *to polu*
material: *hulikos*
material cause: *aitia kata tên hulên,*
hulikê
mathematical: *mathêmatikos*
mathematical objects: *ta*
mathêmatika
mathematics: *ta mathêmatika*
matter: *hulê*

matrix: *ekmageion*
measure (v): *metrein*
unit of measurement: *metron*
medicine, science of: *hê iatrikê*
memory: *mnêmê*
mind (Anaxagoras): *nous*
mixture: *migma, mixis*
model: *paradeigma*
modification: *pathos*
moist: *hugros*
moisture: *to hugron, hugrotês*
moon: *selênê*
mortal: *thnêtos*
motion: *kinêsis*
motionless: *akinêtos*
imparting motion: *kinêtikos*
mould: *tupos*
move (v.tr.): *kinein*
move (v. intr.): *kineisthai*
movement: *kinêsis*
multiplicity: *plêthos*
musical scale: *harmonia*
myth: *muthos*
mythologists: *theologoi*

narrow: *stenos*
natural: *phusikos*
natural philosophers: *hoi phusikoi*
natural philosophy: *hê phusikê*
philosophia
natural things: *ta phusika*
nature: *phusis*
by nature: *phusei*
contrary to nature: *para phusin*
in accordance with nature: *kata*
phusin
be by nature: *phuein*
necessary: *anankaios*
necessity: *anankê*
of necessity: *ex anankês*
negation: *apophasis*
not-being: *to mê on*
note, musical: *phthongos*
notion: *ennoia*
number: *arithmos*
even, odd: *artios, perittos*
ideal: *eidêtikos*
square: *tetragônos*
numerically one: *hen tôi arithmôi*

object of appetite: *to orekton*
object of thought: *noêma*
objects, mathematical: *ta*
mathêmatika
obvious: *dêlos, enargês*
octave: *harmonia, sumphônia, dia*
pasôn
odd (math.): *perittos*

of the same kind: *homoeidês*
one (a): *heis*
  the One: *to hen*
  the One itself: *to hen auto, autoen*
  one in kind: *monoeidês*
  the one-over-many: *to hen epi pollôn*
  numerically one: *hen tôi arithmôi*
opinion: *doxa*
  forming opinions: *doxastikos*
opportunity: *kairos*
opposed, be: *antikeisthai*
  opposed (a): *antikeimenos*
  opposite: *antikeimenos, enantios*
  opposition: *enantiôsis*
order, ordering: *taxis*
  regular order: *eutaxia*
  in an orderly way: *tetagmenôs*
other: *allos, heteros*
own (a): *oikeios*

part (n): *meros, morion*
  partless: *amerês, ameristos*
  particle: *meros*
participate: *metalambanein,
  metekhein*
  participation: *metaskhesis,
  methexis, metokhê, metousia*
particular: *kath' hekasta*
passion: *pathos*
  subject to passion: *empathês*
  without passions: *apathês*
passive: *pathêtikos*
per accidens: *kata sumbebêkos*
per se: *kath' hauto*
perceive: *aisthanesthai*
  perceptible: *aisthêtos, phainomenos*
  sense perception: *aisthêsis*
perceptive intuition: *nous*
perfect: *teleios*
  perfection: *teleiotês*
perish: *phtheiresthai*
  perishable: *phthartos*
phenomena: *ta phainomena*
philosopher: *philosophos*
  natural philosophers: *hoi phusikoi*
  the ancient philosophers: *hoi
  arkhaioi*
  philosophy: *philosophia*
  natural philosophy: *hê phusikê
  philosophia*
  theoretical philosophy: *hê theôrêtikê
  philosophia*
place (n): *topos*
plan: *logos*
plane: *epipedon*
planets: *hoi planêtes asteres*
pleasure: *hêdonê*
plurality: *plêthos*

point (math.): *sêmeion, stigmê*
posit: *tithesthai*
position (math.): *thesis*
  without position: *athetos*
possession: *hexis*
posterior: *husteros*
potentially: *dunamei*
power: *dunamis*
  by one's own power: *automatôs*
practical: *praktikos*
  practical wisdom: *phronêsis*
predicate (n): *to katêgoroumenon*
  predicate (v): *katêgorein*
  predicate essentially: *katêgorein en
  tôi ti esti*
premise: *protasis*
  first, immediate, indemonstrable
  premises: *hai prôtai, amesoi,
  anapodeiktoi protaseis*
preserve: *sôzein*
primary: *prôtos*
principle: *arkhê*
prior: *prôtos*
privation: *sterêsis*
produce (v): *poiein*
  productive activity: *poiêsis*
proof: *apodeixis, deixis*
  prove: *apodeiknunai, deiknunai,
  sunagein*
proper: *idios, oikeios*
  in the proper sense: *kuriôs*
property: *to idion*
proportion: *analogia*
proximate: *engus, prosekhês*
pure: *katharos*
puzzled, be: *aporein, diaporein*

quality: *to poion, poiotês*
  without qualities: *apathês*
quantity: *to poson*

rare: *manos*
  rarefaction: *manôsis*
ratio: *logos*
rational: *logikos*
  rationally: *kata logon*
reality: *hupostasis, ousia*
reason (n): *logos*
  reason why: *aitia*
  reasonable, reasonably: *eulogos,
  eulogôs*
reasoned account: *logos*
reasoning, reasoning process:
  epikheirêsis, logismos, logos
reduce: *anagein*
reference: *anaphora*
reflect: *ennoein*
regular order: *eutaxia*

Greek–English Index

This is a general lexicon to Book 1 of the commentary. Although excluding particles, a number of adverbs, and a few terms of no philosophical import that occur frequently, it is a quite comprehensive guide to Alexander's vocabulary in this book, an area for which the *Index Verborum* appended to Hayduck's edition of the Greek text is simply inadequate. Cognate terms are grouped together, so that the listing of terms does not always follow strict alphabetical order. Only the first occurrence of less important terms is cited, the citation being followed by *passim*; but all significant occurrences of key philosophical terms are listed. This index is confined to a listing of citations; for the relevant philosophical topics contained in these citations, the Subject Index should be consulted. In cases in which a key term (e.g. *arkhê*, principle) occurs so frequently that its uses must be distinguished, the reader is referred to the Subject Index for the citations, which are there grouped according to the various contexts in which the term is used. A number in parentheses after a term refers to the footnote in which that term is discussed. Page and line references are to the Greek text.

barus, deep (sound): 39,27
  barutês, heaviness: 36,25; 72,36;
    73,6
basanizein, test: 78,3
[bathus] to bathu, the deep:
    118,11.12; 127,14
  bathos, depth: 118,9
bebaios, certain: 26,17
  bebaioun, confirm: 3,1, *passim*
  bebaiôsis, confirmation: 23,3
beltion ekhein, have greater
    certainty: 13,1
biaios, forced: 36,24–5
blepein, look: 43,3.5; 44,2; 103,24
boêthein, aid, assist: 12,19; 70,1;
    96,31
  boêthêma, remedy: 5,8
boulesthai, desire, wish: 14,15,
    passim; aim at, intend: 68,8;
    70,1; 73,7; 88,16; 131,1
  boulêma, boulêsis, intention:
    28,11; 68,9
bouleuesthai, to, (act of)
    deliberation: 3,11; 7,23
  ta bouleuta, objects of deliberation:
    3,11
[brakhus] to brakhu, the short:
    117,28; 118,11.25; 120,8; 127,13
brontê, thunder-clap: 6,7

deiknunai, point out, show: 2,1,
    passim
  deiktikos, showing: 6,15; 21,2;
    77,11; prove: 9,4; 11,18; 12,22;
    13,3; 78,5; 84,21
  deixis, proof: 13,6
dekas, dekad: 39,3; the number 10:
    40,28
dekhesthai, accept: 83,12
  dektikos, capable of receiving:
    58,14
dêlos, clear, evident, obvious: 5,19,
    passim
  dêloun, make clear, point out,
    show: 4,21, *passim*
  dêlôtikos, indicating, expressing,
    revealing: 21,34; 41,21; 69,14;
    106,5
dêmiourgein, fashion (v): 1,19
deisthai, need, require: 2,7, *passim*
  to deon, that which ought: 78,18
deuteros, secondary: 11,18, *passim*
dexios, right (adj): 42,1
diaballein, discredit: 101,17
diagignôskein, distinguish: 4,4
diagogê, way of life, pleasant life:
    8,17; 17,2–3
diairein, break down: 127,2;

distinguish: 3,4; 34,7; 128,18;
    divide: 35,11; 57,5; 64,5
diairetos, divisible: 98,6; 127,18
diairesis, distinction: 7,14;
    disjunction: 92,30; division: 9,5;
    19,17; 35,16; 55,2.5–6; 57,6
diakrinein, pierce: 20,18.21;
    segregate: 35,8–23; 67,21–2; 68,1
  diakritikos, piercing: 20,15.20
  diakrisis, separation: 27,17.19.25;
    28,18; 35,9.17; 65,18; 66,13
dialambanein, deal with: 9,31; 50,1
dialektikos, dialectical: 55,13
  ho dialektikos, dialectician: 55,3
  hê dialektikê, dialectic: 55,1.3
dialuesthai, be dissolved: 123,25
  dialusis, dissolution: 123,23; 124,2
diamenein, remain constantly: 67,11
diametros, diagonal (math.): 18,20;
    92,4
dianoia, good sense: 33,7; thought:
    26,26; 33,19
diapherein, be superior: 5,26; 6,7.17;
    differ: 10,16, *passim*
  diaphora, difference: 1,22; 36,5.10;
    92,2.4.9.10; differentia (log.):
    112,8–12; 116,24; 117,19;
    122,17.19; 123,1
diaphônein, be out of conformity:
    40,24
diaporein, be puzzled: 16,8; 120,8
  to diaporoumenon, difficulty: 96,1
diarthroun, articulate: 68,9; 135,4
  diêrthrômenôs, articulately: 61,3
diasaphein, make clear, state clearly:
    26,22; 121,8.9
diathigê, mutual contact: 36,6.7
diatribein, spend time: 121,28
didaskein, teach: 6,9, *passim*
  didaktos, can be taught: 133,9
  didaskaleion, school: 46,8
  didaskalia, teaching (n): 10,7;
    13,13.16; 129,23; 130,5.14;
    131,1.3.5
didosthai, be conceded: 102,4; 125,16
dielenkhein, refute: 85,6
diereunasthai, examine critically:
    71,3
dikaiosunê, justice: 38,10
dikhopoios, dividing into two:
    58,11.12
dioratikos, seeing clearly: 17,8
diôrismenôs, with proper
    distinctions: 135,6
diplasios, double: 133,2.3
  to diplasion, the double:
    48,20.24.25; 56,11.12.23–30

erôs, love (n): 32,23.25; 33,3.4.7.8; 61,30; 62,5.7.8

êremein, be at rest: 42,2

ergon, function: 9,26; work: 27,28; 79,6

erga, actions: 72,28

eruthros, dark red: 2,1

eskhatos, final: 20,7–21,36 *passim*

êthika, ta, ethical questions: 49,23

ethos, practice (n): 9,19; 15,32

eu, to, good (n): 60,20.24; 124,5

euelenktos, easily refuted: 97,20

eulogôs, rationally, reasonably, with good reason: 3,1, *passim*

euporos, well prepared: 136,9.10

euporia, prosperity: 17,18

eustrophia, versatility: 3,15

eutakton, to, right order: 104,8.15

eutaxia, regular order: 104,14

eutelês, unsophisticated: 28,3

euteleia, triviality: 26,25

[euthus] to euthu, the straight: 42,2; 129,4; 130,5

euthunein, censure, refute: 48,21, *passim*

exarithmêsis, numerical order: 46,15

exêgêsthai, explain: 3,19, *passim*; interpret: 68,13

exêgêsis, explanation: 85,10

exetazein, examine critically, scrutinize: 64,19; 94,16; 132,5; 134,19

exetasis, critical inquiry, examination: 55,1; 71,7; 76,3

existasthai, abandon: 124,4

gamos, marriage: 39,8.9

gê, earth: 28,20; 31,14.23.25; 39,2; 40,30.32; 45,6; 65,13.27.–66,4

gennan, generate: 29,4, *passim*

genêtos, generated: 45,5; 71,5

genos, class, kind: 83,32; 127,21; genus: 12,12; 55,6; 77,21; 81,7; 84,4; 118,11.12.21.22; 119,1.2.5–8; 126,2–37

geômetrês, geometrician: 12,1.2

gêometrikos, geometrical: 12,3; 120,3

geômetrein, be a geometer: 130,2

geômetria, geometry: 7,7; 11,25; 79,13; 130,3

gignesthai, come to be, into being; be generated: 24,2 *passim*

to gignesthai, genesis (93), becoming, coming-into-being, generation: see Subject Index: generation

ta gignomena, the things that come into being: 22,14, *passim*

gignôskein, know: 1,5, *passim*

gnôsis, knowledge: 1,4; 2.11.16–21; 4,5; 5,16–15,12 *passim*; 12,17–20; 13,17–31; 15,28–32; 129,15–21

gnôstikos, capable of knowing: 4,2, *passim*

gnôstos, knowable: 11,9; 96,24

gnôrizein, know, 1,16, *passim*; recognize, understand: 4,3; 14,5; 131,5

gnôrimos, knowable, known: 7,19, *passim*; familiar: 46,25; 131,9; understood, intelligible: 76,1.11

gnôrimôs, in a way that can be understood: 24,11

gônia, angle (math.): 75,29

gramma, letter (of alphabet): 133,2.24

grammê, line: 11,26; 18,21–19,2; 55,23.24; 117,28–119,12 *passim*; 120,5–15

graphein, paint: 83,2; 101,6.18

ta gegrammena, pictures: 83,2

grapheus, painter: 101,5

hê graphikê, painting (art of): 80,4

hairein, do away with: 131,4.5

haireisthai, choose: 10,11

hairetos, chosen, to be chosen: 2,5.9.12; 10,13; 13,21–4; 17,11

hamartanein, be mistaken: 64,21; 66,17; fail: 78,12

hamartia, error: 64,23

haplous, simple: 11,11; 55,22; 87,19; 92,18

haplôs, in the unqualified sense, without qualification: 2,16, *passim*

haptesthai, apprehend, grasp: 44,6.8; 61,4.8; engage in, touch on: 17,13; 33,10; attempt: 35,21; be contiguous: 35,21–23

harmozein (intr.), be applicable: 73,2

hêrmosmenos, harmonious: 104,9

harmonia (123), concordance, concordant interval: 39,19; 40,1.22.24; 89,4; musical scale: 38,22; harmony (Pythag.): 40,1

hêdonê, hêdos, pleasure: 6,22.23; 7,2

hêmiolos logos, to hêmiolon: the ratio 3:2: 39,21; 41,26; 108,16; 109,19

heis, one: 4,26, *passim*; single, sole: 65,12; 81,4; 82,12; 83,17

to hen, the number 1: 47,12; 57,9; The One: see Subject Index: one

hugrotês, moisture: 73,6
hulê, matter: see Subject Index:
    matter
hulikos, material: 28,23; 52,19;
    54,5; 57,26; 116,3
    hê hulikê aitia, the material cause:
    see Subject Index: causes
hupagein, bring, place, under:
    119,17; 120,7; 124,9; 125,2;
    126,35
hupallêlos, subordinate (adj): 118,12;
    119,2.6
huparkhein, belong: 11,6; 13,19;
    88,18; 129,2; be, exist: 16,21;
    33,8; 89,3; 118,17; be predicated:
    48,14.19.21
    huparxis, existence: 11,8; 36,1
huperekhein, be preeminent: 17,24;
    exceed: 112,3
    to huperekhon – to
    huperekhomenon, that which
    exceeds, is exceeded: 56,17–27
    huperokhê, excess: 54,8; 56,16;
    122,19.23; 123,2.7.8
huphistasthai, huphestanai,
    subsist: 52,16.17; 68,22; 83,25;
    84,28; 97,23; 110,11
    hupostasis, actual existence,
    reality, substantial being: 83,22;
    92,19; 110,13
hupoballein, make substrate: 54,14
hupodekhesthai, receive: 101,29
hupokeisthai, be assumed: 86,3; be
    subject (log.): 26,3; be substrate,
    underlie: 47,24; 73,1
    hupokeimenos, underlying: 31,21;
    48,7
    to hupokeimenon, substrate:
    24,12.14.16; 29,7; 53,19; 100,10;
    109,1.3; 129,8
hupolambanein, assume, suppose:
    10,1, *passim*
    hupolêpsis (33), judgment: 7,19;
    supposition: 10,20; 16,22
hupomenein, remain: 100,10.15
hupoteinousa, hê (pleura),
    hypoteneuse: 75,30
hupotithenai, make substrate: 48,1;
    53,14
    hupotithesthai, assume: 23,16,
    passim

iasthai, treat: 5,25
    iasis, cure: 15,32
    hê iatrikê, medicine: 79,11.24
ideai, hai, the Ideas: see Subject
    Index: Ideas
idios, characteristic, distinctive,

peculiar: 42,11; 49,19; 67,9.18;
    72,22
    to idion, property: 38,10; 73,5
    idiai, kat' idian, by itself, in its
    own right: 35,20; 63,26; 84,28;
    110,22
iris, rainbow: 16,6
isarithmos, equal in number:
    76,10.14.20, *passim*
iskhus, force: 76,22
isos, equal, equivalent: 25,20, *passim*
    to ison, the equal, equality:
    56,13–16; 83,7.10
    isotês, equality: 48,17; 73,3
    isakis isos, equal-times-equal
    (math.): 38,12; 48,17.26–49,8
Italikoi, hoi, the Italians: 46,7–14

kainoprepesterôs, in more modern
    fashion: 69,1
kairos, opportunity, season:
    38,17.21.22; 49,14; 78,4; 75,23
[kakos] ta kaka, evil things:
    33,16–25; 51,2; 77,8; 104,15
    to kakon, evil: 33,24.25; 47,18.19
kalos, beautiful: 50,2
    to kalon, the beautiful: 32,25; 50,2
    kallos, beauty: 1,19
kampulos, curved: 42,2
katagignesthai, be concerned (with):
    2,13; 8,5
katakermatizein, cleave: 35,19
katalambanein, apprehend: 76,16
kataleipein, leave: 32,26; admit,
    include: 73,14; 76,4
katallêlos, consistent, corresponding:
    37,20; 54,13
kataphaskein, affirm: 81,15.17.21
    kataphasis, affirmation: 81,18.20;
    130,17
    kataphatikos, affirmative: 25,19
katapheresthai, have recourse: 23,2
katarithmein, enumerate: 23,6; 44,5;
    64,19
kataskeuazein, establish: 78,9,
    passim
katastolê, control (n): 2,9
katêgorein, katêgoreisthai,
    predicate, be predicated: 9,11;
    26,1.3; 69,7; 80,8–81,10 *passim*;
    82,12–83,10; 83,34–84,2;
    84,22–85,3; 85,22; 87,4.6;
    88,17–20; 91,18–31; 93,5.25;
    115,19; 126,15–19
    en tôi ti esti katêgoreisthai, be
    predicated essentially: 119,7
    to katêgoroumenon, predicate (n):
    82,13; 114,22

kath' hauto, essentially: 90,1;
  independently: 24,17; 52,15;
  68,22; 83,25; 86,7; 97,4.23; 98,20;
  110,11; 120,11
kath' hauto – kata sumbebêkos,
  per se, per accidens: 89,10–91,31
  passim; 129,2–3
katharos, pure: 69,13
katholikos, general, universal: 4,24;
  10,25
katholou, to, the universal: 8,13;
  12,10.12.13; 50,1.8; 55,12; 131,1
katholou (adv), in general: 1,1,
  passim
keisthai, be assumed: 13,21, *passim*
keklasmenos, crooked: 130,5
kenos, meaningless: 101,17; 121,8
kenologein, use empty words:
  101,3.21
to kenon, the void: 35,27; 36,1–4;
  60,7; 61,20
khairein, delight (in): 1,10
khalepos, difficult: 10,3; 11,8–11
khaos, chaos: 65,29
kharaktêristikos, characteristic:
  83,21
kheimôn, winter: 18,19
Khimaira, Chimaera: 82,6
khiôn, snow: 20,15
khôra, role: 61,16; 63,18; 107,10
khoros, choir: 18,3
khôrizein (169), distinguish: 69,12;
  separate: 3,4; 35,11; 52,16; 54,25;
  55,4.11; 68,1.18.21.23; 80,12.14;
  84,15.23; 85,22; 96,26;
  97,1.23.25; 105,30; 106,1
kekhôrismenos, separated: 55,11;
  80,12.14; 84,23; 96,26.33; 115,19;
  126,25
khôristos, separable, separated:
  85,22; 97,25; 98,20
khôrismos, separation: 27,17;
  68,22
khreia, need: 16,17; 17,17.20;
  usefulness: 2,24
khreiôdês, satisfying needs:
  6,21.23; 7,11
khrêsimos, useful: 5,4; 6,17; 17,4;
  23,2
khrêsthai, employ, use: 5,5, *passim*
khrêsis, practice: 5,24; need: 8,17
khrôma, colour: 1,22; 69,8; 94,14;
  119,8
khronos, time: 9,24
khrusos, gold: 98,9
khumos, taste: 69,8
kinein, impart motion: 62,17; 106,17
kineisthai, move (intr.): 18,18; 32,20;

103,19; shift: 83,8; tend: 44,5; be
  inspired, led, motivated: 32,23;
  33,15; 49,20
to kineisthai, movement: 64,26
kinêtikos, imparting motion,
  moving: 31,24; 33,9; 67,18
kinêsis, motion, movement: 4,9;
  22,8.16; 30,4; 32,18; 36,23.24.29;
  37,1.2; 39,16; 40,6; 45,26; 52,17;
  64,28; 72,9.18.22–32; 96,1–15;
  103,19.20.39; 104,14; 121,3;
  126,4–6.13–14
koinos, common, commonplace,
  popular: 3,10, *passim*
koinai prolêpseis (33), common
  conceptions: 5,27; 9,20.29; 15,14
to koinon (243), the common thing,
  common predicate: 77,7.21–4;
  79,19; 83,19; 85,21; 93,3.11.18;
  114,23; 115,1.3.10–16; 116,32
koinôs katêgoreisthai, be
  predicated in common: 81,9–11;
  83,35; 84,3; 93,4–5.25; 94,2
koinônia, community (abstr.): 94,9;
  119,6; 125,6.7; 126,23.27
koinein, have in common: 126,11
koinousthai, join: 106,9
koinopoiein, make common cause
  with: 83,30
kôluein, hinder, prevent: 13,6, *passim*
kosmos, universe, world: 41,4; 45,5;
  73,15.17; 75,12.22.23; 77,26;
  103,6.8.11; 124,2
kouphotês, lightness: 72,36; 73,6
krasis, blending: 135,14
krisis, decision: 74,9; 75,25
krouesthai, knock (intr.): 36,22
kuôn, dog: 4,1; 110,9
kurios, proper (sense): 9,11; 121,16;
  sovereign, supreme: 15,4; 123,19;
  124,6; 131,16.18
kuriôs, in the primary, proper
  sense; properly so called: 3,10,
  passim

lalein, babble: 33,23
lambanein (intr.), assume, postulate,
  suppose: 8,1; 41,3; 44,13;
  124,17.22
lanthanein, be unaware: 132,2.4
legesthai pleonakhôs, pollakhôs,
  be said in several, many, ways:
  22,23; 79,3; 116,13.18.22; 117,16;
  126,32.36; 128,15–17
leptos, leptomerês, subtle: 65,22.34;
  66,7
leukos, white: 1,23; 20,20; 44,14; 69,7;
  81,13; 97,3.5

83,5; Ideas as models: see Subject
Index: model
paradekhesthai, accept: 81,3; 120,2
paradidosthai, explain: 7,14
  paradosis, explaining (n): 10,9
paragesthai, be dragged in: 35,2
paragignesthai, comes (to): 20,2; be
  present: 45,14
paraiteisthai, dismiss, reject:
  26,23.24; 70,13; excuse: 76,3
paralambanein, include: 29,4
paraleipein, leave out: 63,17; 64,25;
  neglect (v): 121,2
paralogos, against all reason: 132,1
paraphuas, offshoot: 83,33; 86,10
paraskeuē, provision: 16,19
paratithesthai, add, bring in: 9,6;
  11,24; 16,9; 24,23; adduce, cite:
  1,10; 13,28; 28,3; 32,24
  parathesis, reference: 72,31; 76,26
parekhein, confer: 89,15
  parekhesthai, provide: 2,20
  parektikos, conferring, providing,
  supplying: 58,29; 62,19; 63,15;
  92,5.9.12–13
parepesthai, be concomitant: 7,3
parerkhesthai, arrive: 6,19
paristanai, present (v): 6,10
parthenos, virgin: 39,8
[*pas*] *hē dia pasôn (harmonia,
  sumphônia)*, octave: 39,20.21;
  108,15
  to pan, the universe: 30,2;
  31,1.3.10.12
paskhein, be acted on: 129,1
  peponthos, taking on a property:
  53,19
  pathētikos, passive: 31,21
  pathēmata, phenomena: 16,9
  pathos (11), passion: 2,6.8;
  modification: 23,20; 24,6; 36,8;
  38,2; 41,21–8; 68,21; 73,12; 74,16;
  75,7; 97,5
pauein, put an end to: 15,28; 114,18;
  cease, terminate: 20,16; 21,7.9
peira, experimentation: 5,5
  peirasthai, attempt: 10,20, *passim*
peptesthai (211), be concocted: 66,7
peras, limit: 118,5.6; 120,11.12
  peratoun, limit (v): 43,7
  peperasmenos, limited: 28,4.5;
  40,16; 41,11.29; 43,6; 44,3;
  47,11.13; 58,10; 61,16
  to peperasmenon, limit, the
  limited: 47,20–48,2; 72,24
periekhein, provide: 32,5. enclose:
  75,29
perilēpsis, comprehension: 5,1; 8,13

perilēptikôs, comprehensively:
  9,31
periousia, store: 4,5
peripatein, walk: 84,9–14
periphora, orbit: 40,9
peristasis, annoyance: 17,14
perittos, refined: 6,21; odd (math.):
  see *artios*; profound: 10,6; out of
  the ordinary: 10,2
  hoi perittoi, those who excel: 17,24
pezos, walking (adj): 130,32
phainesthai, be obvious: 23,4,
  passim; appear, seem: 25,20,
  passim
  phainomenos, apparent,
  perceived, perceptible: 16,4;
  31,13; 40,28; 58,6; 70,9
  ta phainomena, phenomena: 45,3
  phaneros, obvious: 30,4; 40,23;
  72,4; 121,1.6
phaios, grey: 1,23; 69,8
phantasia, imagination: 3,17; 4,9;
  82,4; imaginings: 3,14
phantasma, image: 3,16; 82,4
pharmakon, medicine: 5,3
pherein, offer: 74,10; 78,5
  pheresthai, be superior: 2,19; move
  (intr.): 39,25,26; 41,6
  phora, motion: 72,28
philia – neikos, friendship – strife:
  see Subject Index: friendship
philomuthos, lover of myths: 16,13
philosophos, lover of wisdom: 16,15
  hoi philosophoi, philosophers:
  262,26; 27,1
  philosophia, philosophy: 1,18;
  15,21.33; 16,20; 24,9.21; 60,30;
  122,4; 135,8.10
  philosophein, philosophize:
  15,26–16,1.3–18; 122,6
  to philosophein, philosophy:
  121,27
philtron, charm: 17,12
phônē, sound (n): 3,21; 133,26
phôs, light (n): 42,2
phronimos, intelligent: 3,9–4,9,
  passim
  phronēsis (39), practical wisdom:
  3,11–15; 4,19
phrontizein, ponder: 45,11
phtheiresthai, perish: 82,2; 123,25;
  be destroyed: see Subject Index:
  destruction
  phthartos, perishable: 82,2; 88,8;
  93,19
  phthora, destruction: 123,23
phthongos, note (mus.): 109,2.6.25
phthonos, jealousy: 18,3

spoudazein, be eager, enthusiastic: 16,13.15; 121,27

stasis, stationariness: 62,17; 96,15

[stenos] to stenon – to platu, the narrow – the wide: 118,1.11.25; 127,14

[stereos] to stereon, solid (math.): see Subject Index: solid

sterêsis, privation: 92,17

stigmê (317), point (math.): 55,24; 112,13; 119,14; 120,1.13

stoikheion (174), element: of things, see Subject Index: element; of the alphabet: 133,3

sullogismos, syllogism: 25,15; 26,11; 44,12; 130,18; 131,6; 133,5

  sullogizesthai, come to a (correct) conclusion: 26,11; 78,6.8.22; prove: 81,8; 82,6

  sullogistikos, syllogistic: 7,19

sumbainein, happen: 5,25; 63,22; turn out: 5,22; 49,5; be agreed: 6,6

  ta sumbainonta, phenomena: 72,15

  to sumbebêkos (58), accident, attribute: 12,14.16–19; 47,21; 48,2; 68,21; 88,20; 94,17; 126,4

  kata sumbebêkos, *per accidens*: 5,24; 128,23; 129,1 (see also *kath' hauto*)

sumballesthai, contribute: 2,24; 95,8; 96,8

summetros, commensurable: 18,23–19,4; 79,14; 92,24

sumpaskhein, be affected: 1,20

sumperasma, conclusion (of syllogism): 7,19

sumphanai, agree: 135,27

sumpherein, be beneficial: 5,4

sumphônos, in agreement: 28,10

  sumphônôs, in harmony: 9,28

  sumphônia (273), harmony: 89,4; 108,12–15.21–109,2

sumphutos, innate: 14,13; 131,14; 132,1.2.6.7

sumptôma, accidental attribute: 52,19

sunagein, assemble, bring together: 35,18; 97,29; 98,24; conclude, prove: 21,19; 25,12; 44,19; 68,10; 78,6

sunakmazein, flourish at same time: 37,10

sunanaireisthai, be destroyed along with: 55,22

sunanakirnasthai, be blended together: 35,21

sundesmos, conjunction (gramm.): 68,24

sundiarthroun, articulate carefully: 68,26

sunedreuein, sit with: 45,11–14

sunekhein, maintain: 35,7

  sunekhôs, continually: 83,9; 96,11

sunepesthai, be sequel: 136,13

sunerithos, co-worker: 122,4

sunesis, understanding: 7,15

sunêthês (n), associate: 49,21; (adj) accustomed: 55,13

sunethizesthai, be habituated: 55,2

sungramma, writing (n): 26,17

sunistanai, establish: 5,26, *passim*; sustain: 65,30

  sunistasthai, be constituted, consist in: 42,14; 73,15; 74,7; 108,8

  ta phusei sunestôta, the things constituted by nature: see *phusis*

  sustasis, composition: 16,7

sunkeisthai, be composed: 39,19; 42,14; 54,16

  sunkeimenos, combined, composed, constituted: 36,26; 39,20; 41,24; 48,9; 53,23; 72,34; 98,14; 105,6

sunkephalaiousthai, summarize: 15,6; 69,16

  sunkephalaiôsis, a bringing together: 5,2

sunkhôreisthai, concede, grant, permit: 72,32; 102,15; 105,18; 107,12; 126,23

sunkrinein, aggregate, combine: 35,8–23; 67,21.22; 68,1

  sunkrisis, aggregation, combination: 27,17–25; 28,18; 35,8–23; 65,18; 66,13

sunodos, coming together (n): 27,16; 28,16.18; union: 39,9

sunônumos (146, 166), synonymous: 50,23; 51,4–18; 77,12–15

sunoran, recognize: 5,5

sunteinein, pertain: 136,8

suntelein, contribute: 4,6, *passim*

  sunteleia, contribution: 96,35

suntithenai, combine: 58,8; 104,2; 110,6–9.20

  sunthetos, composite (adj): 109,24; 110,17

  to suntheton, combination, composite (n): 110,10.14.21

sustoikhiai, columns (of opposites): 41,32; 47,16–19

sustolê, a drawing together: 5,1

[tapeinos] to tapeinon, the shallow:
118,11.12; 127,14
tassein, rank (v): 127,5
tetagmenos, fixed: 103,32.29;
104,6.17
tetagmenôs, in orderly sequence:
32,17; 88,20; 103,4
taxis, arrangement, order: 1,19; 3,2;
32,3.4; 36,5.12; 41,3; 74,10; 75,15;
103,36; 104,1; 127,6.13.24;
position: 63,21; role: 33,15;
101,28
tautotês, identity: 124,4; 126,5
têide, ta, the things here below: 76,19,
passim
teinein, point (to): 3,6
tekhnê, art (29, 36, 39): see Subject
Index: art
tekhnitês (17), artisan, expert in an
art: 5,11.21.25; 13,9; 58,18; 107,9
to tekhnêton, artefact, product of
an art: 55,9; 77,8; 107,3
tektonikê, hê, carpentry: 80,3
telos, end: 1,6; 2,4; 7,2; 14,16; 15,1.2;
22,11.16.18.19; 59,30; 63,3.4.6;
104,1; 121,14.22; 122,3
telikon aition, final cause: see
Subject Index: causes
teleios, complete, perfect: 2,27;
3,3.5.8; 6,18; 15,33; 38,17; 40,27;
41,34; 66,2; 100,4
teleiotês, perfection: 1,4–7;
maturity: 38,18
teleiousthai, be perfected: 66,7;
100,17
tenizein, fix one's gaze on: 1,18
terêdôn, grub: 104,8
têrein, insure: 26,7
têrêsis, observation: 7,5
tetarton, to, the fourth: 56,29
tetragônos arithmos, square
number: 38,14.16
to tetragônon, square (n): 52,23
tetraplasios, quadruple: 56,28
thaumazein, admire: 6,17; 32,10;
wonder (v): 15,24.26.33;
16,2.4.8.12.15; 18,14.16; 19,5.6.13
thaumastos, admirable: 6,16;
astonishing, wonderful: 18,22;
87,21
thaumatapoios, creator of
marvels: 18,16
thelein, wish: 117,27
thêlu, to, female (n): 39,9–12; 58,22;
107,10
themelios, foundation: 66,4
theos, ho, (76) god: 18,10; 44,9

hoi theoi, the gods: 2,7; 25,9; 35,2;
92,25; 104,5.7.10.12
theios, divine: 1,16; 17,15;
18,2.5.6.8; 22,2; 96,4.9
to theion (73), the divine: 17,19;
18,3.7
hê theologikê pragmateia,
theology: 18,11
hoi theologoi (99), mythologists:
25,10; 26,9
theôrein, contemplate: 1,18
theôria, recognition: 8,14;
speculation: 16,20; 55,13; 120,21;
121,28; theoretical inquiry,
knowledge: 1,5; 2,10; 6,20; 7,2;
17,5.6; 123,14 (see also Subject
Index: knowledge)
theôrêma, consideration: 55,13
theôrêtikos, theoretical: 8,9;
13,12–17; 15,3.6–12
thermos, hot: 20,14
to thermon, heat: 2,1; 24,25–29;
31,22; 91,3
thermainein, heat (v): 20,13.15
thermantikos, capable of heating:
20,14
thermotês, heat (n): 73,6
theros, summer: 18,19
thesis, position (local): 36,7.12
(math.): 11,26; 12,1; 37,15;
112,12; positing, thesis: 87,3;
120,3
thnêtos, mortal: 18,2
ti, dia, the question 'Why?':
20,11–21,36, *passim*
ti esti, ên einai, to, essence: see *einai*
timios, estimable: 2,2, *passim*;
honorable: 21,15–26,7 *passim*
tithesthai, hold, posit: 24,27, *passim*
tode ti, this something: 56,30; 97,21
tolma, daring: 74,13
topos, place: 9,23; 74,11–75,10 *passim*
tragôidia, tragedy: 35,2
trauma, wound: 104,16
trephesthai, be nourished: 24,27
trophê, nourishment: 24,23.24
trigônos, triangle: 36,15; 52,23; 75,28
triplasion, to, the triple: 56,28
triton, to, the third: 56,28
tropê, solstice: 18,19; turning: 36,7
tropos, type: 23,3; 64,9; 65,20; mode,
way, procedure: 65,14; 99,10;
100,30; 124,10
tunkhanein, be, happen to be: 1,23,
passim; chance to be: 42,7
to tukhon, chance thing: 68,19
tukhê, chance: 5,12
apo tukhês, by chance: 103,32.36

tupos (23), impression: 3,17; mould: 57,6

xanthos, auburn, 1,23
xêros, dry: 2,1
    xêrotês, dryness: 73,6
xenikos, strange: 71,13

zêtein, inquire, investigate, seek: 7,1, *passim*
zêtêsis, inquiry, investigation, search: 6,20, *passim*
zôion, animate being: 2,6; animal: 2,26.27; 3,4.5; 32,12; 33,15; 51,23; 80,9; 92,11; 104,16; 105,2.8–22; 110,10–13.16–19.23; 119,5–11; 124,1.17–21; 130,22

Subject Index

This index lists topics of interest, including the names of, and citations to, the philosophers whom Alexander mentions. The textual references in this Index duplicate those given in the Greek–English Index, but in this index the citations are distributed according to the multiple contexts in which a term occurs. In cases in which a key term (e.g. *arkhê*, principle) occurs so frequently that its uses must be distinguished, all citations are found in the Subject Index. Page and line references are to the Greek text.

abstraction, *aphairesis*, origin of numbers: 37,22
    things abstracted are intermediates: 113,15–17
    (see also Separate)
accidents, *ta sumbebêkota*, being of: 134,10–14
    knowledge of things having few or none: 12,16–20
    sciences of: 88,9–13
    similarity based on: 126,1–17
    the unlimited, limited, as accident: 47,19–48,4
    the one-over-many predicated of: 88,19–20
    and substance: see Substance
    Ideas of: see Ideas
    per accidens – per se: see Participation, Predication
action, *praxis*, is referred to an end beyond itself: 2,3–9
    inferior to knowledge: see Knowledge
activity, *energeia*, that proper to the gods: 18,5–8
    of imagination: 3,15–18
    of the stars: 72,31–2
aggregation – segregation, *sunkrisis – diakrisis*, Empedocles: 27,15–25; 35,8–23
    Anaxagoras: 28,16–18
    in generation of the primary bodies: 65,17–66,13
air, *aêr*, as element, principle, in early philosophers: 26,22; 27,5–7;

45,15–17; 115,11; 116,32–5; 122,16–18
    in Anaximander: see Intermediate Nature
    as compound (Anaxagoras): 28,19–20
    as passive principle: 31,24–6
    as unlimited: 47,19–22
Alcmaeon: 42,3–11
alteration, *alloiôsis*, def.: 24,6
    not true change: 23,23–24,11
Anaxagoras, doctrine: 27,28–28,21.24; 29,12; 31,19; 32,9–21; 33,2.10.27; 34,11; 35,1–6; 45,26–46,4.17–19; 60,25; 61,30–62,10; 63,8; 97,14; 134,4; 136,5
    critique: 68,6–70,9 *passim*; 97,21–7
Anaximander: 45,18; 47,23; 60,8; 61,12
Anaximenes: 26,22; 27,6; 29,12; 45,18.22
animal, *zôion*, capacity for learning: 3,19–4,4
    possessing intellect: 32,11–13; 33,14–15
    man in relation to lower: see Man
    as Idea in Platonic 'exposition': 124,16–20
    as genus of man: 51,23; 105,2–22; 110,8–24; 119,4–11; 130,22
    rational–irrational as differentiae of: 51,23; 92,11–17
appetite, object of, *to orekton*, is the good: 33,2–5

participates in experience: 4,16–20

not operative in natural generation: 103,37–104,10

reduction, *anagein*, of the question 'Why?' to final definition: 20,10–21,21

of all things to numbers (Pythagoreans): 38,8–41,35

to equality – inequality, i.e. the indefinite dyad (Plato): 56,13–20; 117,24–118,1

to the One (Platonists): 124,9–125,4

relatives, *ta pros ti*, def.: 86,8–10

have their being in relation to one another: 83,25–6

no Ideas of: 51,1–2; 83,22–6

resemblance: see Similarity

rest–motion, Pythagorean opposites: 42,2

rhythm, *rhusmos*, i.e. *skhêma*, of the atoms: 36,4–7

right–left, Pythagorean opposites: 42,1

sciences, *epistêmai*, have universal as their object: 79,18–19

their own end: 2,10–12; 13,17–21

other sciences depend on wisdom: 19,24–20,3

divine, i.e. theology: 18,4–13

mathematical: 7,3–9; 72,8–12

more authoritative, exact: 11,13–24; 12,16–20; 14,3–15,5

practical – theoretical: see Knowledge

of accidents as well as substances: 88,9–13

Platonic argument 'from the sciences': 79,1–80,6; 88,9–13

scientific knowledge, *epistême*, def.: 7,17–21

is knowledge of the cause: 13,25–14,2; 19,24–20,3; 20,10–21,36 *passim*

equated with, distinguished from, art: 4,27; 7,26–28

relation to experience: 4,26–8

most excellent: 131,16–20; 133,9–11

segregation, *diakrisis*: see Aggregation

sense perception, *aisthêsis*, contributes to knowledge: 2,24; 4,4–7

a form of learning, possesses truth: 4,7; 7,15–16

in relation to experience, imagination: 8,12–15; 4,9–10

not wisdom: 10,4–6

is innate: 132,1–2

sense power, sense(s), *aisthêsis*, love for: 1,9–12; 2,23

their ordering: 3,2–4,10

their object sensible particulars: 6,10–12; 133,29–30

possibility of knowledge without: 133,22–134,7

separation, *khôrizein*, *khôrismos*, *kekhôrismenos*, of elements from the One,

the mixture (Anaxagoras, Empedocles): 27,15–25; 28,16–18; 35,8–23; 68,15–25; 97,21–5

of accidents from substance: 68,20–2; 97,25

of species from genus: 110,10–24

of mathematical objects from matter, motion: 52,15–17

of Ideas from sensibles: 54,25–6; 55,4–11; 80,8–14; 96,32–3; 98,19–20; 105,30–106,1

sequence, *akolouthia*, in natural generation: 32,2–5; 101,25–31; 103,36–104,10

shallow, the, *to tapeinon*: see the Deep

shape, *skhêma*, of the atoms: 35,4–12

common to mathematical and natural bodies: 73,2–4

short – long, the, *to brakhu* – *to makron*, principles of the line (Platonists): 117,28–119,12 *passim*; 120,8; 127,13

sight, sense of, *hê horatikê (aisthêsis)*, superiority of: 1,12–2,2

similarity, *to homoion*, *homoiôma*, *homoiotês*, recognition of: 4,23–5,6; 8,12–15

by reference to form: 51,15–23

based on genus, species: 126,1–37

result of participation in same thing: 84,1–2; 88,4–5

does not require an agent: 102,3–103,1

of things to numbers (Pythagoreans): 37,22–41,4 *passim*

of likenesses to their models (Platonists): 82,12–83,6.12–17

simple, *haplous*, things farthest from the senses: 11,10–11

simple things first in nature: 55,22–23

simplicity of the Ideas: 87,19–20; 92,1–8; 105,6